THE
SIEGE
OF
MECCA

Also by Yaroslav Trofimov

·

Faith at War:
A Journey on the Frontlines of Islam,
from Baghdad to Timbuktu

THE FORGOTTEN

UPRISING IN ISLAM'S

HOLIEST SHRINE AND THE

BIRTH OF AL QAEDA

Yaroslav Trofimov

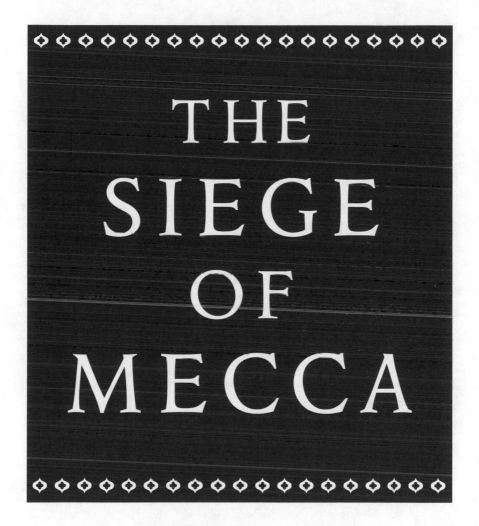

THE
SIEGE
OF
MECCA

DOUBLEDAY

New York   London   Toronto   Sydney   Auckland

PUBLISHED BY DOUBLEDAY

Copyright © 2007 by Yaroslav Trofimov

All Rights Reserved

Published in the United States by Doubleday,
an imprint of The Doubleday Broadway Publishing Group,
a division of Random House, Inc., New York.
www.doubleday.com

DOUBLEDAY and the portrayal of an anchor with a dolphin
are registered trademarks of Random House, Inc.

Book design by Kathryn Parise

LIBRARY OF CONGRESS CATALOGING-IN-PUBLICATION DATA
Trofimov, Yaroslav.
The Siege of Mecca : the forgotten uprising in Islam's holiest shrine and the birth of al Qaeda /
By Yaroslav Trofimov.—1st ed.
p. cm.
Includes bibliographical references and index.
1. Mecca (Saudi Arabia)—History—Siege, 1979.   I. Title.

DS248.M4T76 2007
953.805'3—dc22

2007007520

ISBN 978-0-385-51925-0

PRINTED IN THE UNITED STATES OF AMERICA

1 3 5 7 9 10 8 6 4 2

First Edition

To Nicole, Jonathan, and Susi,
with love

Cast of Principal Characters

(Positions as held in 1979)

SAUDI ARABIA

Prince Abdullah: Commander of the Saudi National Guard.

Prince Bandar bin Sultan: Son of Prince Sultan, future Saudi ambassador in Washington.

Abdelaziz Bin Baz: Chairman of Saudi Arabia's Department of Scientific Research and Guidance, a ministerial-level clerical body in charge of interpreting Islamic law.

Salem Bin Laden: Head of the Bin Laden construction company that expanded the Grand Mosque in Mecca; Osama Bin Laden's brother.

Brigadier-General Faleh al Dhaheri: Commander of the Saudi Army's King Abdelaziz Armored Brigade.

Mohammed Elias: A senior Egyptian preacher who participated in the Mecca uprising.

Crown Prince Fahd: Saudi Arabia's day-to-day ruler.

Faisal Mohammed Faisal: One of the most senior Saudi leaders of the Mecca uprising.

Colonel Nasser al Homaid: Commander of the Saudi Army's Sixth Paratroop Battalion.

Nasser Ibn Rashed: Most senior cleric in charge of the Holy Mosques in Mecca and Medina.

Mohammed Ibn Subeil: Imam of the Grand Mosque in Mecca and Ibn Rashed's deputy.

King Khaled: King of Saudi Arabia.

Prince Nayef: Minister of the interior of Saudi Arabia.

Major Mohammed Zuweid al Nefai: Operations officer of the Saudi Interior Ministry Special Security Force.

Mohammed Abdullah al Qahtani: Juhayman al Uteybi's brother-in-law and the alleged Mahdi.

Lieutenant Abdulaziz Qudheibi: Platoon commander of the Sixth Paratroop Battalion.

Hassan al Saffar: Religious leader of Saudi Shiites in the Eastern Province.

Prince Sultan: Minister of defense and aviation of Saudi Arabia.

Prince Turki al Faisal: Chief of Saudi Arabia's General Intelligence Directorate.

Juhayman bin Seif al Uteybi: retired corporal in the Saudi National Guard and chief leader of the Mecca uprising.

Ahmed Zaki Yamani: Saudi Arabia's minister of oil.

Mohammed Abduh Yamani: Saudi Arabia's minister of information.

UNITED STATES

Zbigniew Brzezinski: President Carter's national security adviser.

President Jimmy Carter: President of the United States of America.

Herbert Hagerty: Chief political officer at the U.S. embassy in Pakistan.

Mark Hambley: Political officer at the U.S. embassy in Saudi Arabia.

Ralph Lindstrom: U.S. consul general in Dhahran, Saudi Arabia.

Jack McCavitt: Central Intelligence Agency station chief in Tripoli, Libya.

Cyrus Vance: U.S. secretary of state.

Ambassador John C. West: U.S. ambassador to Saudi Arabia.

FRANCE

Captain Paul Barril: Deputy commander of the French commando unit Groupe d'Intervention de la Gendarmerie Nationale (GIGN). Head of the GIGN mission dispatched to Saudi Arabia during the Mecca uprising.

President Valéry Giscard d'Estaing: President of the French Republic.

Count Alexandre de Marenches: Head of French intelligence agency Service de Documentation Extérieure et de Contre-Espionage (SDECE).

Christian Lambert: Member of the GIGN mission dispatched to Saudi Arabia.

Captain Christian Prouteau: Commander of the GIGN.

Ignace Wodecki: Member of the GIGN mission dispatched to Saudi Arabia.

OTHER COUNTRIES

Mehmet Ali Agca: Turkish militant who tried to assassinate Pope John Paul II.

Leonid Brezhnev: Leader of the Soviet Union.

Colonel Moammar Ghadhafi: Revolutionary leader of Libya.

Babrak Karmal: Soviet-installed leader of Afghanistan.

Ayatollah Ruhollah Khomeini: Leader of the 1979 Islamic revolution in Iran.

General Mohammed Zia ul Haq: President of Pakistan.

A Note on Arab Names

Names in Arabia usually consist of four parts: the given name and the names of the father, of the grandfather, and of the tribe or family. They are separated by the prepositions "bin," "ibn," or "al," which usually, but not always, mean "son of."

Mohammed bin Abdullah, Mohammed al Abdullah, Mohammed ibn Abdullah, and the preposition-less Mohammed Abdullah are different ways of identifying the same person, Abdullah's son Mohammed. Abdullah in this example could also be known simply as Abu Mohammed, with "abu" the Arabic for "father."

As it would be too unwieldy to use the full Arabic names throughout the book, I followed the common usage, which, sometimes without much logic, varies from case to case. On some occasions, this meant employing just the first two parts of a name; on others, the first and the last. Spellings were simplified to make proper names more easily recognizable to non-Arab readers.

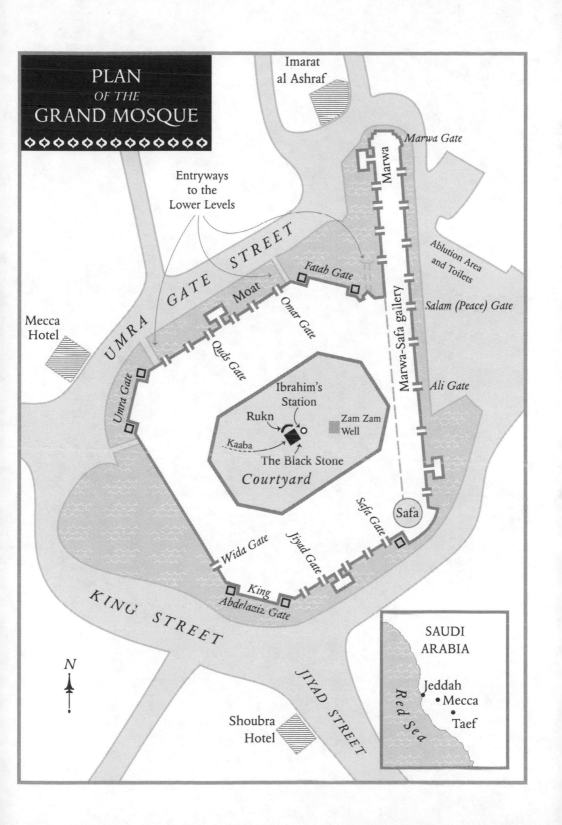

PLAN
OF THE
GRAND MOSQUE

◇◇◇◇◇◇◇◇◇◇◇◇◇

Imarat
al Ashraf

Marwa Gate

Marwa

Entryways
to the
Lower Levels

*Ablution Area
and Toilets*

UMRA GATE STREET

Moat

Fatah Gate

Marwa-Safa gallery

Salam (Peace) Gate

Mecca
Hotel

Omar Gate

Quds Gate

Ibrahim's
Station

Rukn

Zam Zam
Well

Ali Gate

Umra Gate

Kaaba

The Black Stone

Courtyard

Widda Gate

Jiyad Gate

Safa Gate

Safa

King
Abdelaziz Gate

KING STREET

JIYAD STREET

N

Shoubra
Hotel

SAUDI
ARABIA

Red Sea

Jeddah
• Mecca
• Taef

THE
SIEGE
OF
MECCA

INTRODUCTION

The holy city of Mecca looked deceptively calm as the first dawn of the new century started to break behind craggy mountains.

Splashing his face with cold water, the Grand Mosque's bearded imam fastened a beige-hued cloak over his shoulders and muttered praises to the Lord. The time to lead the morning's first prayer was minutes away.

Under his window, the mosque's floodlit courtyard was filling up quickly. The hajj pilgrimage season, when this stadium-size enclosure was traversed by more than a million worshippers, had already ended. Yet Mecca remained jam-packed with the faithful. Many of them had spent the night inside Islam's holiest shrine, curling up on wool carpets in the Grand Mosque's multistory labyrinth of nearly a thousand rooms.

As usual, these worshippers camped along with their bundles, mattresses, and suitcases that nobody had bothered to check. Following custom, many hauled in wooden coffins, hoping that the imam would bestow on decomposing relatives inside the precious blessings that can only be received in such a sacred precinct.

Today, some of these coffins contained an unusual cargo: Kalashnikov assault rifles, Belgian-made FN-FAL guns, bullet belts, and an assortment of pistols.

The men who had smuggled this arsenal into the mosque sought an ambitious goal: to reverse the flow of world history, sparking a global war that would finally lead to Islam's total victory and to a destruction of arrogant Christians and Jews.

The date was the First of Muharram of Islam's year 1400—which in calendars kept by infidel Westerners corresponded to November 20, 1979.

For the natives of Mecca, a city that lives off the flood of humanity that has coursed through its shrines since time immemorial, this Tuesday morning promised a particularly joyful occasion: New Year's day is when, according to tradition, the Meccans make a pilgrimage of their own to the Grand Mosque.

In darkness, thousands trekked to the outskirts of the city, shedding everyday clothes after a shower and returning in the pilgrims' snow white *ihram* outfits—two towel-like garments that symbolize purity and leave men's right shoulders exposed.

Mixing in with the locals were as many as 100,000 visitors from all over the world—Pakistanis and Indonesians, Moroccans and Yemenis, Nigerians and Turks. Some were stragglers left behind after the hajj, entrepreneurial pilgrims who, year after year, try to offset the cost of their passage by reselling in Mecca's bazaars exotic wares from their remote homelands. Others had arrived in Mecca just to witness the turn of the century—a once-in-a-lifetime event.

Hidden in this human sea were hundreds of grim-faced rebels, many of them sporting red checkered headdresses. Some had been inside the mosque for days, reconnoitering its maze of corridors and passageways. Others were bused in during the night by a friendly religious academy. Yet others drove their own cars to Mecca this morning, arriving at the last minute and accompanied by children and wives to allay guards' suspicions.

Most of these conspirators were Saudis of Bedouin stock, though their ranks also brimmed with foreigners, if such a word had a meaning for men who believed in the single citizenship of Islam. They even included African American converts, inspired by a new faith and hardened by race riots half a world away.

The color of the cloudless sky just started to turn from grayish to pink when the dawn ritual began, as it does that time of the year, at 5:18 a.m. *"La ilaha ila Allah,"* the deep-voiced prayer call rang from new loudspeakers affixed atop the mosque's seven towering minarets: "There is no god but Allah."

Barefoot, worshippers knelt in the Grand Mosque's marble-paved courtyard. Clearing his throat, the imam picked up the microphone and read out the blessings. On his cue, the faithful prostrated themselves on the ground, in a vast succession of concentric circles that radiated from the Kaaba, an ancient cube draped in black silk embroidered with gold that looms in the center of the enclosure.

Then, just as the imam concluded the prayer with wishes of peace, gunshots rang out. The crackling sound reverberated in the courtyard as in an echo chamber. Stunned worshippers spotted a young man, a rifle in his hands, walking briskly toward the Kaaba. Another shot sent into the air flocks of panicked pigeons that usually graze on the plaza outside the Grand Mosque.

Rumors quickly swirled through the crowd. What could all this be? What was all that noise? Maybe there is an innocuous explanation, one man opined. Maybe the gunmen were bodyguards for some senior prince, or even the Saudi monarch, King Khaled, himself? Maybe the gunfire was just some peculiar Saudi way to celebrate the New Year?

More knowledgeable worshippers shuddered. Firing a weapon in the Grand Mosque, they knew, was a grave sin. They couldn't recall the last time such a sacrilege had occurred. Pilgrims watched with angst as more and more gunmen closed in on the Kaaba, carrying weapons that had been extracted from uncrated coffins. The Grand Mosque's own police force, armed with nothing more threatening than sticks for beating misbehaving foreign pilgrims, melted away once two guards who attempted resistance fell dead by the gates.

Amid this commotion, the rebels' leader, Juhayman al Uteybi, emerged from the depths of the mosque. A forty-three-year-old Bedouin preacher with magnetic black eyes, sensual lips, and shoulder-length hair that seamlessly blended into a black curly beard, Juhayman conveyed a sense of immediate authority despite his slender stature. Emulating a piety first displayed by Prophet Mohammed himself, he wore a traditional Saudi white robe that was cut short at midcalf to signal the rejection of material goods. Unlike his fellow gunmen, he was bareheaded, with only a thin green hair band keeping his unruly locks in check.

Flanked by three militants armed with rifles, pistols, and daggers, Juhayman started to elbow his way across the courtyard, toward the sacred Kaaba and the Grand Mosque's imam. The cleric, who had just turned his face away from the Kaaba and toward the distressing tumult among the believers, noticed that he was standing right next to a coffin. This one contained a real cadaver; the dead child's relatives, oblivious to the mounting upheaval, were imploring the imam to bless the tiny corpse.

As the cleric obliged, reciting the sacred lines, recognition flickered on his face. He realized in these moments that Juhayman and some of the other gunmen, who now got disconcertingly close, had attended his lectures on Islam here in Mecca. This feeling turned to horror seconds later, as Juhayman unceremoniously pushed the cleric aside and seized the microphone. When the imam tried to wrestle back the mike, one of the intruders raised a sharp curved dagger and screamed at the top of his lungs, ready to stab.

A fright swept the crowd.

Picking up shoes, thousands rushed toward the enclosure's gates, only to find all fifty-one of them chained shut. Ragged-looking gunmen, muzzles staring into the crowd, barred all exits. Unsure of how to behave, some worshippers started chanting *"Allahu Akbar"*—"God is Greatest"—the Muslims' invocation of faith in a moment of adversity. The gunmen unexpectedly joined in this chorus and it became louder and louder, spreading throughout the packed mosque until it turned into a deafening roar.

When this chanting subsided, Juhayman barked into the microphone a series of clipped military commands. Following his instructions, scores of his well-trained followers dispersed throughout the compound, setting up machine-gun nests atop the shrine's seven minarets. Trapped pilgrims were gang-pressed into aiding the rebels. Some had to roll up the thousands of heavy carpets inside the courtyard and prop them up against the chained gates. The fittest were forced at gunpoint to climb the steep staircases to the tops of the minarets, carrying water and crates of ammunition. The takeover of Islam's holy of holies was swift and complete.

At their 89 meters (292 feet) of height, the mosque's minarets over-looked much of downtown Mecca, providing rebel snipers with a vast field of fire. Trigger fingers caressing the cold metal, they scanned neighboring streets for potential foes. "If you see a government soldier who wants to raise his hand against you, have no pity and shoot him because he wants to kill you," Juhayman instructed these snipers in his guttural desert accent. "Do not hesitate!"

Under the minarets, even Saudis—proficient in the local dialect—had a hard time understanding what was going on. The crying of women, the coughing of elders, and the shuffling of bare feet filled the Grand Mosque's courtyard with an anxious hum. Many foreigners among the tens of thousands of hostages spoke no Arabic at all and stood trans-fixed in the turmoil, asking better-educated countrymen for explanation in a multitude of tongues.

The conspirators were prepared for linguistic problems, and wanted to be comprehended. Soon they grouped Pakistani and Indian pilgrims on one side of the mosque, with a Pakistani-born rebel interpreting the announcements in Urdu to bewildered compatriots. A cluster of Africans was provided with a speaker of English. "Sit down, sit down and listen," Juhayman's gunmen yelled, rifle-butting those pilgrims who dared to disobey.

As cowed worshippers finally settled in fearful attention, the mysterious group indicated that its authority now extended well beyond the Grand Mosque to Saudi Arabia's commercial capital and to the second of the country's two holy cities. "Mecca, Medina, and Jeddah are now in our hands," the rebels declared through the shrine's public-address system, so powerful that their words could be heard throughout central Mecca.

Then Juhayman handed the microphone to an aide better versed in classical Arabic speech. It was high time to explain the purpose of this daring venture.

For the next hour, the Grand Mosque's loudspeakers relayed the uprising's shocking message to the world's one billion Muslims, announcing that an ancient prophecy had been fulfilled at last and that the hour of final reckoning was being struck. By the time this speech, occasionally interspersed with gunshots, was over and the loudspeakers fell silent, panic infected the whole of central Mecca. Even waiters at the outdoor cafés near the mosque had all run away.

Thus began a drawn-out battle that would drench Mecca in blood, marking a watershed moment for the Islamic world and the West. Within hours, this outrage would prompt a global diplomatic crisis, spreading death and destruction thousands of miles away. American pilots and European commandos would all have to be involved in restoring the shrines of Islam to the House of Saud. Soon, American lives would be lost, and America would find itself more isolated than ever in the increasingly hostile Muslim universe.

The consequences of this forgotten crisis—which remains blotted out of history books in Saudi Arabia and many other Muslim lands—last to this day.

In tackling Juhayman's brazen attack on its holiest shrine, the Saudi government showed sickening arrogance, cruel incompetence, and bewildering disregard for the truth. The royal family's image was sullied forever. Many Muslims in Saudi Arabia and beyond, including the young Osama Bin Laden, were so repulsed by the carnage in Mecca that their loyalty started to fracture. In following years, they drifted toward open opposition to the House of Saud and its American backers. The fiery ideology that inspired Juhayman's men to murder and mayhem in Islam's holy of holies mutated with time into increasingly more vicious strains, culminating in al Qaeda's death cult.

By a coincidence of global events, it is precisely this ideology that American policy makers—and the House of Saud—found right after the crisis in Mecca to be of great value on the Cold War battlefronts. Instead of being suppressed, Juhayman's brutal brand of Islam was encouraged and nurtured as it metastasized across the planet since 1979. Today, hordes of his spiritual heirs are busy blowing up airplanes, tourist hotels, and commuter trains on four continents, self-satisfied smiles of true believers curling their lips.

The significance of the Mecca uprising was missed at the time even by the most sharp-eyed observers. Too many other threats preoccupied the West. The seizure of the Grand Mosque—the first large-scale operation by an international jihadi movement in modern times—was shrugged off as a local incident, an anachronistic throwback to Arabia's Bedouin past.

But with the benefit of hindsight, it is painfully clear: the countdown to September 11, to the terrorist bombings in London and Madrid, and to the grisly Islamist violence ravaging Afghanistan and Iraq all began on that warm November morning, in the shade of the Kaaba.

ONE

The territory that Juhayman and his men occupied in Mecca was literally the center of the Muslim universe. It is toward the Kaaba, the black-clothed cubical building also known as House of God, in the Grand Mosque's courtyard, that Muslims worldwide turn in prayer five times a day.

Every Muslim who can afford it must visit the Kaaba during the annual hajj at least once in a lifetime, donning the two-piece *ihram* and performing seven counterclockwise circumambulations around the building. A swirl of women and men circles the Kaaba day and night, as constant—until Juhayman's interruption—as the movement of planets around the sun. According to the Prophet Mohammed, a prayer at this sacred spot, the axis between Heaven and Earth, is worth a hundred thousand prayers elsewhere. Even in death, Muslims are buried with their faces turned toward the Kaaba.

This simple stone structure, measuring some sixteen meters in height and twelve meters in length (about 52.5 feet × 40 feet), is believed by

Muslims to have been built many millennia ago by Prophet Ibrahim, the patriarch of Arabs and Jews who is known as Abraham in the Bible. In Christian and Jewish tradition, Abraham's rightful heir is Isaac, the forefather of Jews, born to Abraham's wife, Sarah. For Muslims, Ibrahim's legacy instead went to Ishmael, the forefather of Arabs and the son of the Egyptian slave girl Hagar.

According to Muslim canon, Ibrahim had left Hagar and the infant Ishmael all alone in Mecca—then just a barren desert valley without a well in sight, carpeted by fine sand among occasional shrubs and sharp-edged rock outcroppings. The anguished mother, seeing baby Ishmael dying of thirst, ran seven times between the two hills of Marwa and Safa, searching for water. As she nearly abandoned hope, a spring miraculously burst out from the ground. This was the holy source of Zam Zam, adjacent to the Kaaba and still supplying the taps in the Grand Mosque. Its water, which is said to be streaming directly from Paradise, is avidly collected in bottles and plastic containers by pilgrims and then transported all over the world as a precious cure against bad luck and disease. While in Mecca, worshippers reenact Hagar's seven races between Marwa and Safa. The path between the two rocky hills is now paved and sheltered by a covered gallery attached to the Grand Mosque's outer perimeter.

Ishmael and his mother are said to be buried next to the Kaaba in a low C-shaped wall known as *Rukn*. A boulder preserved beneath a golden dome nearby is marked with what is believed to be the impression of Ibrahim's feet. According to tradition, Ibrahim stood on that spot while erecting the Kaaba atop the foundation of an even more ancient house that had been constructed on God's own direction by Adam, and modeled by the first human on a building he had admired before his expulsion from Eden. The Kaaba from its very beginning was meant to be a shrine, a sanctuary where prayers could be offered in absolute safety.

There is little independent knowledge of the site's history, other than that over the centuries the current structure has been repeatedly destroyed by cataclysms and floods, just to be rebuilt on the very same spot. Long a place where Arabian tribesmen worshipped idols, the building displays in its southeastern corner a polished black stone. Probably of meteoric origin and credited with magical powers, the sacred Black Stone is encased in a broad silver band. It is said to have been originally white and to have turned black after absorbing the sins of millions of worshippers who touch and kiss it every year.

A Meccan tribe, the Quraysh, had been guarding the Kaaba and its idols for centuries before the advent of Islam, earning a comfortable living from the pilgrim trade. This arrangement almost ended in 570 CE when the shrine's growing prominence attracted the wrath of a Christian Abyssinian viceroy of Yemen named Abraha. Riding a fearsome elephant into battle, Abraha—who wanted Arabian pilgrims to visit his newly built church instead—approached the city and announced his plans to raze the Kaaba to the ground. Once the terrified Meccans withdrew into nearby hills, placing the Kaaba's safety into God's hands, flocks of strange birds appeared in the sky and proceeded to shower the Abyssinians with pea-size clay stones. This bombardment infected Abraha and his Army of the Elephant with deadly disease, causing his heart to burst and his fingers to fall off one by one; the unlucky Christian invaders, the Muslim scripture says, were "rendered like straw eaten up." Explaining this narrative, an Arab chronicler suggested that the House of God had been saved thanks to a provident outbreak of smallpox and measles.

The very same year, a boy named Mohammed was born to a Quraysh subclan in the city. Once he grew into adulthood, the Muslim canon holds, Mohammed started receiving from Angel Gabriel the final word of God—the Quran, or literally, "recitation"—which corrected mistaken beliefs of Christians and Jews. Mandating obedience to a single God, this religion of Islam also declared the local custom of idol worship a mortal sin. Prophet Mohammed's demands to purge the Kaaba of totems and fetishes earned him the enmity of his hometown. In 622, he had to flee north to a city now known as Medina, establishing there the world's first community that lived under the new laws of Islam. It was this migration, known as *hijra* in Arabic, that marked the first year of Islam's 354-day lunar calendar.

Prophet Mohammed returned home at the head of a victorious Islamic army eight years later, throwing the despised idols out of the Kaaba and decreeing that infidels henceforth should be barred from setting foot in Medina and Mecca, the two holy cities where the Quran had been revealed. This injunction is still in effect—Saudi government checkpoints ring approaches to Mecca, and travelers of any non-Muslim religion, which is marked on their IDs, have to bypass the city on a circuitous deviation signposted as the "Non-Muslims' Road."

Mecca, which flourished as an unrivaled pilgrimage center once Islam conquered lands from Indonesia to Spain, has remained firmly under Muslim control ever since. The closest it came to falling into infidel hands since the elephant-riding Abraha was in 1182, when Crusader prince Reynaud de Chatillon led a marauding expedition down the Red Sea from his fortress in what is now Jordan. Attempting to sack the two holy cities of Islam, he captured pilgrim caravans heading to Mecca and sent his marines inland to Medina with a mission to steal Mohammed's body, which is buried there. But de Chatillon's men never reached the shrines. A few years later, Salaheddin, the Muslim conqueror of Jerusalem, punished the Crusader prince's insolence by severing his head.

The only people who actually managed to seize by force and desecrate Mecca's Grand Mosque before Juhayman's uprising of 1979 were fellow Muslims. In the year 929, members of Islam's fringe Karmatian sect pillaged the Kaaba and purloined the magic Black Stone. They took it to their tribal homeland in eastern Arabia, near the city of Qatif, in a mistaken belief that such usurpation would generate a profitable influx of pilgrims. This tourism-promotion scheme never worked. Twenty years later, the Karmatians gave up and returned the stone, damaged in the process, to its rightful place.

In following centuries, Bedouin nomads who roamed the vast emptiness of Arabia, living off camel-herding and predatory raids on rival tribes, relapsed into many of the same pagan practices so roundly condemned by Prophet Mohammed. While nominally Muslim, they worshipped again the graves of ancestors, holy rocks, and old trees.

Then, in the mid-1700s, they encountered a fiery new breed of preachers. Dubbed Wahhabis by their numerous foes, these bearded clerics followed the creed of a man of religion named Mohammed Ibn Abdel Wahhab.

His teachings were not complicated: they demanded a return to a pure and harsh faith of the kind once practiced by Prophet Mohammed and his early companions. Outraged by the loose ways and European influences that had begun to corrupt the lands of Islam, Ibn Abdel Wahhab rejected the vast wealth of culture and sophisticated philosophy accumulated by the Muslim world in the previous thousand years as a harmful and heretical innovation, *bidaa*.

With its stress on simplicity and rejection of luxuries such as tobacco, gold jewelry for men, silk clothes, music, and dancing, the Wahhabi idea stoked Bedouin pride. After all, it proclaimed the superiority of their simple desert customs over the confusing ways of uppity townsfolk in cities like Mecca or Basra.

To Wahhabi preachers spreading this new gospel, a holy war of jihad was the only possible attitude toward Christian powers that already were encroaching upon Muslim lands. Miscreant Shiites—adepts of the smaller of the two main branches of Islam that dominates Iran, south Iraq, and parts of Arabia's Gulf coast—were also treated as legitimate prey, subject to conversion or extermination.

Like most Muslims worldwide, Wahhabis belong to the Sunni community that parted ways with the Shiites in the early days of Islam because of a succession dispute. After Prophet Mohammed's death in 632 the future Shiites demanded that leadership of the Muslim world be inherited by his son-in-law Ali, and then by the Prophet's grandsons Hassan and Hussain. The future Sunnis refused, installing in power other companions of the Prophet. Resulting wars caused a theological schism that lasts until this day.

Shiite towns on the edges of the Arabian deserts weren't the only quarry of Wahhabi raiders. Fellow Sunnis, too, were considered infidels in disguise—unless they embraced all the rigors of the only true faith, precisely as interpreted by Ibn Abdel Wahhab.

This fiery ideology provided a powerful economic incentive for joining the new sect. For Ibn Abdel Wahhab's Bedouin converts, pillaging non-Wahhabi neighbors stopped being simple banditry: it turned into doing God's work.

Ibn Abdel Wahhab's early supporter was a tribal sheikh named Mohammed al Saud from the central Arabian highlands of the Nejd. The combination of al Saud's military prowess and Wahhabi religious zeal quickly turned this new Saudi state into a major power in the Arabian Peninsula. Mohammed al Saud's heirs even dared to challenge the mighty Ottoman Empire, whose Istanbul-based sultan held the title of Caliph of all Muslims and considered himself Arabia's rightful suzerain.

In the year 1802, a terrifying force of al Saud's camel-riding Wahhabi warriors emerged from the desert outside the city of Karbala in Ottoman-ruled Iraq. A center of Shiite learning and pilgrimage centered around the gold-domed tomb of Prophet Mohammed's grandson Hussain, Karbala was a city of incredible treasures that had been ferried there over the centuries by the faithful from Persia, India, and beyond. It was also poorly defended.

As they set Karbala's mosques and academies ablaze, the Wahhabi invaders showed no mercy for the despised Shiites. According to a contemporary account, some four thousand of Karbala's citizens perished. The Bedouin invaders had a particular predilection for disemboweling pregnant women and leaving their fetuses atop bleeding corpses. Four thousand camels were reportedly needed to carry the plunder back into the barren badlands of the Nejd.

The following year, it was Mecca's turn. Well aware of the wholesale slaughter in Karbala, the Meccans chose to surrender without a fight. The Wahhabis promptly forbade smoking of tobacco, burning all pipes on a main square. In line with their distaste for opulent graves, they also destroyed the mausoleums that had been built over the tombs of prominent Muslims. When they seized Medina shortly thereafter, the Wahhabis engaged in another round of grave-smashing, going as far as desecrating Prophet Mohammed's own tomb.

It wasn't until 1813 that an Egyptian expeditionary corps recaptured Mecca from al Saud's Wahhabis on behalf of the Ottoman Empire. It took the Egyptians another five years of war to seize and raze al Saud's capital city of Dirraiya, just outside what is now Riyadh. The defeated Saudi monarch was brought in a cage to Istanbul and beheaded in front of St. Sophia amid fireworks and a public celebration.

When the twentieth century began, few people outside Arabia remembered al Saud. The family's elders lived as exiles in Kuwait, their ancestral lands of the Nejd governed by rival tribes. In the Hejaz coastal region that encompasses Mecca and Medina, the Hashemite dynasty that would later provide the kings of Jordan and Iraq was firmly in control.

Then, in January 1902, a young al Saud chieftain named Abdelaziz led a small raiding party to the desert near Riyadh. The raiders numbered only six dozen men. At night, they climbed above an unrepaired wall and found refuge in an old supporter's home. Patiently, they waited for the local governor to emerge from Riyadh's mud fort and head for the morning prayer in the town mosque. Once the fort's heavy wooden gate finally opened and the governor stepped outside, Abdelaziz's men struck without pity.

A shot fired by Abdelaziz himself felled the governor. A spear launched at the same time by another raider lodged in the gate, its tip still visible there. The hapless garrison was put to the sword. Riyadh, where many townsfolk entertained fond memories about al Saud's past glory, and about the wealth once brought by raiding neighboring lands, was under Saudi rule again. A new empire began.

News of al Saud's stunning victory in Riyadh spread through Arabia like wildfire. In skirmish after skirmish, Abdelaziz defeated nearby

tribes and gained authority across much of the Nejd, just as his ancestors had done more than a century earlier.

Conquered tribes were forced to adopt the Wahhabi way of Islam,
with bearded instructors making sure that the five daily prayer times
were strictly observed and that no music or smoking occurred in al
Saud's new domains. Al Saud's proselytizers deeply resented the very
appellation of Wahhabis—a label that suggested they didn't quite belong to mainstream Sunni Islam. Far from considering themselves a separate sect, the Wahhabi clerics insisted that they merely enforced strict
obedience of the *tawheed*—uncompromising monotheism—that had
been commanded by Prophet Mohammed since the dawn of Islam.

There was one problem to overcome: rigorous discharge of Islamic
rituals requires ablutions before prayers and is therefore ill suited for a
nomadic lifestyle in the waterless desert. Al Saud and the Wahhabi
clergy came up with a piece of social engineering that combined political control with religious indoctrination. They encouraged—and occasionally forced—the Bedouin of the Nejd to forgo their roamings and
to settle once and for all in the new oasis communities based on strict
Wahhabi rules. To highlight the parallel with Prophet Mohammed's
abandonment of pagan Mecca on his *hijra*, or migration, to Medina,
these utopian settlements were also called *hijras.* The men who settled
there swore an oath to one another and adopted the name Ikhwan—
brothers—that would soon instill horror all over Arabia.

The Ikhwan knew little about farming and had a hard time sustaining themselves with the meager crops that could sprout from the *hijras'*
dry land. But they were very proficient in warfare—and, like most neophytes, were powered by infinite zeal. They cut short their robes and
often painted their beards with red henna. Faithful to the bigoted Wahhabi view that considered other Muslims as infidels, the Ikhwan refused
to answer greetings by those who were not fellow brothers, let alone
Christians.

This fanaticism turned the Ikhwan into the shock troops of al Saud's
conquests. Moving swiftly across the Arabian Peninsula, they seized town
after town in a war of expansion that lasted decades. By 1913, the pre-

dominantly Shiite Gulf coast, where giant oil riches remained undiscovered, had fallen to al Saud. In 1924, after failing to capture the Jordanian capital city Amman, the Ikhwan battled their way into the town of Taef, perched atop a mountain escarpment near Mecca. The slaughter was brutal. Some four hundred Taef citizens were bludgeoned by the Ikhwan, who—just as the Wahhabi raiders had in Karbala a century earlier—enjoyed slicing open pregnant women's wombs. Showing contempt for Taef's urban luxuries, the Ikhwan smashed mirrors and ripped out window frames, using the wood for campfires. Mecca surrendered later in the year, after Abdelaziz promised the Meccans that the Ikhwan would not be allowed to plunder their city.

By the late 1920s, Abdelaziz had secured his rule over most of the Arabian Peninsula, becoming the absolute ruler of a country as large as the United States east of the Mississippi. The Ikhwan Frankenstein ran out of room to loot and ransack. Iraq, Jordan, Kuwait, and smaller Gulf sheikdoms on the new kingdom's borders were now protected by Britain, and King Abdelaziz could not afford a major war with what was still a mighty empire on which the sun never set. He also wanted to be recognized as the legitimate custodian of Mecca and Medina by the entire Muslim world—and this meant that the Ikhwan could no longer be allowed to harass non-Wahhabi pilgrims to the holy sites.

The Ikhwan, on their part, were already incensed by al Saud's decision to spare the unrepentant Shiites of the eastern coast. King Abdelaziz's new demand to stop the jihad against the heretics and infidels was seen in Ikhwan encampments as a blatant betrayal of God's word. In a final insult, the king began introducing devil's inventions never seen in Arabia before—the telegraph, the telephone, the radio, and the car. The Ikhwans' *hijras*, fat with fresh booty no more, were boiling with discontent.

Defying the king in 1927, the Ikhwan attacked British-ruled Iraq and then tried to storm the prosperous port of Kuwait, also under Britain's tutelage. Soon the Wahhabi warriors felt the pain of another devil's invention—the airplane. With King Abdelaziz's agreement, Britain's Royal Air Force flew bombing sorties against Ikhwan camps and the *hijras*. Hundreds of men, women, and children were killed, strafed from the air.

In March 1929, the weakened Ikhwan faced al Saud's loyalist troops for a decisive battle near the wells of the Nejdi oasis of Sbala. As King Abdelaziz's sons led royal detachments, the two armies—mounted on horses and camels—galloped toward each other under the cries of *"Allahu Akbar."* The Ikhwan were commanded by two tribal leaders of legendary authority, Faisal al Duwaish and Sultan al Bijad.

Luck was on al Saud's side: in the first moments of fighting, Duwaish was gravely wounded in the stomach. Demoralized, his kinsmen began a retreat that quickly turned into a rout. Minutes later, their ranks cut down by al Saud's heavy machine guns, Bijad and fellow Uteybi tribesmen also abandoned the field. By the end of that year, the last pockets of the Ikhwan movement were destroyed in the Nejd, the Ikhwan's arms had been confiscated, and both Duwaish and Bijad languished in jail, where they quickly died.

In the gutted *hijras*, many Ikhwan families found themselves orphaned by the fighting, and deeply shocked by the sudden collapse of their world. Among the hardest hit was the small *hijra* of Sajir north of Riyadh, peopled by many survivors of the great battle of Sbala. One of the veterans nursing grievances there was Mohammed bin Seif al Uteybi, who had fought side by side with the great chief Bijad and who fondly remembered the legendary sheikh's final words: "Never give up." Seven years after the rout at Sbala, Mohammed celebrated the birth of a son. The baby seemed to grimace a lot, and so the father decided to name him "the scowler."

In Arabic, the name was Juhayman.

TWO

By the time Juhayman al Uteybi became old enough to start growing a beard, as every good Muslim should do, the huge country assembled by King Abdelaziz was barely recognizable. A famine-prone backwater for centuries, Saudi Arabia was suddenly thrust into global limelight and unimagined wealth. The reason: a discovery that the kingdom sat atop one-quarter of the world's irreplaceable and increasingly precious commodity, oil.

American explorers tapped the first oil well in eastern Saudi Arabia in 1938. Seven years later, recognizing the kingdom's strategic importance, President Franklin Delano Roosevelt dined with King Abdelaziz aboard the USS *Quincy* in Egypt's Great Bitter Lake, bestowing on the elderly monarch the gift of a spare wheelchair and sealing a lasting strategic alliance between the two countries. Aramco, the Arabian American Oil Company, then under complete American ownership, became the monopoly operator of the Saudi oil industry.

Soon, thousands of American oil experts, construction engineers—

and military men—started pouring into the kingdom, building the first modern roads, power lines, and airfields. Though these Western infidels were usually sheltered from Saudi eyes, living inside walled compounds, their very presence ran against the core of Wahhabi teachings and was perceived as an affront by many religious luminaries.

One of the more virulent early protesters against American penetration was an up-and-coming scholar named Abdelaziz Bin Baz. In a fiery fatwa that he signed in the 1940s and that earned him the admiration of surviving Ikhwan, Bin Baz spelled out the same objections against Western presence in Saudi Arabia that al Qaeda militants are voicing today.

Blind since his teenage years, Bin Baz was already greatly respected for his intricate knowledge of Prophet Mohammed's sayings, the hadith—a fundamental source of Islamic law. And the hadith, Bin Baz said, extended the traditional ban on infidel presence in Mecca and Medina to the entire Arabian Peninsula.

"It is illicit to employ a non-Muslim servant, whether male or female, or a non-Muslim driver, or a non-Muslim worker in the Arabian Gulf, for the Prophet . . . commanded that all Jews and Christians be expelled, and only Muslims remain," Bin Baz wrote. "The presence of infidels, male or female, poses a danger to Muslims, their beliefs, their morality, and their children's education."

Offended by the fatwa's bluntness, King Abdelaziz, who had grown to appreciate the income provided by American oilmen, jailed Bin Baz for daring to oppose royal policy. Then the monarch impressed on the cleric that such public dissent could undermine the Islamic legitimacy of al Saud's Wahhabi state, opening the floodgates to the far worse evils of Communism and secularism. Bin Baz learned the lesson: in a lengthy career that took him to the pinnacle of the Saudi religious establishment, he would always temper his criticism of modernization by backing the Saudi regime in its times of adversity.

Saudi Arabia's founder, King Abdelaziz, died in 1953, leaving behind scores of sons who would take turns as his successors. These were precarious years: fellow monarchies on Saudi Arabia's doorstep collapsed one after another in bloody revolutions, swept away by the nationalist fervor that followed the Arab armies' humiliating defeat by the nascent Israeli state in Palestine. Egypt's king was ousted in a 1952 coup that brought the revolutionary dictator Gamal Abdel Nasser to power. Iraq's king and his family were slaughtered in 1958. Yemen's ancient monarchy collapsed in 1962.

Nasser's ideas of secular Arab nationalism, which viewed Saudi Arabia as a feudal relic that should dissolve into a single pan-Arab state sharing oil riches equally among all its citizens, presented a mortal danger to al Saud. There was only one viable alternative to this pan-Arab dream—the idea of a global Islamic nation, the *ummah*.

King Faisal, the fruit of a marriage between King Abdelaziz and a woman descended from the great Ibn Abdel Wahhab, became an eloquent champion of this pan-Islamic ideology. He rejected talk of unity among all Arabs—many of whom, after all, were inferior Christians—as ungodly. Wouldn't it make more sense, he argued, to seek an alliance sanctified by a shared faith and embracing all Muslims, be they Arabs or Turks, Nigerians or Malays?

This stress on Islamic identity permitted Saudi Arabia to claim a global leadership role. A marginal player in Arab politics at the time, the kingdom couldn't compete with the bustling centers of modern Arab culture in Cairo, Beirut, or Baghdad. But Saudi Arabia was unquestionably the birthplace of Islam, and the only nation where Islamic law still reigned supreme. The royal family's control over Mecca and Medina, Islam's two holiest sites, allowed it to influence how the faith itself was practiced around the world.

The advent of commercial air travel attracted ever-growing numbers of pilgrims to these two shrines. The Grand Mosque in Mecca underwent expensive enlargement and renovation, courtesy of the royal family's loyal servant and trusted adviser, a construction magnate named Mohammed Bin Laden. Gaudy new colonnades, marble domes, and prayer halls lined with artificial stone replaced much of the ancient structure. Between 1956 and the late 1970s, the Grand Mosque expanded sixfold in size, growing to occupy 180,850 square meters, or almost forty-five acres. Historic neighborhoods in the vicinity were torn down without mercy to make room for concrete hotels, public latrines, and asphalted parking lots necessary to handle the pilgrim traffic. In a sign of royal gratitude, key thoroughfares in Jeddah and Mecca were called Bin Laden Street; they carry this name even today.

As part of his pan-Islamic outreach, King Faisal also invited into the kingdom thousands of members of the Muslim Brotherhood, the secretive fundamentalist organization that preached the destruction of secular Arab regimes. The Brotherhood, whose armed "Secret Apparatus" had unsuccessfully tried to assassinate Nasser, was outlawed and persecuted in Egypt and Syria; its chief ideologue, Sayyid Qutb, still revered by Islamic radicals worldwide, had been hanged in Cairo.

By contrast, Qutb's brother Mohammed was welcomed with open arms in Saudi Arabia, which awarded him and other Brotherhood exiles plum teaching jobs in the kingdom's new universities. Among their students were many of Juhayman's future aides—as well as Mohammed Bin Laden's young son, Osama.

King Faisal's international prominence as a defender of Islamic causes provided him the legitimacy to remove some of the more anachronistic Wahhabi strictures at home, dragging a reluctant and mostly illiterate Saudi Arabia closer to modernity. Shunting aside the guardians of Wahhabi orthodoxy, Faisal outlawed slavery in 1962. The following year, he ignored street protests and went ahead with his plans to introduce education for women. And, in a 1965 move that ended up costing him his life, Faisal created Saudi television.

These first TV broadcasts sparked bloody riots in Riyadh by religious conservatives who contended that the satanic innovation violated Islamic prohibitions against graven images. The king's own nephew took part in these protests and was subsequently killed in a shootout with police.

Despite their private misgivings about Faisal's reforms, leading Wahhabi clerics couldn't openly challenge the king. The reason was an enormous surge in Faisal's popularity following the 1973 Israeli-Arab war. Outraged by the U.S. airlift of weapons to the Jewish state, which had seemed about to buckle under a surprise assault by Egypt and Syria, King Faisal orchestrated that year an Arab oil embargo against America and Israel's European allies. This was an immensely profitable initiative. As the price of crude soared, the kingdom's oil revenues—at some $1.2 billion in 1970—shot up to $22.5 billion in 1974, and then kept climbing to nearly $100 billion a year at the end of the decade.

This flood of money transformed Saudi lifestyles virtually overnight. Housing developments mushroomed in the kingdom's dusty main cities, drawing in Bedouins who had never seen a gas stove or a toilet bowl and who often moved into new apartments with their livestock. Hospitals and schools sprouted in remote towns, cars rather than camels became the main method of transport, and countless government jobs opened up for the kingdom's proud citizens. A classified CIA intelligence assessment opined: "The Saudis are flush and have few rational options to dispose of their income."

Since hardly any Saudis were sufficiently qualified—or disciplined—for private-sector employment, the already sizable infidel community had to be expanded as well. A myriad of laborers disembarked from the Third World: Muslim Pakistanis, Egyptians, and Turks, but also non-Muslim Indians, Koreans, and Filipinos. By the late 1970s, these foreigners were visible in every corner of the kingdom, accounting for a stunning half of the country's labor force and one-third of its six million inhabitants.

In March 1975, King Faisal—at the zenith of his popularity—prepared to welcome a Kuwaiti delegation that arrived to pay its respects. Hidden among the Kuwaitis in Faisal's Riyadh palace that day was a nephew, the brother of the prince who had been killed following the 1965 television riots. When his turn came for a customary kiss on the monarch's nose, the nephew extracted a pistol from the folds of his robe and unloaded it in King Faisal's head. Declared deranged, the assassin was promptly beheaded.

Replacing the late king Faisal on the throne was his brother, King

Khaled. A simple man with little formal education, Khaled was already stricken by debilitating illnesses and, by most accounts, appeared far more interested in his camel farm than the affairs of the state. Real power for more than two decades to come dropped into the lap of another sibling—the crown prince, and later king, Fahd.

THREE

Prosperity generated under King Faisal took a long time to reach out-of-the-way Bedouin settlements like Juhayman's former *hijra* of Sajir. For the young men who lived in this jumble of mud houses set on a dry gravelly plain, far away from the booming oil fields, few opportunities existed outside the ancient business of herding camels and growing dates. There was one exception, however: the Saudi National Guard.

A praetorian force of the Saudi regime, the Guard existed to protect al Saud from internal unrest. In the age of military coups, this meant above all counterbalancing the regular military. The Saudi Army and Air Force were staffed by ambitious young officers from cosmopolitan coastal cities who often nurtured Arab nationalist and socialist ideas. The Guard—which since its early days absorbed the defeated Ikhwan—was immune to such alien thoughts. The force was infused with Islamic orthodoxy and always preferred to recruit among the conservative tribesmen of the Nejd. Juhayman enrolled at the age of nineteen.

The Guard's role as a foiler of coups meant that it had to operate outside the Ministry of Defense and the normal military chain of command. It reported directly to Prince Abdullah, who was respected by the Bedouins because of his desert upbringing and matrilineal descent from one of the mightiest tribes of the Nejd, the Shammar. Still a direct commander of the National Guard, Abdullah succeeded King Fahd in 2005 and reigns in Saudi Arabia today.

When Juhayman was a Guardsman, service in the force—also known then as the White Army because its men wore the traditional white Arab robes and bandoliers across the chest instead of khaki uniforms—was hardly an arduous task. While some Guardsmen belonged to modern mechanized units, a large proportion of the men—including Juhayman—collected their pay for occasional soldiering in a part-time tribal militia that cared little about military discipline. The militia units were organized based on the tribal origins of the troops, and training was haphazard when it occurred at all; many of the Guardsmen, who ranged from teenagers to white-haired elders, never bothered to show up when summoned for exercises.

For those willing to work the system, the Guard offered avenues of rapid social advancement. The example was set by members of Juhayman's immediate family. The brother of Juhayman's first wife, a court poet who penned flowery Bedouin-style odes to the senior princes, made a brilliant career in the force, earning general's crossed swords on his shoulder straps; he can still be seen orating paeans on Saudi TV.

Juhayman himself never showed such ambition. Raised on memories of the Ikhwan defeat at the battle of Sbala, he did not forgive al Saud the indignities that had been inflicted on his kin. Like most orthodox Wahhabis, Juhayman did not smoke, considering tobacco consumption a sin. But his disgust with the Saudi state and its laws outweighed such qualms: he supplemented his modest Guard pay by dabbling in the lucrative trade of smuggling cheap cigarettes from Kuwait.

Like many fellow Bedouins, who learn how to handle firearms from childhood, Juhayman was a good marksman. He also nurtured ties with numerous cousins, relatives, and friends dispersed throughout the force and other Saudi security agencies. But in his eighteen-year Guard career, he never rose above the rank of corporal, and the most responsible assignment he ever received was driving a water truck.

What Juhayman picked up in the Guard, however, was exposure to Saudi Arabia's new religious education, on the rise thanks to the oil boom and King Faisal's import of Muslim Brotherhood cadres from Egypt and Syria. At first, Juhayman—whose Guard job afforded him plenty of free time—attended lectures on Islam in Mecca, with clerics like Sheikh Mohammed Ibn Subeil, the imam of the Grand Mosque, among his tutors. After retiring from the service in 1973, he settled in a small white-washed home in a poor neighborhood of Medina, where lectures by the blind cleric Bin Baz now drew enraptured crowds at the new Islamic University.

By then, true to the opinions he had aired in the 1940s, Bin Baz towered as the leading critic of the dizzying pace of Saudi Arabia's modernization. The liberal ideas brought home by thousands of Saudis who returned from travel abroad, new shopping malls, and—albeit heavily edited—American soap operas that were now broadcast on TV simply outraged a scholar who still insisted that the Earth was flat.

The rot seemed to come from above. Unlike the pious King Faisal, the country's new de facto ruler, Crown Prince Fahd, was gaining a reputation as a pro-American playboy. Following Fahd's example, slews of lesser princes—and these now numbered in the thousands—had taken to escaping Wahhabi restrictions in the French Riviera or Spain's Costa del Sol, where stories proliferated about their gambling, drinking, and whoring exploits.

Bin Baz didn't shy away from raising his voice in defense of tradition. He boldly attacked the government practice of displaying royal portraits on official buildings. "It is not permissible to hang pictures on a wall . . . Instead, it is compulsory to obliterate these pictures. Hanging

a picture may lead to exalting or worshipping it, particularly if the picture is that of a King," Bin Baz ruled in one decree.

Cigarettes—legally sold in the kingdom—were as illicit as pork and
alcohol, he ruled in another. Barber shops were supposed to be prohibited too, Bin Baz decreed. Even clapping hands was forbidden behavior
because it emulated Western ways.

The cleric reserved his harshest vitriol for the budding emancipation
of Saudi women. They had just begun to emerge from age-old seclu-
sion and were appearing in the workplace, some even becoming news-
casters on government-run TV. Though Bin Baz, being blind, couldn't
watch TV news, he was infuriated by such lassitude. In one ruling, he
lashed out at a proposal in one of the newspapers that women teachers
be allowed to work in boys' elementary schools. "This suggestion has
been inspired by Satan or some of his deputies . . . and is pleasing to
our enemies and the enemies of Islam," Bin Baz struck with his usual
bluntness. "This is because, when a boy reaches ten years old, he is considered an adolescent. He naturally becomes inclined toward women.
Someone like him can even get married and do what men do."

Bin Baz's protests about such ghastly developments seemed to fall
on deaf ears. While treating the cleric with deference, the Saudi government felt secure enough to ignore his advice. So, trying to force
change from below, Bin Baz used his position as the dean of Medina's
Islamic University to launch a new missionary movement that would
reinvigorate Wahhabi devotion across the kingdom. The movement was
called Dawa Salafiya al Muhtasiba—a name best rendered in English as
"Islamic outreach that follows the ways of the Prophet's companions,
and that is carried out with charitable goals."

Supervised by Bin Baz and other senior clerics, most of whom were
on the payroll of the state, this missionary network rapidly spread
throughout the country. And, in recruitment to the true path of God, it
produced wonders of showmanship.

One way of saving impressionable souls at the time was to offer
poor youngsters a cheap desert weekend. For two days, participants
would listen to religious lectures in the stifling heat, fed only dry flat-

bread flavored with vinegar. "Pray to Allah, and he will deliver," they would be urged, again and again. Then, at the end of interminable sessions of prayer, a "miracle" from God would be arranged to reward the believers for their strengthened faith. Suddenly, exhausted participants would stumble upon a surprise spread of steaming lamb, saffron rice, and sour yogurt, inexplicably laid out for them in the middle of the desert. "It's Allah's gift!" a teacher would proclaim. Allah was usually so thoughtful as to throw in enough ice-cold Pepsi for everyone. (Coke, blacklisted in most of the Arab world at the time for selling its beverages in Israel, was not an option.)

Juhayman, with his desert upbringing and charismatic demeanor, proved a natural for such indoctrination trips. Soon, he rose in Dawa al Muhtasiba's hierarchy, becoming the main coordinator for the movement's outings and traveling to recruit allies across the country. At the hajj of 1976, he was already an established authority, supervising the camp for Dawa al Muhtasiba's adepts making a pilgrimage to the Grand Mosque. A young student, Nasser al Hozeimi, was introduced to Juhayman in Mecca that year. As befitted a true leader, Juhayman could only be met after lengthy preparations where the neophytes would learn about the man's greatness. When the time came, Hozeimi was shepherded by Juhayman's aides into the meeting room. He immediately sensed the former corporal's magnetism. "Why don't you go with us for outreach work?" Juhayman asked, scrutinizing the newcomer. Hozeimi, a diminutive olive-skinned man, meekly nodded in agreement, awed by the attention bestowed on him. Soon, like hundreds of fellow missionaries, he started traveling from one desert settlement to another, spreading God's word.

As the new movement flourished, Bin Baz left the Islamic University of Medina and moved to the capital Riyadh, gaining nationwide authority at the helm of the Department of Scientific Research and Guidance. This innocuous-sounding clerical body held enormous power: it was in charge of interpreting Islamic law, the only law valid in the country, and of delivering fatwas, the binding religious opinions on all facets of life in the kingdom. In Saudi Arabia, where the regime's very legitimacy is based on its Islamic credentials, Bin Baz's new position as chairman of the department carried a senior cabinet minister's rank. Every week from then on, the blind cleric would appear on TV solemnly sitting next to the king and discussing affairs of the state in an opulent palace room, a visible proof that men of the only true faith remained four-square behind al Saud.

In providing such a religious shield to the ruling family, Bin Baz and the other leading ulema—scholars of Islam—embodied a contradiction that keeps exploding in Saudi Arabia again and again. After all, the Wahhabi clerics never moderated the original ideology that had prompted the bands of Ikhwan to slaughter and pillage across the peninsula in the 1920s. Hatred of non-Muslims and all signs of social change was still taught in the fancy air-conditioned new Islamic universities of Riyadh and Medina just as it had been drilled into pupils' brains in the old baked-mud madrassas of the desert half a century earlier.

But, taking to heart a lesson that King Abdelaziz had imparted on Bin Baz back in the 1940s, the senior ulema made sure that theory and practice stayed apart: their rejection of modern ways never crossed the line into open opposition to the royal family. It was fine to criticize proposed reforms, but not the established government. Despite the reports of their drinking and gambling in Europe, the Saudi royals were still seen by these ulema as the only bulwark of Islam in an increasingly secular world; opposing the established rulers, official Wahhabi clerics taught, was a cardinal sin.

Juhayman—who, unlike the ulema, didn't receive a fat government salary—was unwilling to be so forgiving. Molded by Bin Baz's teachings of what a true Islamic society should be, he couldn't understand the growing gap between Islamic theory and Saudi reality without questioning the very foundation of the regime. In Medina, he witnessed the coddling that Muslim Brotherhood exiles, who openly denounced the Egyptian and Syrian governments as infidel, received in the Saudi kingdom. But if it was religiously permissible for the Egyptians to oppose their authorities because they weren't sufficiently Muslim, why did the ulema deny such a right to the Saudis?

Wasn't it clear, Juhayman wondered, that the ubiquitous royal portraits—still displayed everywhere in spite of Bin Baz's fatwa—were a sign of un-Islamic behavior that positively veered into idolatry? The king's bearded likeness even graced the Saudi currency, the riyal!

By 1977, as Juhayman debated this quandary with sympathetic clerics in Medina and Riyadh, his allegiance to Bin Baz and the establishment ulema began to erode. Soon, he started to pen a series of treatises that would lead hundreds of followers to a deadly showdown in the Grand Mosque and inspire future generations of jihadis.

Brimming with commonsense irony, these epistles highlighted the contradictions of the Saudi state, ridiculing its Islamic credentials at a time when, as Juhayman noted, "worship of the riyal" took hold of the land and imported movies and books poisoned young minds.

Even the official body that enforced Islamic propriety and had long made liberals chafe, the Committee to Promote Virtue and Prevent Vice, was nothing but a sham, Juhayman argued. "What is the meaning of [the committee] when we have cinemas, clubs and art shows?" he asked. "What is the meaning of spending money on both things? Isn't that a comedy? A way of satisfying the lustful while deceiving the great sheikhs?"

There was simply no way to reconcile Islam's innate superiority with the surging numbers of foreigners and Saudi Arabia's shameful dependence on America and other Western nations. "How is it possible to declare jihad against the states of the infidels when we have ambassadors in their countries and they have in ours ambassadors, experts and professors?" Juhayman wondered. "We should not be deceived by the ornaments. How can we propagate Islam when our professors are Christians? Is it possible to raise the flag of jihad when the banner of Christianity is flapping next to the banner of the faith of One God [Islam]?"

He was especially upset by the insufficiently harsh treatment reserved for Saudi Shiites. In the radical Wahhabi worldview, the Shiites are apostate polytheists because they revere Ali and Hussain, the Prophet's son-in-law and grandson, in the same way Christians worship Jesus alongside God the Father.

Back at the dawn of the Saudi state, the leading ulema of Riyadh issued a fatwa asking King Abdelaziz to destroy Shiite mosques and to force these heretics to adopt Sunni Wahhabi Islam on pain of expulsion. But, for reasons of realpolitik, this draconian ruling has never been implemented. Despite pressure from the Ikhwan in the 1920s, Shiite clergy were allowed to operate on the country's Gulf coast and Saudi authorities, while discriminating against the Shiites, considered them fellow Muslims.

"This country calls itself the state of One God!" Juhayman scoffed. "But then . . . it accepts the Shiites to be called Muslims, and fights those who disagree with this, and opposes those who combat the heretical worshippers of Ali and Hussain!"

As Juhayman attracted a following of disaffected young students, his vociferous views started to draw unwelcome attention. Sometime in 1977, the question of Juhayman appeared on the agenda of a large meeting of senior clerics in Medina. Juhayman himself was not present at the encounter, held in a large reception room with bare walls. But his opinions were defended by supportive scholars such as Muqbil al Wadii, a Yemeni preacher who would later become a spiritual guide of al Qaeda fighters in his homeland. On the opposing side were Bin Baz's representative in the city and several Islamic judges and professors from the Islamic University.

The meeting, watered by multiple cups of sweet tea and fruit juice, proved acrimonious. Whenever establishment clerics chastised Juhayman's invective, defenders pointed out that the retired National Guard corporal simply repeated the teachings of revered Wahhabi scholars and applied them to current Saudi conditions. "What they have said, Juhayman says," argued Wadii. After all, hatred of infidels and Shiites and the prohibition of images were all to be found right there in the holy books. One just had to read the fatwas of Bin Baz himself!

Finally, one of the senior clerics agreed that, theologically, there was little fault with Juhayman's thought. The issue was simple common sense at the time of rising Communist threat. "Communism would destroy Islam, and al Saud are much better than the rest," he explained.

At the end of the meeting, another of the official clerics issued a warning for Juhayman: "The state," he said, "has opened its eyes, and it is watching you."

For Juhayman and his hard-core allies, this exchange marked a formal break with the official guardians of Islam. The learned ulema, he concluded, had betrayed the faith, siding for reasons of political expediency with a regime they clearly knew to be violating Islamic rules. "Those who really know the Sunna [Prophet Mohammed's teachings and actions] are few, and one of them is Bin Baz," Juhayman wrote. "But he is now just an administrative employee. [The al Saud] take from him only what suits them. If he disagrees with them, they will have no problem in disagreeing with what he says."

Soon Juhayman openly crossed the line into sedition, proclaiming Saudi Arabia's monarchy itself to be illicit. "You should know that a ruler and leader of Muslims should satisfy three conditions: be a Muslim, be a member of [Prophet Mohammed's tribe of] al Quraysh and be a man who applies the religion," Juhayman wrote, pointing out that al Saud, being not of Quraysh descent, did not qualify on at least two counts.

Rulers of other Muslim lands were equally illegitimate, Juhayman added, challenging the respected ulema to oppose these usurpers: "Have you condemned evildoers in public? Such a testimony has to be obvious and not hidden in your hearts. Have you told the presidents, emirs, ministers and kings that they contradict the faith? Have you warned the people, as Prophet Mohammed has warned, not to work as policemen, tax collectors and servants for those who befriend the evildoers?"

Then, with unnerving foresight, Juhayman pondered his own fate. His father and other Ikhwan, he recalled, had been labeled "kharijites" by al Saud. The term, which means a deviant from religion, was originally used to name the radical Kharijite sect whose adepts assassinated Prophet Mohammed's son-in-law Ali in the year 661.

In modern Saudi Arabia, Juhayman noted, a scholar of Islam had three options: to agree with al Saud, to keep silent, or to oppose the regime. He himself had no intention of taking the first two options, Juhayman wrote, and then concluded: "If you disagree with them, they will kill you, and then they will call you a kharijite."

FOUR

Though estranged from Bin Baz and the senior Saudi ulema, Juhayman found plenty of eager recruits among a younger generation. Displaced by the country's breakneck modernization, many of these men hailed from similar Bedouin backgrounds and, lured by the post-1973 economic boom, flocked from the deserts to the shining lights of Riyadh.

Weaving a network among fellow Uteybi tribesmen, National Guard veterans, and students of Islam, Juhayman assembled a secretive organization that numbered hundreds of members. This group of starry-eyed Muslim idealists sought to follow God's word to the letter, adopting short-cut robes, shunning material luxuries, and forswearing any use of photographs and other graven images. Eerily similar to hippies in the West, they let their hair and beards grow unchecked. They blotted out with black ink the king's portraits on the banknotes that passed through their hands. Considering the Saudi state to be illegitimate, they also destroyed their government-issue identity cards, which are mandatory to carry in the kingdom. Among the Saudis, none had passports for travel abroad.

Though many adepts had their own homes, Juhayman established communal-style quarters in cities such as Riyadh, Medina, and Mecca. There, the movement's men could eat and sleep on the cheap, praying and studying Islamic religion together.

Proselytizing, preferably away from the ears of the senior ulema, remained the main goal. Hozeimi, the youngster who had met Juhayman during the 1976 hajj in Mecca, rose through the ranks of the group as he continued crisscrossing the country and spreading the former corporal's teachings.

University campuses in Medina, Mecca, and Riyadh at the time overflowed with foreign students, brought to Saudi Arabia on generous government stipends and indoctrinated in the spirit of Wahhabi Islam. Muslim Brotherhood sympathizers abounded among Egyptians and Syrians. They, like many young Yemenis and Kuwaitis, eagerly embraced Juhayman's creed.

The Saudi kingdom—which would end up overseeing a large share of Islamic activities in the United States—in those years also began its outreach to the American Muslim community, then almost exclusively black.

The Nation of Islam, a movement that mixed vaguely Islamic precepts with black racism, had been started in 1930 by a Detroit preacher who went by the name Master W. Fard Muhammad. That group, seen as heretical by mainstream Muslims, believed that the white race had been created by evil scientists and that American blacks should separate themselves from the rest of the country into a state of their own. (Ironically, Master Muhammad, of partial Polynesian descent, appears to have had no African blood himself; he was classified in U.S. law enforcement records as "Caucasian.")

In the 1960s, as America went through a paroxysm of racial violence, Malcolm X became national spokesman for the Nation of Islam. In 1964, he met an Egyptian-born Saudi representative in New York. On the man's urging, later that year Malcolm X traveled to Mecca for the hajj. This was a life-changing experience. Treated as a state guest by one of King Faisal's sons, Malcolm X—unaware that just two years earlier Africans had still been legally enslaved in the kingdom—was "rendered speechless and spell-bound" by Saudi Arabia. The kingdom was infused with "a spirit of unity and brotherhood that my experiences in America had led me to believe never could exist between the white and non-white," he wrote in his autobiography. Paving the way for tens of thousands of other American blacks, he abandoned the Nation of Islam for the mainstream Muslim faith, made even more appealing by anti-American feelings already prevalent in the Middle East. "The American passport," Malcolm X wrote, "signified the exact opposite of what Islam stands for."

In 1975, after the death of the Nation of Islam's leader, Elijah Muhammad, his son and successor, Wallace, also embraced Saudi-style Islamic orthodoxy. Hundreds of black radicals—including former Black Panthers—flocked to Saudi-funded Islamic academies in the United States, and in the kingdom itself. African American students in Mecca in 1978 and 1979 included such prominent converts as Imam Siraj Wahhaj, who thirteen years later would become the first Muslim clergyman to lead a prayer before the start of a session of the U.S. House of Representatives.

Some of these first-generation Muslims were easily swayed by Juhayman's radical ideas, joining his group. Several supplemented their income by teaching the militants the arts of karate and kung fu. Others brought with them even more useful martial skills of urban guerrilla warfare that they had learned in the ranks of the Black Panthers stateside.

In the Saudi universities, Juhayman managed to draw an especially devoted following on the campus of the Imam Mohammed bin Saud Islamic University of Riyadh. The school, which focuses on preparing clerics and religious judges, has long been the ground central of Wahhabi hardliners, many of them nostalgic for the Ikhwan.

There, Juhayman developed close ties with a Saudi student in his early twenties named Mohammed Abdullah al Qahtani. With an unusually fair skin, long straight hair, and honey-colored eyes, Mohammed Abdullah hailed from a small Bedouin settlement in the southern province of Asir, one of the poorest parts of Saudi Arabia and home to many of the hijackers who would participate in the September 11 attacks of 2001. Sensitive and shy, Mohammed Abdullah was given to dreamy silences and wrote passionate poetry in flowery classical Arabic. Unlike Juhayman, who had attended religious lectures without ever passing exams, Mohammed Abdullah was a full-time student who was nearing the completion of a four-year college degree.

Like many members of the new movement, Mohammed Abdullah had reasons to dislike the Saudi state. By one account, prior to enrolling in university he was employed as an administrative worker in a Riyadh hospital. Suspicion fell on Mohammed Abdullah when money disappeared from the hospital safe. Saudi police, whose main investigating technique tends to be torture, pulled the young man's fingernails until he confessed to the crime. He was cleared and released from jail only after the real culprit was accidentally caught with the stolen cash later.

Settling in Riyadh's conservative Manfuha neighborhood, an area of squat cinderblock houses peopled by many recent arrivals from the desert, Mohammed Abdullah often delivered sermons in the local Ruweil mosque. His two brothers, Sayid and Saad, were frequently in attendance. The young student seemed very special—something about the way he looked and talked made people think that the pale-skinned Mohammed Abdullah had been singled out by God. Neighbors agreed that he was destined to become a great man of Islam, and they often offered him food and gifts.

The mosque attracted crowds of youngsters eager for more religious education. Mohammed Abdullah, like other followers of Juhayman, charted a new path: he often refused to accept established clerics' religious rulings without first seeing the evidence. "But why is it so?" he frequently argued. "Where is it written in the hadith?"

The science of hadith, of course, is extremely complicated. There are thousands of hadith narratives recounting Prophet Mohammed's examples and words, all written down much later and grouped in four categories according to the reliability of the chain of narrators: genuine, fair, weak, and fabricated. It takes years of assiduous scholarship to navigate this maze—scholarship that Mohammed Abdullah, who now often disappeared in the library to research old hadith collections, simply didn't possess.

Establishment clerics have long discouraged such independent research. They felt that only the learned ulema could interpret hadith, placing every saying of the Prophet in its appropriate context. Turning to these primary sources without supervision was a challenge to authority, a step down the slippery slope.

By early 1978, as his movement gained momentum, Juhayman felt that he had to publish his own writings, reaching out to new audiences and making sure that his ideas were not being distorted. There was, of course, no hope that the tightly controlled Saudi presses would agree to print such inflammatory literature. Instead, Juhayman turned his sights north, to Kuwait.

Juhayman's representatives smuggled their teacher's manuscript across the porous desert border. There, they were introduced to the local publishing industry by a helpful Kuwaiti Muslim Brotherhood activist who would later become one of the emirate's most prominent Islamist politicians. *Al Qabas,* Kuwait's leading newspaper, asked for an astronomical sum. Other commercial printing presses refused to touch the material, fearful of jeopardizing their Saudi business relationships.

The only willing partner was a small press named Dar al Talia', or House of the Vanguard. This was no ordinary publisher—Dar al Talia' was affiliated with Iraqi-backed Saudi dissidents and propagated the nationalist ideology of Saddam Hussein's Baath Arab Socialist Party. The secularist and often Shiite militants of Dar al Talia' had virtually nothing in common with Juhayman's aggressive strain of Wahhabi-inspired Sunni fundamentalism. Except, of course, their hatred of the Saudi royal family. Acting on the principle that my enemy's enemy is my friend, Dar al Talia' sent back a message that it would publish Juhayman's work, charging only its own printing costs.

Soon a 170-page green and white booklet titled "The Seven Epistles" was being smuggled back into Saudi Arabia. Only four of the seven chapters—the ones with the most political content—were signed by Juhayman himself. One carried the name of Mohammed Abdullah. The authors of the two remaining chapters identified themselves only as "A Student of the Teacher." Saudi authorities—already alerted by some of Medina's official clerics about the rebellious nature of Juhayman's clandestine network—now had the incontrovertible proof. It was time to act.

In late spring of 1978, shortly after the illicit book rolled off the presses, Hozeimi, the young missionary, rested in Juhayman's modest home. The house, in the Hara Sharqiya neighborhood of Medina, did not possess such temptations as television or radio; an electric light bulb was the single concession to modernity. Women's quarters were strictly separated upstairs; even his closest friends did not know the names of Juhayman's wives, let alone ever engage them in conversation. As a precaution, a hidden back door was in place, to facilitate escape in times of trouble.

And trouble was at hand. One night, an agitated local post office worker knocked on the door. He was a member of Juhayman's Uteybi tribe, possibly a distant relative. Following Bedouin tribal codes of honor that require protection of fellow kinsmen from authority, he came with a warning. A telegram had just arrived, with government orders to arrest scores of men. Juhayman's name, the tribesman had noticed, was on the top of the list.

"Come with me," Juhayman ordered Hozeimi after hearing the news.

The youngster agreed without hesitation. Picking up a small bag, the two raced out through the back door.

After scrambling into a battered pickup truck, they sped off north to the desert, away from people and roads. For seven days, Juhayman used his Bedouin tracking skills to navigate by the stars, moving through the emptiness. The two fugitives fed themselves with a few dates and the meat of an antelope Juhayman had managed to shoot.

On the seventh day, the pickup arrived at an isolated hamlet, home of one of Juhayman's trusted men. Juhayman and Hozeimi stayed there for another five days while a messenger was dispatched to the oases north of Riyadh, in the Uteybis' tribal homeland near Sajir, to find out the precise details of the government crackdown.

The picture was gloomy. On the orders of Prince Nayef, the powerful minister of interior and a full brother of Crown Prince Fahd, some twenty-five of the most senior members of Juhayman's network had been arrested. The detainees included Mohammed Abdullah, the fair-skinned poet-student in Riyadh. The movement seemed all but crushed.

A sympathizer in the security services provided Juhayman with the list of all those who were still sought for arrest. After glancing at the paper, Juhayman summoned a tense Hozeimi: "Your name is not here. You have nothing to fear—go home to Riyadh."

In the following days, Juhayman used all his energies to reach the only man who could help—his former teacher, the blind cleric Bin Baz. As a supervisor of the Saudi judiciary and the interpreter of Sharia, or Islamic law, Bin Baz now possessed an authority that the royal family could hardly ignore, especially in this kind of affair.

Juhayman still had the ear of clerics in Medina and Riyadh who had defended him in the debate with the older ulema. Contacted by them, Bin Baz took interest in the case.

After a conversation with Prince Nayef, Bin Baz insisted on personally questioning the young poet Mohammed Abdullah and others among Juhayman's arrested followers. The investigation did not take long. From the standpoint of Wahhabi theology, Bin Baz could find no reason for punishing the detainees. True, the devout youngsters may have used intemperate language against al Saud, and against Bin Baz himself. But they seemed to have had the best of intentions in upholding public morals and spreading the true faith. All they wanted was to make the country more pious. What was the harm?

After a few days, Bin Baz recommended that all the detainees be released. His words usually carried great weight. One Saudi businessman witnessed this influence while sitting in Prince Nayef's office in that period. As the ministerial telephone rang, Prince Nayef picked up the heavy receiver. Suddenly he straightened his back and listened attentively, uttering, "Yes, sir, yes, sir" between ornate expressions of respect. The businessman thought that the interlocutor was King Khaled or Crown Prince Fahd but didn't dare to ask. Then, after carefully hanging up with both hands, Nayef punched a phone number and angrily rolled off the names of students at the Islamic University of Medina who had been detained by police. "I have just spoken with Sheikh Abdelaziz [Bin Baz]," Prince Nayef barked instructions to an aide. "You must free these men immediately."

Bin Baz's advice to Prince Nayef appears to have been followed with equal speed in the case of Juhayman's supporters. All the men were released forthwith, free to continue their work in the path of Allah. A year and a half later, chastened by the Grand Mosque debacle, Crown Prince Fahd recalled this decision with palpable regret. "We had earlier taken action against them, but some people intervened for their release, out of good intentions," Saudi Arabia's de facto ruler mused. "Those who interfered believed that perhaps they were something useful for the propagation of Islam."

Energized by this support from the ulema—and radicalized by the beatings they suffered in Prince Nayef's jails—Juhayman's militants emerged from their ordeal with a strengthened faith. The miraculous rescue must have been God's divine work! In the following months, the movement ballooned, drawing in new adepts across Saudi Arabia, in Kuwait, and farther away.

In Egypt in particular Juhayman's ideas found fertile ground. There, after Nasser's death in 1970, "President-Believer" Anwar Sadat

switched alliances from Moscow to Washington and, wrapping himself
in the mantle of Islam, hastened to release imprisoned Muslim Brotherhood activists. Just as was the case with American diplomats and spies,
he considered Islamic radicals far preferable to pro-Soviet leftists. As in
Saudi Arabia, a religious revival—partially inspired from above—swept
Egypt's university campuses. It became fashionable for young men to
grow beards and for female students to wear Islamic veils.

This embrace of piety was remarkably similar to the Saudi missionary movement that had been started by Bin Baz at the University of
Medina. And, just like in Saudi Arabia, it soon spun out of control.

Paralleling Juhayman's split from Bin Baz, radical Egyptian students
and graduates moved away from the mainstream Muslim Brotherhood,
creating a web of secretive cells all over the country. That loose network, especially strong on the campus of Cairo University, became
known as Gamaat Islamiya, or "Islamic groups." Using intimidation and
outright violence, its activists attacked leftists and enforced Islamic
morality. Like Juhayman, they demanded a ban on art shows and secular cultural events and insisted on strict segregation between women
and men. Little by little, they started accumulating firearms that, in following years, would drench Egypt in blood.

Sadat's 1977 surprise trip to Jerusalem, which paved the way for
Egypt's American-sponsored peace talks with Israel, further radicalized
the young firebrands. As the Saudi Ikhwan had done in the 1920s, they
embraced the practice of *takfir*, declaring fellow Muslims with whom
they disagreed to be apostates who could be killed at will.

No longer a "president-believer," Sadat, reviled in clandestine leaflets
as a new "pharaoh" who had deserted Islam, was now seen as a prime
candidate for such an unnatural death. An even more secretive offshoot
of Gamaat Islamiya, the Islamic Jihad, set to work on assassination
plans.

Prominent among these militants was a recent graduate from Cairo
University's department of medicine, Ayman Zawahiri. He and others
shared their thoughts in the clandestine reading groups that developed

on campus and in the mosques. Juhayman's "The Seven Epistles"—smuggled from Kuwait—was by then widely circulated, and admired, in that milieu.

Egyptian radicals were in total agreement with Juhayman that the current rulers of the Arab world—be it the Egyptian president or the Saudi king—were no longer legitimate because of their failure to defend the true faith and to stand up to the West. In 1979, a magazine affiliated with the Egyptian Muslim Brotherhood and widely read by Gamaat Islamiya supporters, al Dawa, even dedicated an issue to how the Saudi kingdom was supposedly succumbing to decadence and vice. The article's target—just as Juhayman's, or, for that matter, Bin Baz's—was Saudi television and radio.

"Where is Saudi Arabia heading?" the magazine wondered, enumerating recent outrages. In one TV series, it complained, a female hero had been shown planting a kiss on a man who was not her husband. On a recent radio program, male and female anchors "exchanged sweet words on air while it was clear that the doors behind them had been closed." Even Saudi taxi drivers had started misbehaving, no doubt influenced by American movies. All in all, the magazine complained, Saudi children, instead of dedicating their lives to Islam, now chose as role models "the American six-million-dollar man" and "Superman" Steve Austin!

Such infidel contamination, in Saudi Arabia or Egypt, was condemned with particular eloquence by Mohammed Elias, a popular cleric in his thirties who taught Islam to Gamaat Islamiya members at Cairo University. Elias was especially touched by Juhayman's writings. At first he merely repeated Juhayman's ultraconservative views in his own sermons, which were taped and distributed illegally across Egypt. Then, in 1979, Elias began planning a trip to Saudi Arabia, to meet this inspiring new guru.

FIVE

Like most Saudis at the time, Juhayman was vaguely aware of the Islamic revolutionary movements that were gathering strength around the region, including the Gamaat Islamiya in Egypt and the religious revival that steadily sapped the Shah's secular monarchy in nearby Iran. But these foreign developments exerted only limited influence on his thinking. Juhayman definitely never watched TV and rarely browsed newspapers. Whatever happened in Iran, he thought, didn't deserve much attention because the Iranians were Shiites, incorrigibly stuck in their miscreant beliefs.

Raised on Wahhabi tradition, Juhayman was trained to look for all answers in Islam's glorious past, in the actions of Prophet Mohammed and his righteous companions. So, as Juhayman contemplated his movement's next steps, he burrowed deeper and deeper into the big dusty volumes of the hadith. There, he stumbled upon a powerful concept of Islamic theology that seemed just right for these turbulent times—the Mahdi.

The idea of a Mahdi has fueled Muslim imagination for centuries. There is no mention of it in the Quran itself. But Prophet Mohammed, according to some narrators, had forecast that God will one day dispatch a redeemer—a Mahdi—to command the Muslim world and establish an ideal society, after an apocalyptic clash with the forces of evil. This Mahdi cannot be killed by mere mortals—at least not during the first seven years of his reign. In that time, he will "fill the Earth with peace and justice as it will have been filled with injustice and tyranny before then," the prophecy says.

Shiite Muslims believe the Mahdi had already emerged in the ninth century and then vanished to return at the end of the world. Several claimants to the status of Mahdi appeared among the Sunnis in the meantime, including the Sudanese rebel Mohammed Ahmed Sayid Abdullah, whose followers routed the mighty British army and captured Khartoum in 1885, killing General Charles Gordon.

Juhayman dedicated to the Mahdi's imminent arrival one of the seven epistles. Before the promised Mahdi emerges, Juhayman noted in the text, "great discord will occur, and Muslims will be drifting away from the religion"—a condition that, to him, was already painfully obvious.

Once revealed, Juhayman wrote, the Mahdi will become the only just ruler on Earth. All true Muslims will pledge him *baya*, the religious oath of allegiance, abandoning loyalty to their current presidents and kings. An army of the Mahdi's enemies will be swallowed into the opening ground between Medina and Mecca.

Then, the prophecy held, the hour will sound for the great showdown. The world's Christian empires, dead-set in their arrogant ways and their hatred of the true faith, will dispatch a never-seen-before force to Arabia. Forty thousand short of a million Christian soldiers will disembark, bringing their fearsome weapons and intent on desecrating the shrines of the Muslims and defeating God's servants.

One-third of the assembled Muslim force will be stricken by fear and flee when confronted by Christians in the battlefield, Juhayman wrote, citing the hadith; these men would be condemned to eternal damnation. Another third will be martyred, fertilizing the land with their precious blood. But the remaining third will triumph in battle, seizing all Christian cities with the cries of *"Allahu Akbar."*

The elimination of the Christian world will not be the end of events, however. That's precisely the moment when the devil will show his ugly hand, sending Dajjal—the Antichrist sorcerer and deceiver— to Earth. To await his arrival, the Mahdi will first travel to the al Aqsa Mosque in east Jerusalem, restoring it to Islam. Like Moshe Dayan, the Israeli general who was defense minister in the 1967 conquest of east Jerusalem, the Antichrist will be missing one eye. And—in another re- minder of the Arabs' current predicaments—he will be accompanied by an army of Jews, 70,000 of them.

Overwhelmed by the Antichrist's powers, the Mahdi will flee to Damascus, where the Muslims will be besieged behind the city's thick walls, some hadith explained. In this trying hour, the Mahdi will kneel in prayer and Jesus Christ will be returned to Earth, carried by two white angels. (Jesus, in Muslim tradition, is a prophet but not a son of God; much of Christian dogma is therefore viewed by orthodox Mus- lims as a distortion of Jesus' true teachings.)

Appearing in front of the Mahdi and extending his comfort, Jesus will rejoice at the elimination of Christians and take over command in the battle against global evil. The Antichrist, or Dajjal, will be promptly slain by Jesus, who will stab him with a lance borrowed from one of the Muslims; the devil's envoy will dissolve like salt in water. After this, the Jews will be slaughtered just like Christians had been and the hour of redemption will finally sound. "Not a single infidel will survive the breath of [Jesus'] air," Juhayman wrote longingly.

The hadith were fairly precise about the Mahdi's features and details of his coming. The redeemer will look like Prophet Mohammed, with a broad forehead and a prominent nose, one narrative said. He will have a fair complexion and a large birthmark on his cheek. He will be tall. And, crucially, he will carry the same name as the Prophet and descend from the same tribe of Quraysh.

In due time, the Mahdi will receive the oath of *baya* on the holiest of grounds: near the Kaaba in Mecca, between the C-shaped wall containing Hagar's and Ishmael's graves, the *Rukn*, and the boulder with the impression of Ibrahim's feet, the *Maqam*. Even the time was foretold in the prophecies—right after the hajj, at the turn of a new Muslim century.

In November 1978, after members of Juhayman's movement were released from jail, hajj season arrived. In the calendar of Islam, year 1398 was turning to 1399. Juhayman summoned his men on a pilgrimage to Mecca's Grand Mosque, the place where the great revelation should happen. The world was twelve months away from the tumultuous events that would cover the mosque's marble courtyard with blood, spilled guts, and severed limbs.

On the long trip to Mecca from Riyadh five hundred miles away, Hozeimi rode wrapped in a woolen blanket on the roof of a dented Mercedes sedan. Next to him, shielded by another blanket from howling winds that blasted the vehicle with sand, lay Mohammed Abdullah's younger brother, Saad. The two chitchatted about the upcoming hajj. Then, startling Hozeimi, Saad blurted out: "Did you ever notice that my brother has all the features of a Mahdi?"

"What do you mean?"

"Well, he has the same name as the Prophet—Mohammed, son of Abdullah," Saad explained. His brother was also fair and tall and had a broad forehead, a prominent nose, and a big red mark on his cheek. Bouncing on the car's roof, Hozeimi mulled over these words. But wasn't the Mahdi, according to the hadith, also supposed to come from the same bloodline as the Prophet?

This was a clear contradiction. The Arab race comprises two branches—the Adnanis, who trace their lineage from Prophet Ibrahim's son Ishmael, and south Arabia's aboriginal Qahtanis. How could Saad's brother, Mohammed Abdullah al Qahtani, possibly be a descendant of Prophet Mohammed if the Prophet's own tribe, the Quraysh, was of Adnani origin?

Saad smiled. "You see, we're not really Qahtanis," he confided. In the previous century, his great-grandparents had taken up residence on the lands of the Qahtani tribe in what was now southern Saudi Arabia. Following Bedouin custom, they eventually adopted the tribe's name as their own. But the family's blood came from a very different source. Saad's ancestors, he said proudly, were actually Turks of noble origin who traced their lineage directly to Prophet Mohammed, and therefore to the Quraysh. In the days of the Ottoman Empire, the family lived for generations in Ottoman-ruled Egypt and then was settled in Arabia by government officials eager to strengthen Ottoman control of the peninsula.

Hozeimi remained unconvinced. The world outside Arabia was full of Muslims who claimed descent from Prophet Mohammed, often on fanciful grounds. The Bedouins of Saudi Arabia usually took such pretensions with a large pinch of salt, especially if this alleged lineage involved the inferior blood of Turks and other non-Arabs. By the time the Mercedes arrived in Mecca, Hozeimi had put the whole conversation out of his mind.

After the hajj, Juhayman started preparing for what he now believed would be an inevitable showdown with the kingdom's illegitimate rulers. Almost permanently present in the Grand Mosque, his adepts began to pop up among crowds of worshippers, treating them to short improvised sermons about the rigors of Islamic observance and the duty to fight unbelief.

They didn't just talk. The true believers, Juhayman now taught, had to prepare themselves for the worst. They should be able to defend themselves if the hypocritical Saudi state chose to strike God's servants again.

The idea seemed right to everyone, especially those rattled by the beatings and the abuse they had received in jail. In small groups, Juhayman's followers took long desert trips, perfecting there their marksmanship. There was no shortage of trainers. Many of the organization's Saudi members were, like Juhayman, fellow veterans of the National Guard. Much of that training appears to have happened on the remote bases of the Guard's tribal militias.

Some of the weaponry that Juhayman accumulated, too, came brand-new from Guard warehouses. Other guns and ammo had been smuggled across the border from Yemen, or from the battlefields of the Lebanese civil war. The kingdom, after all, was awash with military hardware: in 1978 alone, Saudi border patrols had seized 1,200 smuggled rifles, 481 machine guns, 7,358 pistols, and well over a million rounds of ammunition. Much more remained undetected. All proud Bedouin households in Saudi Arabia owned firearms, if not modern AK-47s then at least ancient British-made bolt action rifles.

In mid-1979 strange things started to happen in the tight-knit community of Juhayman's supporters. After a lull, the Saudi state renewed its crackdown, detaining militants who distributed Juhayman's booklet or collected money for the cause. Juhayman himself was again on the run, moving between desert farms owned by supporters. When visiting cities, he avoided arrest by staying right next to police stations, figuring that his pursuers would never look for him in such unlikely spots.

As more and more members—including Mohammed Abdullah's younger brother Saad—were thrown behind bars, the movement percolated with righteous passion and a burning desire to stand up to the perceived injustice of the Saudi regime.

Then, one after another, hundreds of Juhayman's supporters experienced detailed, vivid dreams. Mohammed Abdullah's sister appears to have been the first, quickly followed by others. In their sleep, they all had the same vision: Mohammed Abdullah standing by the sacred Kaaba in Mecca's Grand Mosque, accepting allegiance as the blessed Mahdi amid multitudes of believers. Militants from as far away as Lebanon who never encountered Mohammed Abdullah in person claimed to have had the same dream.

Much of that dreaming must have been caused by self-suggestion, especially as Juhayman—increasingly obsessed with the coming of the redeemer as the century neared its end—spoke more and more frequently about the divine signs that were supposed to herald the Mahdi's arrival. Yet to most of the faithful, their nighttime experiences seemed a clear sign from God.

In Islam, night dreams, especially when occurring collectively, are not easily dismissed as random stirrings of the unconscious. Prophet Mohammed himself received many of his revelations from God in the form of dreams, and attached great importance to these messages. "The worst lie is that a person claims to have seen a dream which he has not seen," the Prophet is reported to have said.

At first, Mohammed Abdullah, then barely twenty-five, did not take all this seriously; he certainly did not advertise himself as a possible Mahdi. Juhayman, however, seemed deeply convinced that he had now found the redeemer. Even the young man's hesitance was seen as a divine sign: the hadith, after all, had foretold that the blessed Mahdi would be reluctant to accept his new mission. As the year ran its course, Juhayman sent more and more acolytes to whisper into Mohammed Abdullah's ear, convincing the young student that he was the Chosen One.

Shortly before the last hajj of Islam's fourteenth century, Juhayman and Mohammed Abdullah grew virtually inseparable. One uncorroborated account, reported by a Western diplomat after the Grand Mosque takeover, alleged that the two even became homosexual lovers. In any case, they became family: Juhayman divorced his first wife and quietly married Mohammed Abdullah's sister, the one who had had the first dream of the young poet as Mahdi.

The dreams, it was decided in feverish meetings, called for forceful action. The believers, Juhayman said, would do God's duty by converging en masse on the Grand Mosque and fulfilling the prophecy. Casting for wider support, Juhayman in these weeks dispatched an emissary to Bin Baz himself. At a meeting in Riyadh, the blind cleric listened patiently to the theological arguments. But he was not convinced.

First of all, Bin Baz explained to the emissary, he refused to believe that Mohammed Abdullah indeed qualified as the Mahdi. A true Mahdi, Bin Baz said, would spring up on his own, through God's will, without any need for human intervention. Any intrusion of the kind planned by Juhayman, Bin Baz cautioned, had no chance of winning universal acceptance and would result in the sin of provoking *fitna*, discord among Muslims.

The emissary did not mention that Juhayman planned to use weapons while anointing the Mahdi. And so Bin Baz chose not to inform the authorities about this unsettling conversation.

Soon thereafter, Juhayman reclined in a circle of trusted adepts, sharing coffee and yellow dates in a large tent on a farm north of Riyadh. One of the followers present was Sultan al Khamis, a teenage student who had been recruited into the movement while attending Bin Baz's morning sermons at the capital's Faisal bin Turki Mosque. Juhayman was speaking frankly this time: the Mahdi had to be shielded from enemies of the true faith, and the onus was on the believers to provide this protection. On the appointed day, he said, the Grand Mosque will be seized at gunpoint and defended with arms.

Khamis was puzzled. Didn't the Holy Quran and the hadith specifically forbid fighting in the sacred precinct? he wondered.

Juhayman grinned mischievously and responded by citing the hadith about how the army of enemies of the Mahdi will be swallowed into the opening ground. "If we do not bring weapons, this army will not come to Mecca," he said, "and so it will not be swallowed into the Earth." In any case, he hurried to add, the weaponry will be purely defensive: "We will not shoot until they shoot first."

SIX

While Juhayman's clandestine network prepared for the Mahdi's arrival, Saudi princes grew concerned with more obvious perils. Chief among their preoccupations was the rapidly escalating turmoil across the Persian Gulf, in Iran.

For decades, the rulers of Riyadh had maintained cordial ties with the Shah of Iran, Mohammed Reza Pahlavi, bound to him by a common interest of keeping revolutionary fervor and Communist agitation away from the Gulf's warm waters. Both monarchies prospered from oil and were crucial suppliers to America and the rest of what was then called "the Free World." And, for decades, both royal households looked upon Washington to protect them from trouble.

Washington had intervened in the past. In 1953, the Shah was forced to flee to Rome after a confrontation with his elected prime minister, Mohammed Mossadegh, who had expropriated Western oil interests and roused crowds with anti-Western oratory. Using their network of local agents, the CIA and British intelligence at the time organized a countercoup against Mossadegh. Code-named Ajax, this covert operation culminated with the restoration of the Shah to the Peacock Throne of Tehran and Mossadegh's being thrown behind bars.

In Saudi Arabia, America also had flexed its muscles: the U.S. Air Force flew protective patrols in Saudi skies in 1963, when Egyptian forces entered neighboring Yemen, clashing with Saudi-backed Yemeni royalists and encroaching upon the kingdom's own borders.

But all this belonged to the past.

Now, in 1979, America was just emerging from the trauma of Vietnam and had little appetite for foreign entanglements. The White House had been occupied since 1977 by Jimmy Carter, the former Democratic governor of Georgia who was elected on a platform of America's moral rehabilitation and who could still boast that no American serviceman overseas had died on his watch. The U.S. military budget had been slashed. The CIA, tarnished by past involvement in assassinating foreign leaders and spying on American citizens, was on a tight leash following congressional hearings; the agency had lost most of its ability to conduct covert action and found it nearly impossible to recruit new sources.

For Carter's idealistic administration, curbing arms sales abroad and promoting human rights became foremost foreign policy goals. All this meant that the Shah was no longer viewed through the same prism of Cold War balance of power that had ensured him automatic American support in the past.

When Islamist and leftist protesters started rioting against the Iranian monarchy in early 1978, the State Department's new Human Rights Bureau followed Washington's new set of priorities and blocked Iran's request to purchase tear gas—the same chemical that U.S. law enforcement agencies were using for crowd control at home.

As 1978 progressed, student demonstrations, strikes, and clashes with police multiplied in Iran, encouraged by a spreading perception that America was no longer determined to support the Shah's regime.

The Soviet Union's regional ambitions were encouraged, too: America barely reacted in April 1978 when Communists carried out a coup and seized power in neighboring Afghanistan.

Unrest in Iran escalated after Ayatollah Ruhollah Khomeini, the dour seventy-eight-year-old Shiite scholar until then living under tight supervision in Iraq, moved in October 1978 to the relative freedom of France. From the comforts of Neauphle-le-Château near Paris, he assumed leadership of the anti-Shah movement's Islamist component. To Khomeini, the Shah represented a "satanic government" that flouted religion and could be only washed away in "torrents of blood."

In December 1978, as Juhayman first shared his ideas about Mohammed Abdullah being the Mahdi in Mecca, the new Islamic year 1399 began. The first month of the calendar, Muharram, has always been a period of mourning and religious fervor among the Shiites. In Iran, these religious feelings were now harnessed by Khomeini, whose sermons—distributed via cassette tapes smuggled from France—inspired a crescendo of street clashes, protests, and strikes. The Carter administration, prodded by allies, faced a crucial dilemma: what to do next?

The secretary of state at the time was Cyrus Vance, an international lawyer who abhorred violence and believed in the strength of America's moral example. He and much of the State Department bureaucracy believed that promoting democracy and political compromise, rather than rescuing a lifelong ally, were America's ultimate goal in Iran. An overthrow of the Shah, the American ambassador in Tehran predicted optimistically, would lead to the creation of a benign pro-Western government where Khomeini would play a "Gandhi-like" role. When the Shah inquired whether Washington would support a crackdown on increasingly more violent revolutionaries, U.S. officials responded by providing the Iranian monarch with ambiguous encouragements to move toward greater democracy.

Carter's national security adviser, Zbigniew Brzezinski, was incensed by such policies. A Polish-born immigrant, he remembered all too well the perils of appeasement and argued that American policy in

Iran was dangerously naive. "I simply had no faith in the quaint notion—favored by American lawyers of liberal bent—that the remedy to
a revolutionary situation is to paste together a coalition of the contend-
ing parties, who—unlike domestic American politicians—are not moti-
vated by a spirit of compromise but (demonstrably in the Iranian case)
by homicidal hatred," Brzezinski later wrote.

Brzezinski's recipe was to organize a coup by Iran's pro-Western and
American-trained military, something that he felt could quell the revolutionary fervor and stop the slide toward a radical anti-American
theocracy. An American general was duly dispatched to Tehran, on a
mission to assist the Iranian military in retaining cohesion—and, if
need be, liaising for such a coup.

But Vance and the vice president, Walter Mondale, were dead set
against any American encouragement for projects to crush the Islamic
revolution. General Pinochet's American-supported putsch against
democratically elected President Salvador Allende of Chile was still on
everyone's minds, and—as far as American public opinion was concerned—Pinochet seemed a much more evil figure than Khomeini.

In the end, Carter decided to simply wash his hands of Iran. In a
top-level policy meeting on January 3, 1979, he opined, "A genuinely
non-aligned Iran need not be viewed as a U.S. setback." A few days
later, the United States advised the Shah to leave the country. Carter,
unaware that Iran's meltdown would doom his own presidency, went
on repeating the same mantra: "We do not have any intention of inter-
fering in the affairs of Iran."

The Iranian government disintegrated soon after the Shah departed;
he eventually landed in the United States for cancer treatment. On February 1, 1979, Khomeini arrived in Tehran aboard a chartered French
plane, greeted by millions of supporters who jammed the capital's
streets. "I beg God to cut off the hands of all evil foreigners and
all their helpers," Khomeini urged in the airport, whipping up anti-
American hysteria as the dark days of summary executions of counter-
revolutionary suspects began.

Across the Atlantic, even hawks like Brzezinski failed to grasp that the region's upheaval heralded America's global clash with political Islam. "We should be careful not to overgeneralize the Iranian case," Brzezinski advised Carter a day after Khomeini's return. "Islamic revivalist movements are not sweeping the Middle East and are not likely to be the wave of the future."

Other administration officials went as far as to cheer the ayatollah. The U.S. ambassador to the United Nations, Andrew Young, that week praised the "vibrant cultural force" of Islam and predicted that Khomeini "will be somewhat of a saint when we get over the panic."

Viewed from Riyadh, there was little reason for the panic to abate. The rise of an aggressive Shiite theocracy in Iran posed a direct threat to majority-Sunni Saudi Arabia, reviving an age-old hostility between the two sects of Islam and undermining al Saud's claim to leadership of the entire Muslim world. Apprehension over upheaval in Tehran was exacerbated by mounting threats all around the kingdom. In south Yemen, a Marxist regime took power and, with Soviet aid, was destabilizing Saudi allies in north Yemen. Across the Red Sea, Marxist Ethiopia was crawling with Cuban troops and massive amounts of Soviet military hardware, which it used to defeat the Saudis' regional ally, Somalia. Soviet military advisers also grew more and more numerous in Afghanistan.

The delicate task of maintaining America's crucial relationship with Saudi Arabia at this juncture was entrusted to the fifty-seven-year-old ambassador John Carl West. A jovial, bald southern Democrat, he had been elected governor of South Carolina—running on the earnest slogan "Elect a Good Man"—when Carter himself became governor of neighboring Georgia. One of the first prominent Democrats to endorse Carter's presidential ambitions during the primaries, West had been long fascinated with the Arab world. So, instead of settling for a comfortable ambassadorship somewhere in Europe, he specifically demanded a Saudi posting, until then usually occupied by a career diplomat, as his postelection reward. Though West knew precious little about the Middle East, his experience with clannish southern politics made a good introduction to navigating the convoluted relationships within the Saudi dynasty. The Wests entertained prominent Saudis as many as three times a day. Saudi royals, who put a premium on personal ties, reciprocated with access. They valued West's friendship with Carter and knew that the American ambassador frequently bypassed the State Department in his handwritten correspondence with the president.

The Saudis by then were also fully aware of just how much influence they could exert over Washington. In mid-1979, as troubles in Iran disrupted global oil supplies, America was hit by gasoline shortages that made Carter's approval ratings plummet to a dismal 25 percent. Tempers flew as gas lines across the United States snarled traffic; on the first Sunday of summer 1979, a staggering 70 percent of American gas stations closed down after running out of fuel. Begging for help, Carter that month had Ambassador West deliver to Saudi princes a personal handwritten message asking for an increase in oil production.

The Saudis complied, bolstering output to 9.5 from 8.5 million barrels a day and ensuring that American gas lines disappeared. They also made sure the American president didn't forget that he owed them a favor. "Prince Sultan the other day asked me if the increase in production had helped you politically," Ambassador West reported back to Carter in one of his handwritten notes in September 1979. "With a twinkle, he remarked that a million barrels were worth at least a million votes—and if so, the Saudis had done at least something to help with your reelection."

What the Saudis wanted in exchange was an American security umbrella.

In those days, America already provided some military hardware to the kingdom. The Carter administration had just pushed through Congress a controversial deal to supply the Saudi air force with sophisticated F-15 fighter jets. Hundreds of American soldiers were secretly stationed in the country. Since 1975, the Vinnell Corporation—supervised by an

American general—had run a comprehensive training program for the Saudi National Guard. Separately, another American military mission, also headed by a general, was based at the airfield of Dhahran that the U.S. Air Force used from time to time.

Saudi Arabia's key interlocutor with the United States on security affairs was Prince Turki al Faisal, the son of the assassinated King Faisal. Educated at Georgetown University and fluent in colloquial English, the taciturn, soft-spoken prince served from 1977 to 2001 as head of the Saudi General Intelligence Directorate, or GID—the kingdom's equivalent of the CIA.

In response to Saudi requests, even the stunted CIA offered limited assistance to the kingdom. The agency's station chief in Saudi Arabia, George Cave, worked with Prince Turki on training the kingdom's anti-terrorism forces in the latest American techniques. American operatives were based at a special training center in Taef, a mountain town that offers relief from the scorching heat of Mecca or Jeddah and has long served as a summer retreat for Saudi royalty.

The CIA shared its experience on the predictable topics in the age of international bombings and plane hijackings: sharpshooting, explosives handling, tear gas use, hostage rescue. At the end of one such session, Cave mentioned to Prince Turki that—according to the American rule book—a psychiatrist should be on staff of the new Saudi hostage rescue team. "I'll get back to you on this," the prince responded pensively.

The following day, Cave had a reply: conditions in Saudi Arabia differed somewhat from America's. "We can't do this—we only have three psychiatrists in our entire country."

The CIA, despite providing this limited security aid, saw little reason to worry about Saudi Arabia's overall stability. The agency, which found it extremely difficult to procure information in the tightly knit and pathologically secretive Saudi kingdom, had no inkling of Juhayman's agitation, and discounted the Iranian threat. "The modernization of the

[Arabian] Peninsula may have heightened some tensions among local religious elements, although, for now, most appear under control," the CIA opined in its classified April 1979 assessment of Saudi Arabia and neighboring sheikhdoms. "The Shiites in Saudi Arabia are believed to have no particular affinity for Iranian political developments and appear to have gained enough economic ground in recent years to forestall any serious agitation," the document said.

The limited help offered by the small CIA team and the training of the National Guard were by no means enough for the Saudi royals. What Riyadh desperately wanted was a dramatic display of the Carter administration's determination to protect its allies in the region from Khomeini's firebrands and the Soviet menace. Crown Prince Fahd impressed the Saudis' frustration on Ambassador West during a late-night meeting October 2, 1979, in his palace on Jeddah's Red Sea beach. As Fahd saw it, the Soviets, with their support for Khomeini and mischief from Ethiopia to Afghanistan, were making a push for controlling the Persian Gulf, while America manifested "seeming indifference or impotence."

"Instead of pressuring the Shah into bringing his thoughts and actions up to date so as to pull the rug from under the Communist agitators, you let him go," Fahd lamented. "Look at what has happened in Iran! They have killed the cream of their society—the best brains in the military, the professions, and the civil service have all been executed or forced into exile." And after all this, Fahd continued, there had been "not a word of caution to Iran from President Carter."

After Afghanistan, Pakistan might be the next domino to fall, the crown prince predicted, explaining that most of the region—while forced to adopt the newly fashionable anti-American rhetoric in public— yearned for nothing more than a demonstration of American strength. "Three quarters of the Arab regimes are with you, really," Fahd said. "They all await, expect, and hope for their powerful, wise, and morally adroit friend, the U.S., to send out the message loud and clear: enough is enough!"

Taken aback, West argued that "those who insinuated that the U.S.

was not willing to come to the aid of its allies and friends" were mistaken. The crown prince wouldn't relent. All he had received from the United States so far were vague words instead of a "firm, unequivocal stand." The stakes for the kingdom were just too high, he explained, and the dangers seemed far more immediate from Riyadh than from Washington: "To count the lashes is one thing, but to feel them is something else!"

A month after this conversation, the whole world witnessed instead of a show of American strength the humiliating pictures of American weakness. On November 4, 1979, revolutionary students stormed the U.S. embassy in Tehran, seizing sixty-six hostages, who were promptly blindfolded and paraded in front of the cameras. Iran's secular prime minister Mehdi Bazargan, who had just met Brzezinski in Algeria, trying to patch up Iran's relations with Washington, rushed to his office from the Tehran airport.

Bazargan did his best to end the crisis. But Khomeini, by far the more powerful figure, opposed any negotiations with "the Great Satan" that had sheltered the Shah. He immediately endorsed the embassy's seizure; within hours, Khomeini's son personally climbed over the compound's fence to join the hostage takers. Bazargan resigned in protest. Undivided power over Iran now belonged to the ayatollah.

The rest of the region watched, bewildered, as the Carter administration seemed to be taking in stride this ultimate insult—unprecedented in the history of modern diplomatic relations. At the first policy meeting the day after the embassy's seizure, Carter refused suggestions to threaten Iran with military action if the hostages were not released. The Iranians, he muttered, "have us by the balls."

Following standing orders, marines at the embassy in Tehran had offered no resistance to the intruders; not a single bullet was fired. The lack of preparedness for the embassy's takeover was staggering in retrospect: after all, just in February that year, a mob of Khomeini's supporters had surrounded and tried to storm the very same building.

Simultaneously, in neighboring Afghanistan, the American ambassador had been captured by Islamic militants and then shot dead in a botched rescue attempt. Weeks before the November 4 embassy takeover, the top officer at the CIA's Operations Directorate Middle East division had flown to Saudi Arabia specifically to meet the Tehran station chief and warn him of likely trouble ahead.

Once the revolutionary students overran the Tehran compound, they captured along with American diplomats one of the biggest treasure troves of classified information ever lost in history. These reams of secret U.S. correspondence would be published in Tehran in a seventy-seven-volume series called "Documents from the U.S. Espionage Den." In a huge embarrassment to the Saudis, one of the documents in this collection was a copy of Ambassador West's secret cable reporting the frank exchange he had had with Crown Prince Fahd.

SEVEN

The fall of the American embassy in Iran coincided with the hajj of 1979. Saudi royals were frightened that Khomeini's drive to export the Islamic revolution might now prompt the ayatollah to try some spectacular stunt in the Grand Mosque. Trying to buy its way out of trouble, Saudi Arabia even rushed emergency kerosene supplies to Iran in a goodwill gesture that alleviated crippling shortages there. As it happened, the Iranians caused little trouble in Mecca that year, beyond passing around Khomeini posters and leaflets that glorified their revolution. For now, the streets of Shiite towns in Saudi Arabia's Eastern Province remained quiet, too.

Hundreds of Juhayman's followers, from Saudi Arabia and abroad, converged on Mecca that season. They were a disparate lot. The hard core of Juhayman's kinsmen from Bedouin settlements in the Nejd was now complemented by scores of young students from all over the country—including the scions of some of Saudi Arabia's most prominent families, thoroughly infused with the messianic faith of their master. One was the son of a regional governor; a second the son of a Saudi ambassador; a third a teacher of English who had been educated in Britain. Many hailed from villages near Mecca itself. The numerous foreigners included at least two African American converts and the Egyptian preacher Mohammed Elias.

For more than a month, the entire Muslim world, from Indonesia to Africa, had been rife with expectations that something extraordinary would happen in Mecca at the turn of this century. The pilgrim influx was unusually heavy. In October, Meccan clerics dutifully reported to senior ulema in Riyadh that, according to local rumor, the Mahdi was to appear to believers by the Kaaba after the hajj. Coming soon after the Riyadh meeting between Bin Baz and Juhayman's emissary, such a report should have raised alarms. But the ulema took no visible action in response.

The Saudi secret police, the Mabaheth, also did not intervene. It is hard to imagine that the Mabaheth, with its thick network of inform-ers, was completely unaware of Juhayman's plan to proclaim the Mahdi in the Grand Mosque. True, some Mabaheth officers had been reached by Juhayman's followers in their homes and threatened with deadly ret-ribution should they try to oppose the Mahdi's arrival. But the idea of anointing the Mahdi by the Kaaba was shared by then among so many people that it couldn't have been completely hidden from the watchful eyes of Prince Nayef. Then again, the American FBI and CIA also pos-sessed plenty of clues ahead of the September 11 attacks of 2001— and still failed to prevent them.

Only a narrow circle within Juhayman's movement was involved in highly secretive preparations for the actual armed uprising. In explain-ing his vision to senior aides, Juhayman carefully chose his words. He never described his project as a violent occupation of Islam's holy of holies. The burgeoning weaponry stock, he put it gently, was only needed to protect the Mahdi from evildoers. In any case, he predicted with a reassuring smile, it would all end peacefully; the entire Muslim world would quickly accept the Mahdi as its unchallenged leader.

Those who had experienced night dreams about the Mahdi enthusiastically followed Juhayman's instructions. There was no doubting for them: they believed by now that Mohammed Abdullah was the redeemer and that he should be anointed with the oath of allegiance by the sacred Kaaba, as prescribed by the hadith.

Even some of those who didn't fully share Juhayman's theological certitude agreed to take part. Mohammed Elias and fellow Egyptian jihadis in particular were impressed by the arsenal that Juhayman had managed to assemble. Mahdi or not, for them this was an uprising against a puppet regime of American infidels, and Juhayman seemed charismatic and well-connected enough to succeed—possibly even igniting the entire region in the flames of Islamic revolution.

But other senior leaders, including a preacher who helped Juhayman write "The Seven Epistles," remained highly skeptical. Torn between their obedience to Juhayman and the enormity of his venture to capture Islam's holy of holies, many of them quietly peeled away—without, however, informing authorities.

Among such doubters was Faisal Mohammed Faisal, one of the group's most senior members by both age and importance in the organization. A tall, balding man with gaunt cheeks and an aquiline nose, Faisal was in his forties, about two decades older than Juhayman's average disciple. Long active in the Islamic missionary movement, he had studied religion together with the supposed Mahdi's older brother, Sayid Abdullah. Despite Faisal's bitter experiences in Saudi jails during the brief government crackdown on the organization the previous year, he remained a relative moderate, opposing the penchant of some of Juhayman's adepts to practice *takfir* and label those with whom they disagreed as apostates.

In early November 1979, Faisal traveled south, to the mountains near the town of Najran, where he had been born. Accompanied by his wife and children, Faisal stopped over at a farm owned by one of the movement's adepts in the settlement of Amar, north of Riyadh. Juhayman was there as well, waiting for the hajj season to end.

After the usual courtesies, the two shared a meal of rice and lamb, using their right hands to dip balls of rice into the gravy. Then they got down to discussing Juhayman's ambitious plan. Faisal admitted that he himself did not experience the dreams. Was seizing the Grand Mosque the right move? he wondered aloud. How can we be sure that Mohammed Abdullah is indeed the true Mahdi?

Certainty glowed in Juhayman's eyes as he dismissed Faisal's doubts. Wasn't it obvious that the End of Days was near, with corruption flooding the world? Weren't the detailed, vibrant visions of the Mahdi that all other true believers seemed to have nowadays a clear proof sent by God to mankind?

Sensing that Faisal still wavered, Juhayman looked up with a steady gaze that often produced a near hypnotic effect on his followers. "Don't worry, the responsibility for this will be all mine," he said after a long pause. "Everything is on me."

By the end of the day, Faisal's loyalty to Juhayman won over. He was to be counted in. I will continue on my journey south, Faisal told Juhayman that day. But, once I deposit my wife and children in Najran, I will return north and join you in Mecca.

As New Year's day approached, Juhayman also garnered crucial support on the inside. Several among the conspirators studied in the Grand Mosque academy and knew every nook and cranny of the compound. One, Nureddin Sheikh Badiuddin, was the son of one of the Grand Mosque's most powerful clerics, the Pakistani-born Sheikh Badiuddin Ihsanullah Shah. Some other senior clerics—while not actively supporting the conspiracy—chose to turn a blind eye to the unusual doings around them.

The Bin Laden company, which had constructed much of the Grand Mosque anew since the expansion began in 1956, still had a few unfinished work sites in the compound. The company used for access an opening under the Fatah Gate on the northern side of the shrine. Connected with the streets of Mecca by a bridge over a dry moat, this doorless opening led into the Grand Mosque's maze of underground chambers, the Qaboo.

For a modest bribe of 40,000 riyals, members of the Grand Mosque's guard service allowed Juhayman and his aides to drive three pickup trucks—a Toyota, a Datsun, and a red GMC—through the Bin Laden accessway. The trucks, parked in the shrine's basement with the consent of Bin Laden employees, were packed with weaponry, ammunition, and vital supplies of food.

In the last hours of Islam's year 1399, Juhayman and Mohammed Abdullah finally appeared in Mecca. The religious students who usually live in the mosque's basement rooms were given time off to return to their families for the celebrations, so the Qaboo was free of most of its usual occupants. Juhayman and Mohammed Abdullah kept a vigil inside the Grand Mosque that night, lounging under its opulent porticos and talking in hushed voices with fellow conspirators. Their soiled clothes and unwashed faces betrayed an unusual neglect of hygiene and attracted the unwelcome attention of outsiders.

One neatly dressed Iranian pilgrim even berated Mohammed Abdullah for his unseemly appearance that night. "Dress is not important," the Saudi answered impatiently.

EIGHT

At dawn of the First of Muharram, once the rebels seized the mosque, Juhayman concentrated on the military side of the operation. He made sure that the gates were all locked and that his snipers controlled all approaches to the holiest shrine. Someone else was to deliver the uprising's manifesto and to explain these historic events to the world of Islam.

After grabbing the imam's microphone, Juhayman yielded it to the supposed Mahdi's older brother, Sayid, whose smooth classical Arabic testified to rigorous Islamic instruction. With his pitched cadences and melodic intonations, Sayid sounded like a learned cleric, a voice of authority that immediately instilled respect.

The wicked ways of the House of Saud, the silver-tongued Sayid told believers as he stood shoulder to shoulder with Juhayman, were a clear sign to believers that the world was coming to an end and that Islam's final triumph over unbelief was arriving. Prince Fawwaz, the king's liberal brother and the governor of Mecca, was chosen for special opprobrium for his supposed debauchery. Corruption brought by television, the pollution of minds caused by Westerners, and the employment of women sullied Islamic purity in the cradle of the only true faith. And what about the new pagan scourge of soccer that, with government complicity, steered the faithful away from Islam! The kingdom's rulers, pawns of the infidels, were unworthy of true believers' respect. The oath of *baya* that Saudi subjects had given to their king was no longer valid because the royal family demonstrably failed to uphold the laws of Islam.

But luckily, relief was at hand. Citing in detail the relevant hadith, Sayid outlined Juhayman's theory about the Mahdi redeeming the world of Islam. After rattling off divine signs, such as the name Mohammed Abdullah and the red birthmark on the cheek, he paused for effect and made the dramatic announcement: "The good man is here with us, and he will bring justice to Earth after it had been filled with injustice. If anyone doubts, come here to check. We are all your brothers!"

Once this introduction was made, Mohammed Abdullah approached the center of the Grand Mosque's courtyard through a broad passage that militants had made for him in the crowd. A red checkered headdress, worn loosely over his head, flapped in the wind; he was even paler than usual but otherwise showed little emotion. Some of the worshippers gasped at the youth of the man afforded such deference. Holding a submachine gun in his hand, Mohammed Abdullah joined Juhayman at the precise spot that had been described by the prophecies—in the shade of the Kaaba, between the graves of Ishmael and Hagar and a boulder with the impression of Ibrahim's feet.

"In the name of Allah, most gracious, most merciful, here is the awaited Mahdi," Juhayman cried. "Pay allegiance to brother Mohammed Abdullah al Qurayshi," he went on, calling the poet-student by a name that as everyone here knew was also the one of Prophet Mohammed himself.

One after another, Juhayman's gunmen knelt down to kiss Mohammed Abdullah's hand and offer the oath of *baya*—uttering the same words with which early Muslims had pledged their loyalty to

Prophet Mohammed: "We will obey you, in weal and woe, in ease and hardship and evil circumstances...except in what would disobey God."

Clasping their hands, the hostages followed suit, making the same promise. As the pledging went on, the Mahdi's brother, Sayid, sounded almost apologetic. "We have nowhere else to go except the Grand Mosque," he explained through the shrine's public-address system. "All we ask people to do is to return to the ways of the Holy Quran and the Sunna, even though this is against what the government and the ulema are telling you."

By the end of the hour, some of the worshippers seemed to be genuinely convinced. One Yemeni man ran to the supposed Mahdi, screaming that he, too, had seen him in his dreams. Others were too frightened to speak up.

Having pledged the *baya,* senior conspirators ferried crates full of rifles to the center of the enclosure, distributing them to ordinary militants and then to those pilgrims who had decided to join the uprising. "The army will besiege the Mahdi as he will be in the Grand Mosque," Sayid recounted from yet another hadith. "And that army is from the sons of Mohammed—made up not of Jews or Christians, but of Muslims."

In addition to weaponry, stacks of Kuwaiti-printed brochures with Juhayman's writings were passed to the crowd. At this point, some confused worshippers—aware of Khomeini's desire to export the Islamic revolution to Saudi Arabia—shouted questions at Mohammed Abdullah. Was his uprising, they wanted to know, inspired by Iran? Scowling with scorn, the anointed Mahdi answered with a single, emphatic "No!" before walking away. Fellow gunmen hastened to explain that the heretical Shiites of Iran, not being true Muslims, could have no connection with this epochal event.

With the *baya* oath formally switching the allegiance of Saudi worshippers from the royal family to the Mahdi, Juhayman's gunmen began confiscating Saudi identity cards among the crowd and tearing them in half, shoving and insulting their owners. The Saudi state was illegitimate and these documents were a sign of loyalty to Satan, the gunmen yelled. Fearful, many pilgrims rushed to destroy their IDs, littering the courtyard's marble floor with a confetti of embossed paper and torn photographs. Juhayman's supporters also grew enraged at the sight of worry beads, favored by many Meccans but condemned in strict Wahhabi Islam as an alien innovation. Whenever one of the gunmen came nearby, unlucky possessors of these worry beads quickly dropped them on the ground.

In what seemed like a bad omen, Juhayman's men sustained their first casualty in these first moments of the takeover. An unlucky warning shot ricocheted off a column and killed on the spot Mansur al Qahtani, the supposed Mahdi's father-in-law.

Recovering his sangfroid after being shoved away by Juhayman, the mosque's imam, Sheikh Mohammed Ibn Subeil, managed to throw off his distinctive beige cloak and vanish into the mass of pilgrims amid the initial disarray. Running for his life, the fifty-five-year-old imam then headed to his quarters above the Fatah Gate. The office, up a narrow staircase, had windows on both sides of the mosque's main circular body, overlooking the inner courtyard dominated by the Kaaba and the streets of Mecca outside.

The cleric—who also served as deputy chairman of the Saudi religious body in charge of running Islam's two holy shrines in Mecca and Medina—picked up the phone and dialed his superior, Sheikh Nasser Ibn Rashed. After narrating the morning's incredible events, Ibn Subeil looked out the window again and noticed that additional conspirators were entering the Grand Mosque through a passageway from the street below, in one case even driving a vehicle indoors.

Having informed authorities, Ibn Subeil returned downstairs and—trying his best to remain unnoticed—strode to an office of the Grand Mosque police force. The station was located near the King Abdelaziz

Gate, inside the compound, and the officer in charge had already reached a delirious state.

"Have you called your commanders?" Ibn Subeil asked.

"We were told that the Mahdi has come!" the agitated officer replied. Shaken by the killing of two of his men minutes earlier, he appeared to believe that the end of the world was already occurring.

Ibn Subeil did his best to disabuse the officer of that notion. The Grand Mosque's usurpers were familiar to the cleric, as was the missionary movement unleashed by Bin Baz. He even recalled cautioning the parents of some of the youngsters under Juhayman's spell. All in all, Ibn Subeil thought, these wild gun-toting men didn't look like the kind of folk who'd produce the genuine redeemer described in the holy books of Islam.

The officer in charge promised to act, though it was clear he wasn't itching for a fight: to make sure that his rank was not discovered by the rebels, he had already taken off and concealed the upper part of his uniform.

With the Grand Mosque's gates remaining shut, a large crowd of worshippers who wanted to enter for prayers now formed around the shrine. One of them was a fourteen-year-old student in the Grand Mosque's madrassa who will be called Samir in this book. Two of his older brothers were senior members of Juhayman's movement, and Samir himself had already met the great man; his heart had beat so strongly during that encounter that he felt his chest was about to burst apart.

Samir—whose brothers kept him in the dark about preparations for the Grand Mosque attack—had heard through the Mecca grapevine that the Mahdi should appear after the hajj. He had made sure to spend the first few days after the pilgrimage's end in the mosque and was deeply disappointed that nothing happened at the time. Now, two weeks later, he instantly understood what was going on as he heard loudspeakers broadcast the opening words of Sayid's *baya* sermon. He hurried to join his two brothers and the blessed Mahdi indoors.

There was still virtually no police or army presence on the streets around the mosque, and so Samir circled the compound from one closed gate to another until he hit the doorless Bin Laden company accessway under the Fatah Gate. As he ran into the dark opening, his path was barred by two armed gunmen. They recognized Samir from meetings hosted by his brothers in the family home and warmly embraced the teenager: "Brother, come join us."

Another hour or so later, by about eight a.m., the Mecca police finally responded to the crisis. A single police jeep sent out to investigate the disturbance rolled up to the gates. The vehicle was instantly submerged in a hail of gunfire. Bullets fired by Juhayman's snipers from atop a minaret shattered the windshield. The driver, injured and bleeding, fell out of the car.

By then, the rebels had started to let most of the hostages go. Having pledged the *baya* to the Mahdi and having received the seven epistles, these worshippers were now supposed to become the redeemer's envoys, spreading the good news far and wide across the lands of Islam.

A tortuous escape route was provided through raised windows in the lower-level gallery of the mosque. Climbing onto one another's shoulders, civilians could squeeze out through these windows, often twisting limbs in the process and emerging on street level outside the compound. It took well over a day for most of the hostages to trickle out this way.

Ibn Subeil, the mosque's imam, noticed that the conspirators didn't just allow everybody to leave. One young Saudi man next to him looked like a pious believer, with a short robe, a loose headdress, and a curly beard that had never been defiled by scissors. The guards barred his way out: the man's duty, they explained, was to pick up arms and join their jihad. Several other Saudis were similarly turned back.

Realizing that he would have to disguise his appearance, Ibn Subeil pulled down his headdress and wrapped it around his shoulders in the manner of foreigners. He then joined a group of fretful Indonesian pilgrims, trying to blend in. Juhayman had no use for the Indonesians, who spoke no Arabic and couldn't really understand his grand plan. They were let go without harassment, and the Grand Mosque's imam, too, managed to slip out unnoticed.

Officials back at the Mecca police station still did not grasp the extent of the problem at the Grand Mosque. After the first jeep failed to return, a larger convoy of police cars ambled toward another side of the shrine. Their mission bordered on suicidal. In an instant, the rebels riddled these policemen with bullets from the minarets and the upstairs windows, which were covered with intricate latticework providing perfect cover for Juhayman's men.

By one account, eight officers died on the spot; thirty-six were wounded. While the rebels' Kalashnikovs could spray death only about three hundred meters around the mosque, their Belgian-made FN-FAL rifles were sufficiently powerful to kill at nearly double that distance, several city blocks away. Running for cover, the surviving policemen abandoned their vehicles and sought shelter by the mosque's outer walls. Pinned down in a small blind spot area, they were safe from the snipers atop the minarets. But they were also separated from the rest of the city by open ground now littered with bodies.

By now, the desert sun started burning and blood caked up on the asphalt. Gathering courage in the late morning, some Meccan civilians dressed in white robes, the near mandatory clothing for Saudi males, inched behind the disabled police jeep and pulled one hemorrhaging officer to safety. The snipers' guns remained silent: Juhayman had given his men strict orders not to shoot at civilians.

Getting bolder, other men walked toward the bolted gates and surreptitiously threw spare white robes and water bottles toward the policemen who had been trapped in the blind spot by the Grand Mosque's outer walls. One by one, the exhausted officers donned the robes, hid their guns underneath, and walked to safety on the other end of the plaza. If the snipers understood the ruse, they chose not to fire.

Later, there would be claims that King Khaled himself and other senior members of the royal household were expected to attend New Year's dawn prayers in the Grand Mosque. One version, widely reported at the time, held that the entire takeover had been timed by Juhayman in order to take King Khaled prisoner and that only a last-minute throat infection saved the monarch from captivity. Such intentions in fact seemed to have been far away from the minds of the conspirators: senior royals, they knew, were very unlikely to awaken in time to arrive in the Grand Mosque before dawn.

As it happened, some important Saudis—including senior government bureaucrats and forty-five relatives of the powerful oil minister Ahmed Zaki Yamani—did find themselves trapped inside the Grand Mosque Tuesday morning. And at one point Juhayman's gunmen tried to screen the crowd for familiar faces. But, among their tens of thousands of hostages, the conspirators spotted no one of real importance to the House of Saud.

NINE

The morning of November 20, 1979, King Khaled indeed nursed a cold and rested in his Riyadh palace. The country's day-to-day ruler, Crown Prince Fahd, was not even on the same continent. When the sun crept up above Mecca, Fahd dozed in a Tunis hotel suite, thousands of miles and two time zones to the west.

The reason Fahd had traveled to Tunis involved President Carter. Eager to go down in history as a peacemaker, Carter up until then had dedicated most of his energies in the Middle East to reconciling Arabs and Jews. In March 1979, following days of personal mediation by Carter at Camp David, Israel and Egypt finally signed a peace treaty—the first between Israel and an Arab country since the Jewish state's establishment three decades earlier. In exchange for recognition by Egypt, Israel agreed to surrender the vast Sinai Peninsula that it had seized in 1967. But the deal offered no tangible concessions for the Palestinians, whose fate had prompted Arab countries to go to war against Israel in the first place.

Early in the negotiating process, Saudi Arabia had indicated to U.S.

officials that it would support the peace agreement. But with Khomeini's revolutionary fervor inflaming anti-American sentiments in the region, the Saudi royals no longer felt it was safe to do Washington's bidding: the abandonment of the Shah had shown that Carter's America could not be relied upon to protect its allies. So, yielding to pressure from Yasser Arafat's Palestinian Liberation Organization and its hard-line Arab supporters, Riyadh joined a pan-Arab boycott of Egypt. Diplomatic ties with Cairo were ruptured, and the Cairo-based Arab League, having expelled the Egyptians, now moved to new quarters in Tunisia.

On the night of the Islamic New Year, fourteen Arab heads of state and countless lesser officials gathered in Tunis for the Arab League's annual summit, to discuss the thorny problem of Egypt, the unfolding civil war in Lebanon, and the hardening Arab attitudes to America. At the summit, in Tunis's ritzy Hilton Hotel, Crown Prince Fahd was to play a crucial role. In tandem with Iraq's new president, Saddam Hussein, another voice of relative moderation in the region, the Saudi royal had to deflect Iranian-inspired pressure to punish America and the West with a resurrected Arab oil embargo.

That pressure was ratcheted up by the arrival in Tunis of an uninvited Iranian delegation, headed—to the astonishment of the Saudis and the Iraqis—by none other than Ayatollah Hadi al Modarresi, an Iraqi-born Shiite cleric who, after fleeing religious repression in his homeland, had been busy fomenting unrest among Shiites in other Arab Gulf states. Farsi-speaking Iran is not an Arab country and does not belong to the Arab League. Nevertheless, acting on Khomeini's instructions, this Iranian team—abetted by Arafat and Syrian President Hafez al Assad—attempted to gain access to the august proceedings in the Hilton Hotel. The intruders were stopped just a few yards away by Tunisian guards, who, despite their operetta-style helmets topped by white ostrich feathers, could be ruthlessly efficient when necessary.

In Riyadh, the ailing King Khaled first learned the morning's terrible news from Sheikh Nasser Ibn Rashed, the senior cleric in charge of the two holy shrines in Mecca and Medina. A devout Wahhabi who shared Juhayman's repulsion for graven images to such an extent that he always refused to be photographed, Ibn Rashed had personally checked out the Grand Mosque the previous night and found nothing unusual. Then, at about six a.m. Tuesday, he received his first frantic call from the imam Ibn Subeil.

There was no doubt in Ibn Rashed's mind that the matter was of utmost gravity: as Ibn Subeil relayed news from the mosque, frequent gunfire could be heard in the background. Because of his seniority among the ulema, Ibn Rashed enjoyed direct access to King Khaled. So, after hanging up with the imam, he rushed to dial the king's palace in Riyadh. It's an emergency, he insisted to the courtiers: His Majesty must be put on the line right away!

But His Majesty was resting and could not be disturbed, the courtiers tried to object.

Ibn Rashed didn't give up, explaining the perils to which the Islamic sanctities had just succumbed. Minutes later, a groggy monarch picked up the receiver and listened to the shocking report. Jolted awake, he instructed the cleric to wander the streets and see for himself what exactly had just transpired. He also asked Ibn Rashed to try to locate the chief of Mecca's police.

The closest Ibn Rashed dared to approach the Grand Mosque was a barber shop near the Jiyad hospital, just south of the shrine. There he was briefed by a gaggle of excited onlookers. Spotting the police chief in the crowd, Ibn Rashed rushed to tell the officer to get in touch with the king. Then, since there was no way to call the royal palace from the barber shop, Ibn Rashed hurried back to his office.

From then on, King Khaled demanded that Ibn Rashed keep him informed of every development; the cleric ended up phoning the royal palace on some thirty occasions in the course of one hour. Luckily, he had two phone lines in his office, so he could use one to receive updates while keeping the other for communications with his royal majesty.

It occurred to Ibn Rashed in these hectic moments that the

Prophet's Mosque in Medina, the second holiest site of Islam, might be attacked by the same mysterious rebels now usurping the Kaaba. He phoned his representative in Medina, who in turn immediately informed the governor there, Prince Abdulmohsen. On the prince's orders, the Prophet's Mosque was cordoned off by armed police and its golden gates shut.

Pondering how to react, King Khaled had to make do without the two most senior members of the ruling household. Not just Crown Prince Fahd, the day-to-day ruler, was stuck in North Africa. The next in line to the throne, Prince Abdullah—commander of the all-important National Guard—was enjoying a holiday in Morocco. Even Prince Turki al Faisal, the young head of the General Intelligence Directorate (GID), was unavailable; he had gone to Tunis with Fahd.

The task of restoring the Grand Mosque to al Saud's sovereignty fell to Fahd's two full brothers—the interior minister Prince Nayef and the defense minister Prince Sultan. Roused from bed by a succession of increasingly nervous reports, they dropped everything and raced to Mecca, arriving in the Grand Mosque's vicinity by about nine a.m. Joining them was a half brother, Mecca's governor, Prince Fawwaz. Finally getting their act together, Saudi police and security forces started taking up positions on Mecca rooftops and in the streets nearby, even though, amazingly, nobody had thought of stopping the traffic that still flowed right outside the Grand Mosque's perimeter.

In the late morning, the first reinforcements began to arrive from Riyadh. A couple of companies from the recently established Special Security Force, a unit of Prince Nayef's Interior Ministry, flew to Jeddah and then drove up to Mecca. Leading these men was Major Mohammed Zuweid al Nefai, a career army officer and a native of the holy city who, as it happened, belonged to the same Uteybi tribe as Juhayman. Truckloads of men from the National Guard and the Saudi Army also began rolling in.

These new forces started out by establishing a security cordon around the Grand Mosque, stopping traffic in the area and erecting checkpoints in the neighboring streets. The rebels could no longer count on supplies or reinforcements from the outside. The battle lines were drawn.

TEN

Driving straight toward these newly established checkpoints was Brigadier-General Faleh al Dhaheri, commander of the Saudi Army's King Abdelaziz Armored Brigade.

Dhaheri was in a good mood. He looked forward to the day's celebrations and he planned to pray in the Grand Mosque at noon, after a festive meal with his numerous Meccan relatives. Dressed in civilian clothes, Dhaheri passed the familiar streets, where everything looked normal. He rolled by the ancient excavations area near the center and then hit a surprise roadblock. Cursing about road maintenance, Dhaheri tried an alternative street—but it was blocked, too.

"Why are both streets closed?" he asked a traffic policeman.

The officer replied with a cryptic "If you wonder, ask your boss. It's the Grand Mosque."

Puzzled and feeling insulted, Dhaheri pulled away from the checkpoint, determined to get downtown one way or another. Navigating a maze of side alleys, he emerged minutes later on the edge of the plaza facing the Grand Mosque's glistening marble, under brilliant blue skies. The normally bustling area was strangely empty and quiet; the moment of Dhaheri's arrival coincided with a long pause in the shooting.

Spotting a lonely pedestrian, Dhaheri halted him with a burning question: "Tell me, why are the gates of the Grand Mosque closed?"

"God knows," the pedestrian answered meekly.

"Of course, we all know that God knows this. But what do *you* know?"

"There had been some shots," the pedestrian volunteered. "They fired at the soldiers from the Grand Mosque."

"But why?"

"God knows."

Frustrated, Dhaheri moved on. Security officers lurked around a street corner, and he rushed to pepper them with more queries. The officers didn't seem to know much more. Their commander pointed to sniper nests atop the Grand Mosque's minarets. "You're risking your life here," the officer said. "Above all, don't step into the middle of the street." Dhaheri's time, he suggested, could be much better employed by taking a short walk to the luxurious Shoubra Hotel south of the shrine, where the senior princes had just assembled.

Confused, Dhaheri followed the advice. "Where are the princes?" he asked at the entrance to the hotel. Livery men pointed to the first-floor reception area, where gun-toting bodyguards scrutinized all entrants. Mecca's chief of police, an old acquaintance, recognized Dhaheri and waved him through, into a lounge where the three senior princes now held court.

Stunned by the agitation around, and by the illustrious presence of Their Royal Highnesses, the brigadier listened to a short briefing about what was already known: the Grand Mosque had been seized by unknown assailants who appeared to be very successful in shooting police, for motives unclear. With respectful kisses of the royal shoulders, Dhaheri presented himself to Prince Sultan and Prince Nayef. "I am a professional military man," he began, offering his services in planning a quick and decisive raid on the sacred compound. The princes listened with interest, eager for a quick end to this disgrace.

Then the doors of the lounge were flung open. Wide-eyed, one of Dhaheri's friends, a senior Defense Ministry bureaucrat named Saleh, burst inside. The bureaucrat had been to the Grand Mosque for dawn prayers and found himself taken hostage, along with tens of thousands of other worshippers; he had just managed to escape.

Adrenaline pumping through his veins, Saleh told Prince Nayef and Prince Sultan how gunmen had seized the Kaaba. His tale brought into focus the religious nature of the uprising: leading the rebels, he recounted, was a young man who claimed to be the blessed Mahdi and who promised to fill with justice a world gone astray. "What a blasphemy!" Saleh screamed. Dhaheri tried to calm him down, but to no avail. His friend broke down in near hysteria. "These infidels, these blasphemers, these pigs!" he cried. "These murderers! Get rid of them for us, please!"

The religious claims of the rebels confounded al Saud's internal security plans, honed over the years to protect the regime from Socialist or Arab nationalist agitation. As the crisis developed, senior princes decided that the National Guard, rife with ultrareligious Bedouins, could not be trusted to fulfill its primary role of defending the regime—especially as long as the Guard's commander, Prince Abdullah, remained abroad. The traditionally suspect regular army had to be involved in rescuing the royal household from Juhayman's zealots. General Dhaheri's armored brigade, in particular, was to play a key role in the battle ahead.

News about the Mahdi traveled fast as more and more worshippers escaped from the Grand Mosque, some of them carrying Juhayman's epistles. "The Mahdi has arrived," merchants started telling each other with excitement in the Mecca bazaars and down the road in the sprawling conurbation of Jeddah.

Visiting a government office in Jeddah that morning was Sami Angawi, an architect who, as a leading scholar of pilgrimage to the Grand Mosque, headed the Hajj Research Center of King Abdelaziz University. Born into a prominent family of Meccan *ashraf*—direct descendants of Prophet Mohammed—he was something of a rarity in the kingdom. Despite Wahhabi pressure, he retained fidelity to Mecca's millennial tradition of mystical Sufi Islam, which preached love and harmony in the world and shunned the uncompromising zeal of the kingdom's religious orthodoxy. He also defied the Saudi-imposed uniform dress code, favoring an elaborate turban of a kind that used to be worn in Mecca before its conquest by al Saud.

Angawi's appointment was with the director-general for water and sewage affairs, to discuss the maintenance of the sacred Zam Zam spring in the Grand Mosque's courtyard. As he walked into the meeting, radio equipment used for government communications lit up with urgent information. "The Mahdi has appeared," the director-general said by way of greeting.

Angawi thought the bureaucrat was making a joke about his unusual turban, and he grinned in response.

"No, listen, it's for real. I am serious," the man insisted to an astonished Angawi. "The Mahdi has just come, in the Grand Mosque in Mecca."

This information also started to seep across Saudi borders. A Moroccan pilgrim who had witnessed the seizure immediately called to alert the Moroccan embassy in Jeddah. By coincidence, the desk officer who received the call was a captain of Moroccan intelligence. He immediately passed the report to Morocco's King Hassan II.

By another coincidence, when King Hassan II received the decoded message minutes later, he happened to be breakfasting with Prince Abdullah. The commander of the Saudi National Guard didn't deem the news of trouble in Mecca to be sufficiently important to require an immediate return. For now, he stayed put in Morocco.

· · ·

Expecting to oust the usurpers from the Grand Mosque in a matter of hours—and fearful that the takeover was part of a much greater conspiracy guided from abroad—the Saudi royals felt by midmorning that they had to put an end to such information leaks. After all, what could be more embarrassing for Saudi Arabia's standing as a leader of the Islamic world, let alone Fahd's diplomatic mission in Tunis, than a failure to protect the Holy Kaaba? Already there had been occasional calls, in Iran and elsewhere, to take the holy places away from al Saud and to put them under control of a neutral pan-Islamic body.

This was no time for half measures. Before noon of November 20, a Canadian phone company that managed international lines to Saudi Arabia was ordered to impose a total communications blackout. Not a single overseas phone call could be made, telex or telegram sent. Land borders were closed to non-Saudis. For all practical purposes, Saudi Arabia was severed from the rest of the world.

On Saudi radio and TV, not a hint was broadcast about the drama in Mecca. The government kept total silence. This was not surprising—eleven years later, Saudi subjects would have to wait three days before finally being informed that Iraq had occupied Kuwait and had massed an armada on the kingdom's own borders.

In the absence of reliable news, a torrent of fanciful rumors about the Mahdi's arrival engulfed the kingdom. When police sealed the Prophet's Mosque in Medina that morning, the rumor mill churned out what seemed like a most logical explanation: the rebels, it was said, had also captured Islam's second holiest shrine.

Inevitably, many Saudis—including soldiers just deployed to Mecca—started to wonder: What if this is all true? What if the blessed Mahdi has really emerged and the world as we know it is about to end?

This avalanche of theological confusion undermined al Saud's hopes of quickly recapturing the mosque. Absent a clear ruling from the respected ulema on what Islam's requirements are in such a highly unusual situation, many soldiers refused to point their weapons toward the Kaaba. Their oath of allegiance to the king, after all, had the all-important clause of obedience only in things that don't contradict

God's will. But didn't Prophet Mohammed specifically prohibit warfare in the holy precinct and its vicinity, places of peace and devotion? "Fighting in Mecca was not permitted for anyone before me, nor will it be permitted for anyone after me," the Prophet had declared, according to one hadith. "It is not allowed for any of you to carry weapons in Mecca," he was quoted by another. Even in ancient times, didn't the Meccans rely on God, with his disease-spreading birds, to defend the Kaaba from the Army of the Elephant, without defiling the shrine with weapons themselves?

Reconnaissance probes by small units drawn from newly arrived forces quickly ended in several fatalities as the soldiers were picked off from atop the minarets by Juhayman's invisible snipers. Even GID chief Prince Turki, who managed to arrive in Mecca by late Tuesday night, negotiating his way past checkpoints, came close to being shot. At the Shoubra Hotel, located on a street from which one of the minarets could be seen, a bullet shattered the glass front door that night just as the Saudi spymaster turned the handle.

Among ordinary soldiers, mounting casualties compounded the disarray. Will I go to Paradise as a martyr of Islam if I get killed today? some soldiers wondered. Or will I burn in Hell for fighting in the shrine?

One account—probably apocryphal, but indicative of the prevailing mood—tells of the defense minister Prince Sultan growing so frustrated by his men's disintegrating morale Tuesday afternoon that he threw his cloak to the ground in anger. Then the prince reportedly shouted at a group of Saudi soldiers in the mosque's vicinity: "If you do not fight to defend the House of God, who will? Do you want me to bring in Pakistanis to do the fighting in your place?"

There was little that such emotional outbreaks could achieve. Al Saud's authority to govern the kingdom rested on the family's Islamic credentials. With these credentials so dramatically and unexpectedly challenged by Juhayman, the royal family desperately needed its Islamic legitimacy reaffirmed. Such an endorsement could come from only one source: Juhayman's former teacher Bin Baz and a coterie of bearded ulema who happened to share much of the rebels' worldview.

Seeking a fatwa decree that would bless a military assault on the mosque, King Khaled that day issued orders to summon Bin Baz and twenty-nine other senior ulema, including the shrines' supervisor, Ibn Rashed, and the imam who had just escaped from the Grand Mosque, Ibn Subeil, to the Maazar royal palace in Riyadh. The clerics took their time to arrive. And, once they gathered with the king, they made sure to drive a very tough bargain indeed.

ELEVEN

As the Saudi state grappled with its worst security crisis in modern times, the American embassy, like all foreign missions accredited to the House of Saud, operated out of Jeddah instead of Riyadh. For decades, al Saud forbade infidels from staying overnight in the kingdom's conservative desert capital. By the 1970s, this restriction was lifted, but the royal family still preferred to transact most of its business with foreigners in opulent palaces on Jeddah's seashore. The diplomatic community was allowed to transfer to the capital only in 1984—and even then was largely segregated in a special embassies neighborhood.

A sweltering tropical city of anonymous concrete developments, Jeddah spreads along the Red Sea from a maze of crumbling white houses that predate al Saud's rule. Competing with each other in the elegance of their wooden latticework balconies, these mansions are made from coral that remains abundant in local waters; their sophisticated decorations testify to the city's glorious history as a cosmopolitan crossroads.

It is in Jeddah's seaport—and now airport—that most Muslim pilgrims disembark before making the journey to the sanctities of Mecca, and it is through Jeddah that they usually return after the hajj. The drive across a lunar landscape of black rocks protruding from fine yellow sand—and through a checkpoint where the road ahead is marked with a large "Muslims Only" sign—takes only about an hour.

For Ambassador West and other Americans based in Jeddah, the morning of November 20, 1979, started calmly. At a leisurely breakfast with Ohio congressman Tony Hall, West delighted in presenting the visiting lawmaker with Arabian coffee pots and a King Solomon pendant to take home to the wife. To an untrained eye, there was no indication on Jeddah's sunlit, palm-fringed thoroughfares of the violent confrontation beyond the mountain ridge shimmering on the horizon. The first signs of trouble in Mecca that American diplomats received that morning came in anxious phone calls from Danish and British legations: the European diplomats had found themselves unable to communicate with their capitals. A Saudi phone operator told the British that the link to London was out of order and that the embassy should try again in five hours' time.

Alarmed, the Americans immediately tried to phone the State Department and encountered a similar reply. The American embassy in Jeddah and the consulate in Dhahran, however, also maintained an independent, secure cable and phone link with the State Department. Saudi Arabia's communications blackout had a gaping hole.

As embassy staff tried to figure out what had happened, Mark Hambley, a political officer and a rare Arabic speaker among Americans posted to Jeddah, received a tip from a Yemeni employee. The Yemeni, one of scores of non-Americans who worked in the embassy as cooks, drivers, or secretaries, usually commuted from Mecca. As he had left for work, the man told Hambley, he had heard shooting from the area of the Grand Mosque. He did not know the exact reason.

Intrigued, Hambley—whose brief included military affairs—let the

CIA station know about such puzzling developments and then began making inquiries of his own. Saudi contacts in a position to know either were impossible to track down or proffered highly implausible answers. "There's nothing going on in Mecca," said one. "It's just a training exercise," assured another. "There is a typhoid outbreak" went the most imaginative reply.

In different circumstances, an American diplomat or CIA agent would have hopped into a car and driven to the scene of reported unrest, gathering valuable firsthand information. But, though tantalizingly close, Mecca was out of bounds to infidels. And in 1979 neither the CIA station nor the American embassy in Saudi Arabia employed any Muslims who possessed the required security clearances and could be entrusted with such a delicate mission.

As a frustrated Hambley kept scouring for tidbits of news from the holy city, his phone rang. This was an unexpected conversation. The man on the other end of the line had an unfamiliar voice and spoke with an American accent. "I know you; you don't know me," he said. "I have information of great interest."

Whatever he knew was too sensitive to be discussed on an open phone line tapped by Saudi intelligence. The caller, however, was ready to elaborate face-to-face a short time later, at Jeddah's Sands Hotel.

Hambley, a round-faced thirty-one-year-old from Idaho who had already served at American embassies in Yemen and Libya, reflected on whom to take along to this encounter. He decided against involving the CIA. The agency and the State Department were in a perennial rivalry, and Hambley was miffed that the local CIA station had declined to reciprocate his early-morning tip from the Yemeni staffer. Instead, Hambley walked down the corridor and into the office of Lt. Col. Richard Ryer, the U.S. air attaché.

At the Sands Hotel, a prefab building popular with Western expatriates, the mystery caller was waiting for Hambley and Ryer. Once the two

American officials arrived, he started out by establishing his bona fides—as Hambley's blood relative.

In the early twentieth century, Hambley's grandmother broke away from a devoted Seventh-Day Adventist family. Decades later, her example inspired the defection of another relative, in Michigan. Alone among more than a dozen siblings, this man—who shall be called Dan in this book—left the fold and sought a new life outside the church. He flew UH-1 "Huey" choppers during the war in Vietnam. Then, drawn by Saudi Arabia's lucrative expatriate pay, he moved to the kingdom to fly the heavy twin-rotor Chinook helicopters for the Saudi Civil Defense. Dan knew from the grandmother that Hambley was also serving in Saudi Arabia at the time. Now, he told the startled diplomat, seemed like a good time to establish contact with his distant relation.

The Civil Defense Force's task in ordinary times was to deal with fires, crowd control, and natural disasters, especially during the hajj pilgrimage season. Qualified Saudi pilots were scarce, and so the Civil Defense air wing relied on American and British expats. Dan and his colleagues had to undergo a quick conversion to Islam in order to operate within Mecca's sacred boundaries. The conversion process was simple: all that was required of them was to utter in front of a witness the Muslim profession of faith: "There is no god but Allah, and Mohammed is the Prophet of Allah." Dan's new status as a Muslim did not prevent him and most fellow pilots from enjoying single-malt scotch whenever a case could be procured from the American embassy—in spite of Muslim, or, for that matter, Adventist, prohibitions on alcohol.

Dan had been roused this Tuesday morning at six-thirty a.m. at the helicopter wing's Jeddah base. The urgent order was to fly to the Mina area of Mecca, a couple of miles southeast of the Grand Mosque, and to pick up two Saudi intelligence officers for a reconnaissance sortie. Prince Turki's GID lacked an air component of its own and needed the Civil Defense's choppers for a peek behind the Grand Mosque's outer walls. Dan and fellow pilots received only the briefest of explanations. Captain Alwani, the air wing commander, told them that the shrine had been taken over by the "Iranians"—a supposition caused by mistaking the rebels' Mahdist beliefs for the very different invocations of a Mahdi that pervade Shiite Islam.

His Chinook, Dan told Hambley and Ryer, reached the Grand Mosque by nine a.m. The shrine clearly seemed to be under rebel control. Two GID officers peered out of portholes as the chopper made a low pass near the mosque. Some one thousand people remained in the open courtyard near the Kaaba; much larger numbers lurked indoors and in the shadows of the mosque buildings. On the second overflight at around eleven-forty-five a.m., as the chopper approached the northeast corner of the mosque, three distinct rifle shots were fired by the rebels. The aircraft surged skyward, performing evasive maneuvers. The courtyard, Dan jotted down, now for the first time appeared "devoid of humanity."

Dan brought along several photographs from the battle scene. This was most evidently not a typhoid outbreak. Thanks to pure luck and a convoluted family history, Hambley held in his hands a priceless piece of intelligence that would finally supply American policy makers with reliable information.

The pilot was ready to provide more updates, on condition that his collaboration was kept secret from Saudi authorities. The three Americans agreed to meet again the following day, in a different hotel.

By the time the sun rose across the Atlantic on Tuesday, other pieces of the puzzle fell into place. American diplomats managed to get hold of the Saudi military commander for the Western region. American contacts informed the embassy that considerable traffic by C-130 transport planes ferrying troops had been spotted in Jeddah and Riyadh, and that Ministry of Defense hospitals had been put on full alert. Despite the hostage crisis, the United States still officially maintained diplomatic relations with Tehran. The Iranian embassy in Jeddah was contacted, too, to check out whether Khomeini's regime was involved. Iranian diplomats angrily denied all knowledge of the affair.

With America's mission in Tehran already seized by Islamic revolutionaries, Ambassador West's thoughts quickly turned to protecting the American outpost in Jeddah from a similar fate. The Saudi National Guard beefed up its patrols around the embassy, which closed down all peripheral gates to the compound and suspended church services in the chancery auditorium. A lead and a chase car, filled with bodyguards, were added to the ambassador's security detail. Determined not to lose yet another trove of secrets in case of being attacked, American diplomats started to shred classified files.

In Washington, all attention was already focused on Saudi Arabia's neighborhood. Gathering in the White House at four p.m. Eastern time—late at night Saudi time—was a special meeting of the National Security Council dedicated to the escalating hostage standoff with Iran.

Following mediation by the PLO, Khomeini had just released the "lucky thirteen"—five female and eight African American male hostages. The ayatollah magnanimously proclaimed that Islam respected women and that American blacks should not be seen as enemies of Islam because they, too, were being "oppressed" by the Great Satan. As for the remaining hostages, Khomeini threatened to put them on trial for spying, darkly hinting that a likely penalty was death.

The freed embassy workers, flown to Germany, shared tales of harsh treatment that appeared on the front pages of Tuesday morning's American newspapers. They had been kept with their hands and feet bound for two weeks, forbidden to speak, and subjected to psychological torture. Public outrage started to dent Carter's belief in a negotiated solution. The reason the National Security Council convened, two days ahead of Thanksgiving, was to explore ways of using American military might in the region.

The president was ferried to the White House from his Camp David retreat aboard *Marine One* and, precisely a minute before the meeting's scheduled start, strode into the Cabinet Room. America's most senior officials waited for him as they sat in tall leather chairs around an oval mahogany desk that had been donated by Nixon. Vice President Mondale was there, as were the national security adviser, Brzezinski; the secretary of state, Cyrus Vance; and the defense secretary, Harold Brown. Hamilton Jordan, Carter's chief of staff, clutched a folder of secret telegrams he had just received about the newest flashpoint: Mecca.

Carter was shaken by what he viewed as "a spasm of political terrorism" in Saudi Arabia, a country that he had visited the previous year and that had long piqued his curiosity. During that trip, Carter had been charmed by King Khaled, whom he remembered as "quite excited and extremely talkative." On the way into Riyadh, the Saudi monarch had described to Carter his falcon hunting exploits and then fed the American president camel milk and truffles he had personally excavated in the desert. Carter had been duly impressed by the king's common touch: Khaled followed the custom of holding an open court, the *majlis*, where any Saudi citizen could in theory come to state his grievances and where ordinary Saudis were allowed to eat from the royal table.

Among several classified telegrams on the disturbing upheaval in Mecca, a three-page dispatch sent by Ambassador West laid bare the uncertainties. "Embassy is continuing to receive information—some of it conflicting—concerning occupation of the Grand Mosque in Mecca. It is still not known for certain who is occupying the mosque, although it appears that they are very well armed," West wrote, citing testimony by the American chopper pilot. "We have received reports indicating occupiers could be Iranian or Yemeni, although some reports from Saudi sources state occupiers are Saudi tribesmen supporting some as yet unidentified group of Islamic fundamentalists."

This careful, hedged dispatch was superseded by a Defense Intelligence Agency notice issued five hours after West's telegram—and just two minutes before the National Security Council's meeting began. The attack on the holiest place of Islam, the Pentagon's spy service explained categorically, had been perpetrated by a group "believed to be Iranian." The world of Islam "is now entering the month of Muharram, a period of great religious fervor among the Shiites; it is therefore quite likely members of the group holding the mosque are fanatic followers of Ayatollah Khomeini," the DIA said.

A separate telegram by Ralph Lindstrom, the American consul-general in Dhahran, in the predominantly Shiite Eastern Province, appeared to back up this suggestion of Khomeini's involvement, citing the Aramco oil company. The news from Mecca, Lindstrom cabled, "may be related to information we have just obtained from reliable company sources re recent Iranian attempts to agitate Saudi Shiites."

Saudi authorities that year experienced "unusual difficulty" in keeping tabs on Iranians who had entered for the hajj, the consul warned. Iranian pilgrim buses that headed for Mecca routinely arrived with only half the passengers who had crossed into Saudi Arabia at the border; the missing pilgrims turned out to be Arabic-speaking mullahs deployed by Khomeini as agitators, he wrote.

With the lives of American hostages in Tehran on the line and Khomeini looming large as Washington's public enemy number one, it was only natural that the mayhem in Mecca that day was seen by participants at the White House meeting as yet another Iranian provocation. In line with the DIA explanation, the working assumption became that the zealots in the Grand Mosque were Iranians or Iranian-inspired Shiites.

To keep Iran's ambitions in check as Mecca became a war zone, the Pentagon proposed at the White House meeting that afternoon to send to the Persian Gulf USS *Kitty Hawk*, a nuclear carrier with eighty-five aircraft aboard, accompanied by five ships that included a guided-missile cruiser. USS *Kitty Hawk* was to join another battle carrier group led by USS *Midway* and already in the Arabian Sea. Such a huge American presence, Defense Secretary Brown reckoned, would make vulnerable nations like Saudi Arabia feel more secure from Khomeini's Shiite subversion.

Secretary Vance tried to oppose this deployment, arguing that sending USS *Kitty Hawk* to the Gulf would inflame Muslim sentiments and undermine chances of a peaceful solution for the hostage crisis. Carter, who usually sided with Vance's dovish instincts, this time felt compelled to start playing hardball. By late afternoon, the battle group was ordered to start sailing from Subic Bay in the Philippines.

Briefing reporters on the decision, the State Department spokesman Hodding Carter III casually dropped the bombshell about "some kind of disturbance" that had occurred in Islam's holiest shrine. "There has apparently been kind of a seizure of a mosque by a group," he said. To the Saudis' lasting fury, their information blackout on the Mecca uprising was broken—most embarrassingly, by the American government, and without prior warning.

In the Middle East, it was already the dead of night; public outrage wouldn't begin until the morning. Though acknowledging the sketchiness of available information, Carter administration officials who spoke to the media sounded certain about the identity of the perpetrators. "Mecca Mosque Seized by Gunmen Believed to Be from Iran," blared a front-page headline in the next morning's *New York Times*. The article cited an American official, who explained that the militants in Mecca were responding to Khomeini's call "for a general uprising by fundamentalist Muslims."

America's Western allies embraced the same viewpoint. The British ambassador to Jeddah, Sir James Craig, reported that Tuesday in a confidential telegram to the Foreign and Commonwealth Office, "It is widely rumored in Jeddah that a group of Iranians 'stormed and occupied' the Great Mosque in Mecca." In Israel, the Foreign Ministry—citing local Saudi-watchers—also suggested that Khomeini's regime was involved and that the Mecca bloodshed "[did] not signal internal unrest."

This theory fit nicely with the new paradigm that began to take hold and that would dominate Western thinking about Islam for decades, with disastrous consequences. Shiites, because of Khomeini's appeal to this minority sect of Islam, were now deemed to be America's, and the West's, natural enemies. Majority Sunnis—including Wahhabi zealots—were by default seen as benign, if not outright friends.

After Tuesday afternoon's meeting in the White House, President Carter returned from Washington to Camp David. A cinema fan, he watched after dinner with the first lady a movie called *Bloodline*, an international thriller that starred Audrey Hepburn. It wasn't all gloom and doom. The depressing news from the Middle East, so far, had come with a silver lining: despite the humiliation in Tehran, nobody was spilling American blood.

Because of the Mecca events, this would change very soon.

TWELVE

As the news of Mecca unrest broke in Washington, many among the thirty senior Saudi ulema finally assembled in King Khaled's Maazar palace. Rounding them up had been an arduous process; several had had to be transported to Riyadh on special flights from other parts of the kingdom.

Not all could attend. The one member of the ulema council with the most direct involvement in the day's events, the Grand Mosque imam Ibn Subeil, was so traumatized by the upheaval that he stayed put in the holy city.

Shuffling in their leather sandals and adjusting their drooping head-dress, the ulema walked on maroon wall-to-wall carpeting and placed themselves on gold-laced armchairs, exchanging excited comments. Bin Baz, unable to see, had to be helped in by a respectful aide.

King Khaled, after mandatory praises to the Lord, opened the meeting. He recounted how the rebels had bolted the gates of the mosque, demanded allegiance to a so-called Mahdi, and then fired on people inside and outside the shrine, killing innocent Muslims.

Now, the king wanted to know, what should his soldiers be doing? Everyone was aware of the Islamic injunctions against combat in the House of God. What did the learned ulema suggest to preserve the sanctity of the holy place, where the depraved intruders had now stopped the regular prayers and halted the circumambulation of the Kaaba?

Before debating the royal request, the clerics had to make a determination: did the invaders' claim of being led by a Mahdi have any merit?

Ibn Rashed, the sheikh who supervised the Grand Mosque's affairs and who had awoken King Khaled in the early morning, recalled that in previous years he had arrested several "unbalanced" people who had come to the shrine declaring themselves to be Mahdi. The man stirring up trouble in the holy precinct today, he believed, was most certainly an impostor—a real Mahdi, after all, would not be killing and terrorizing innocent worshippers.

Summoning their memory of the hadith, Ibn Rashed and the other ulema agreed that the preconditions of the true Mahdi's arrival, as spelled out by the prophecies, had not yet been fulfilled. Among the missing pieces they noted was that the 70,000 Jews whom the Mahdi and Jesus Christ would destroy had been described by the prophecy as wearing shawls and coming from Isfahan. But Isfahan, in Khomeini's Iran, no longer had such a large Jewish community! And what about the walls of Damascus, with their several gates, behind which the Mahdi would hide awaiting Jesus's aid? Didn't everyone know, Ibn Rashed wondered, that today's Damascus was no longer surrounded by walls!

Having rejected the notion that they might be dealing with a true Mahdi, the clerics moved on to debating King Khaled's request for a fatwa. Unlike the American government, the ulema knew very well that Khomeini's misguided Shiites had nothing to do with the drama in Mecca. It seemed clear by now that the invaders belonged to a Wahhabi missionary movement that Bin Baz and other senior ulema themselves had helped to start. In fact, it was the same movement that had mushroomed under their eyes and that they had determined to be innocuous just more than a year ago.

These idealistic young men couldn't fail to evoke some sympathy among the ultraconservative guardians of Wahhabi propriety. After all, the Grand Mosque's sermon that morning had lamented the kingdom's decaying morale, making the same complaints about spreading infidel mores and tolerance for women's immodesty that the ulema themselves voiced so frequently with the king. And what about the blistering criticism leveled by Juhayman against Prince Fawwaz, the liberal governor of Mecca? Hadn't the ulema also mentioned to His Majesty in the past that Fawwaz sullied the image of al Saud with his tolerance for alcohol and the mixing of sexes, turning the holy city into a den of iniquity? Wasn't it inevitable that such laxity in enforcing the laws of Islam would prompt some hotheaded young men to take matters into their own hands as they sought to uphold the only true faith?

There was only one way forward, Bin Baz and the other senior ulema decided. The House of Saud, despite all its failings, had to be shored up in its hour of need. As King Khaled requested, they would sign a fatwa, reaffirming the regime's Islamic legitimacy. But from now on, the Saudi rulers would have to live up to their Islamic obligations. There should be no more women on TV, no more licentious movies, no more alcohol. The social liberalization that had begun under King Faisal should be halted and, where possible, rolled back. And billions of Saudi petrodollars should be put to good use, spreading the rigid Wahhabi Islam around the planet. Wasn't it Saudi Arabia's duty to dispel the clouds of disbelief, instilling genuine faith among Muslims worldwide and spreading God's word among infidels?

As some Saudi princes described it later, the ulema essentially asked al Saud to adopt Juhayman's agenda in exchange for their help in getting rid of Juhayman himself. As is often the case in the kingdom, this quid pro quo was implied and not necessarily enshrined in clear, unambiguous words. But nobody questioned the meeting's outcome: the royal household accepted the bargain.

It's unclear how much time these negotiations required. It took three long days for the requested fatwa to be composed, signed by all thirty ulema, and released. But King Khaled already felt secure about a commitment from Bin Baz and key clerics by the early morning of Wednesday, November 21. He immediately called Mecca to inform the interior minister, Prince Nayef. Twenty-four hours after the siege of the Grand Mosque began, the Saudi government finally decided that it could tell its own citizens about it. Riyadh radio treated listeners to an unscheduled program of religious poetry and songs, and then, at about five a.m., broadcast a short statement by Prince Nayef's Ministry of the Interior. As Juhayman had predicted, he and his acolytes were described as "kharijites"—a loaded word that referred to the ancient sect that killed the prophet's son-in-law Ali and that would be translated by the Saudis as "renegades," or "deviators" from Islam.

The statement consisted of only four sentences. "A handful of deviators infiltrated the Holy Mosque with arms and ammunition during the early morning prayer Tuesday, the first day of the first month of *Hijra* year 1400. They presented someone to the worshippers in the mosque to perform morning prayers, pretending that he was the expected Mahdi, and urged them at gunpoint to recognize him as such," the document said. "The authorities concerned took all necessary measures to control the situation after procuring a fatwa from the ulema to protect the lives of Muslims inside the mosque. The Ministry of the Interior will issue a subsequent statement on developments in the situation."

The ulema themselves remained conspicuously silent. No word was heard directly from Bin Baz or from other senior clerics.

During the night, while the ulema conferred in Riyadh, Juhayman and his closest aides retreated to an underground area that became their headquarters. These basement-level galleries, the Qaboo, were crammed with supplies. The rebels stocked up on the high-calorie staples of desert survival: dates, flat bread, and a filling dried yogurt paste known as *iqt*. The holy well of Zam Zam provided more than enough drinking water for everyone.

So far, everything had seemed to go well for the conspirators. They were encouraged by the ease of seizing the mosque and the tepid government reaction thereafter. Whatever qualms some may have had about Mohammed Abdullah's status as Mahdi had now disappeared.

From the original tens of thousands of hostages a sizable minority still remained in the mosque. Juhayman's conspirators rounded up scores of poor African pilgrims, men who often stayed behind in Mecca for the lowliest of jobs, and essentially turned them into slaves, tasked with carrying ammunition and water.

One group of 120 Yemeni pilgrims, most of whom failed to understand the Mahdi speech and heard only gunshots during the sermon, was told to sit still near the Kaaba and forbidden to move throughout Tuesday. Their pleas for water or food were ignored. Other basic needs were also difficult to satisfy: public toilets for worshippers visiting the mosque were located outside the compound, in territory now under government control. A few rooms inside the mosque had to be converted into temporary latrines. The stench of urine quickly spread through the shrine's corridors.

Even among those allowed to leave the compound not all could handle the difficult escape route through the windows of the mosque's lower gallery. The old and the infirm had to remain once the main gates were chained shut. "All I can do is lie down," one exhausted seventy-five-year-old Indian pilgrim, Mohammed Staj, told the militants as he refused to move.

With power lines into the compound severed, the Grand Mosque—always bathed in bright light—was plunged into forbidding darkness on Tuesday night, becoming a giant black hole in the heart of the city. Soldiers could no longer see Juhayman's men, while the rebels enjoyed a perfect field of vision into the surrounding streets.

Snipers positioned on top of the minarets continued to score regular hits on government soldiers who tried to observe the goings-on in the sacred compound from Imarat al Ashraf, the tallest building near the mosque, which had now become the military's operational headquarters, and from other vantage points on nearby hillsides.

THIRTEEN

Herbert Hagerty, head of the political section at the American embassy in the Pakistani capital, Islamabad, woke up early on Wednesday, November 21. At seven a.m., as was his habit, he listened to the news on Voice of America. The broadcast made him uncomfortable: items on Carter's dispatch of a naval task force to the Persian Gulf and on the seizure of the Grand Mosque were paired together, with emphasis given to Washington's threats of military action in the hostage standoff. A distracted listener, Hagerty thought, might conclude that the sacrilegious bloodshed in Mecca could have been a result of America's military moves.

Relations between the United States and Pakistan were decidedly frosty at the time. The country's military dictator, General Mohammed Zia ul Haq, rode the region's wave of religious fervor and earlier that year had announced plans to establish "an authentic Islamic order in Pakistan." As Zia canceled elections, he also began implementing Sharia-mandated punishments, such as public floggings and amputations. These policies, combined with Zia's vigorous pursuit of nuclear weapons, provoked a retaliation by Washington. All American assistance and arms sales were suspended, and a flustered Zia started looking toward an Islamic alliance with his revolutionary neighbor, Iran. After all, both countries called themselves Islamic republics—and Islam was the very reason for the existence of Pakistan, a predominantly Muslim part of former British India that had been partitioned off at a huge human cost thirty-two years earlier.

In early November 1979, once the American embassy was captured in Tehran, Iranian diplomats threw daily bonfire parties on their own embassy lawn, brashly urging their Pakistani hosts to launch a similar assault. In the Pakistani media, America was now routinely portrayed as the enemy of the true faith. The *Muslim*, an Islamabad newspaper, that Wednesday morning published a special edition that, like the Voice of America newscast, combined reporting on Mecca events with news of Carter's dispatch of American troops. These, the Pakistani daily charged, were "two hostile actions against the Muslim world . . . by the Imperialists and their stooges."

As Hagerty drove to work, the first radio reports on the violence in the Grand Mosque—a place most Pakistanis either visited or hoped to visit on hajj—brought the nation's hectic metropolises to a standstill. Carnage in the heart of Islam seemed to cause anguish on a visceral, deeply personal level. "People were shocked to hear the news over the radio, and many people broke down in tears. Shops have been closed down as a mark of people's indignation and resentment," a grave-voiced state radio anchorman told Pakistanis on Wednesday. "News of seizure of Kaaba has sent waves of widespread resentment and grief throughout the country."

Hagerty started his day at the embassy by penning an "Immediate" cable that expressed to the State Department his concerns about the Voice of America report and warned of likely anti-American actions in Pakistan. Built at a cost of $21 million six years earlier, the American embassy to Pakistan occupied an elegant modern compound containing a club, a school, and housing blocks. It sat on the edge of Islamabad, overlooking a landscape of fat cows that grazed in well-watered green pastures.

Both the ambassador and the deputy chief of mission were outside the building at about eleven a.m. when Hagerty, the most senior officer remaining indoors, received a phone call from the Australian envoy. The Australian embassy was located about halfway between the Americans and the city center. The allies called in a warning: a crowd of about five hundred youths, shouting anti-imperialist slogans, was heading Hagerty's way.

For diplomats in Islamabad, this was not their first anti-American rally. Surrounded by a wall and guarded by a Pakistani detachment that had been tripled in size earlier that month, the Americans felt relatively secure. They were also protected by a small contingent of U.S. Marines, commanded by Master-Sergeant Loyd Miller, a tall, muscular thirty-eight-year-old from California.

Once the demonstrators arrived, Hagerty dispatched a junior Urdu-speaking officer, David Welch, to meet them at the compound's outer gate. Usually, protesters would hand to the embassy staff a petition outlining whatever grudges they had with American policies and would be on their way after polite assurances that such grievances would be presented directly to President Carter forthwith. The same benign scenario seemed to be unfolding this morning. Welch returned to the chancery with the demonstrators' anti-American manifesto; the youths appeared to be largely leftists. "They're coming your way. I think they are satisfied," Hagerty relayed to the Australian ambassador with relief.

A few minutes later, the phone rang again. "I hate to disappoint you," the Australian warned, "but the bus that had passed us has turned around and is now heading toward you with several more buses from the university." Men clustering on roofs and hanging from the doors of these ramshackle red and blue buses, a much larger mob now rolled toward the diplomatic quarter. Dominated by Islamist firebrands from the capital's Quaid-i-Azam University campus, these young men, dressed in robes and traditional *shalwar kameez*, the matching suits of loose tunics and baggy cotton pants, seethed with uncontrollable rage. As Hagerty feared, a connection between events in Mecca and Carter's decisions had been made in their minds.

Iranian revolutionaries and, before them, the likes of the Muslim Brotherhood in Egypt, have long inundated the Islamic world with self-pitying propaganda that held Westerners—and, in particular, Jews—responsible for all the evils that have befallen the Muslims. In this paranoid worldview, the Americans and the Jews were eternally plotting to undermine Muslim interests and to sully the shrines of Islam. The statement by the Saudi Ministry of the Interior that had aired on Pakistani radio Wednesday morning gave no clue about the identity of the mysterious "deviators" occupying the Kaaba. So, as Pakistanis learned that the House of God had been desecrated by gun-toting invaders, many instinctively blamed the usual suspects.

Even well-educated, seemingly reasonable Muslim intellectuals quickly succumbed to outlandish conspiracy theories. The same happened two decades later, when surprisingly large numbers of Muslims in Pakistan and elsewhere grew convinced that the September 11, 2001, outrage had really been a covert operation by the CIA and the Israeli Mossad.

After hearing about the seizure of the Grand Mosque, one well-known Pakistani newspaper editor jumped to an instant conclusion: an American task force must have launched in Mecca an operation to take full control of the Persian Gulf region. Then he recalled the daring Israeli raid that had rescued hostages in Entebbe, Uganda, three years earlier and decided that the plot wouldn't be complete without the Jews. "Entebbe is on everyone's mind," the editor explained to an American reporter hours later. "People here believed for the last two or three years that Israel is planning such a stroke—to drop paratroopers on Mecca or Medina, or both."

In the following days, it would be a subject of great debate within the Carter administration how precisely such rumors began and whether Khomeini was responsible for the tragedies that ensued.

One thing is clear: Iranian officials, as they awoke Wednesday morning and saw news reports coming out of Washington, did not appreciate being fingered by America—or Israel—as desecrators of the Grand Mosque. Assuming a posture of wounded innocence, Tehran's Foreign Ministry complained that day: "Zionist and U.S. circles have tried to connect this act with Iran . . . The informed people of the world know that the enemies of the true progress and development of mankind use many such tricks."

Then Radio Tehran broadcast a separate communiqué from Khomeini's office in Qom. Turning the tables, it accused the United States and Israel of orchestrating the despicable horrors in Mecca. "It is not far-fetched to assume that this act has been perpetrated by the criminal American imperialism so that it can infiltrate the solid ranks of Muslims by such intrigues," Khomeini's office declared. "It would not be far-fetched to assume that, as it has often indicated, Zionism intends to make the House of God vulnerable."

A *New York Times* correspondent in Tehran reported hearing this incendiary broadcast at eight a.m., which is nine-thirty a.m. Pakistani time, well before any protests began in Islamabad. But the CIA's chief of covert action staff later informed the White House that, according to American radio monitors, Khomeini's statement was first aired early Wednesday afternoon, or two hours *after* Pakistani mobs first encircled the American embassy.

Regardless of whether they had been influenced by Iranian radio or, like the Pakistani newspaper editor, spontaneously blamed America, the militant youths who burst into Quaid-i-Azam University classrooms at about ten a.m., disrupting lectures, seemed to nurture few doubts. American Jews, they announced, had just occupied Islam's holy of holies. For every true Muslim, revenge was a duty.

When these demonstrators converged on the American diplomatic enclave, they were no longer interested in delivering petitions.

. . .

The swelling new throng of protesters started out by burning an embassy vehicle that—with terrible timing—had just pulled up to the compound. In an initial altercation, a student named Asif was shot dead, most likely by police. After that, Pakistani troops who were supposed to maintain order vanished into the mob; some even handed over their guns. Protest organizers shouted that the student, whose bloodied body lay sprawled on the ground, had been killed by Americans firing from inside the embassy. As a battering ram appeared by the wrought-iron gates, embassy staff—realizing how defenseless they had become—rushed to lock up classified files.

Master-Sergeant Miller, a battle-hardened Vietnam war veteran, commanded a total of six marines inside the embassy building. Some were at checkpoint number one, in the main entrance lobby. One marine was at checkpoint number two, the back gate that opened into the cafeteria and the lower-floor area where Pakistani staff worked. And one marine, nineteen-year-old Corporal Steve Crowley from Long Island, was dispatched to observe events from the roof.

"Death to American dogs!" "Avenge the sacrilege in Mecca!" the mob started to chant as the battering ram hit one of the brick columns that supported the compound's entry gate. With surprising ease, the column caved in. The way to the building was open.

Then, all of a sudden, bullets started to fly. The marines hadn't expected to find themselves in a gun battle, and made easy targets. One of the very first shots felled Corporal Crowley, hitting him in the side of his face. He collapsed, unconscious.

Once inside the embassy grounds, Pakistani rioters headed to the motor-pool area in the back of the building, pouring flammables and setting several dozen diplomats' vehicles alight. A new rumor electrified the mob: supposedly one of the students had been captured by the Americans and was allegedly being held prisoner inside. Attackers began to make firebombs out of cloth soaked with petrol and hurl the flaming missiles into the embassy windows. Some landed on the carpeted floor, igniting parts of the embassy itself.

After racing down from the roof, Master-Sergeant Miller dragged

Crowley into the office of the embassy nurse, who desperately tried to revive the hemorrhaging marine with an oxygen mask. The nurse's office sat next door to the embassy vault. Consisting of several rooms in a windowless steel box, the vault is where the most sensitive documents, coding devices, and communications equipment were kept. The vault had its own power generator, and its ceiling was connected via a hatch to the embassy roof—an escape route created for precisely this kind of emergency.

As bullets whizzed by, shattering windows, Master-Sergeant Miller, for the first of many times that day, asked for permission to use firearms to defend the embassy. The request was turned down. Instead, orders sounded: "Everyone to the vault."

Running through smoke-filled corridors, the marines poked their heads into every room, making sure that everyone had heard the instructions. Trying to hold the attackers at bay, the marines—not all of whom even had gas masks—then started to lob tear gas grenades into the crowds that massed by the back and front lobbies.

A total of 137 people—American diplomats, Pakistani staff, and a few guests, including Marcia Granger, a visiting reporter from *Time* magazine—packed the vault by two p.m. Four people were missing: though herded out by the marines, three Pakistani employees and one Spaniard, a builder working on the ambassador's residence, had changed their minds and returned to their offices, hoping to have a better shot at survival separately.

With the embassy now on fire, the air in the vault became unbearably hot. Tear gas also filtered in, prompting bouts of retching. His request for authority to use firearms turned down again, Master-Sergeant Miller pulled all his marines from the lobby checkpoints and into the vault. At 2:23 p.m., a triumphant crowd ran amok through the embassy. Outside, as Pakistani soldiers looked on, demonstrators climbed up the flagpole and tore down the Stars and Stripes. Having torched the American flag, they hoisted up in its place the white Muslim crescent and star on the green Islamic background that make up the banner of Pakistan.

.　.　.

The same white and green banner was being carried with pride at this very moment by troops accompanying General Zia on a four-hour "meet the people" tour of Rawalpindi, a large, chaotic city ten miles south of the wide, empty boulevards of Pakistan's purpose-built capital. Moving at first in an open jeep, and then on bicycle, the Pakistani dictator was showered with flower petals by women strategically positioned on balconies along his route. Whenever Zia stopped, aides handed out bags of rice, cash, and copies of the Quran.

At a teeming Rawalpindi marketplace, Zia made a speech that was carried live on Pakistani radio and TV. Haranguing his subjects about the need to become better Muslims, Zia promised to turn Pakistan into "an impregnable fortress of Islam." Then he expressed his pain over an unfolding tragedy—the one in Mecca, not Islamabad. "The situation in Kaaba is extremely sad," the Pakistani leader said. "Muslims must pray to God Almighty to bestow His blessings and mercy on the Muslim world."

Ever since the attack on the embassy began, hours before that speech, American officials had been trying to get Zia to intervene. From the vault, Hagerty, the most senior diplomat inside the embassy, was in permanent radio contact with Ambassador Arthur Hummel, who remained at home not far from the embassy and who kept calling the Pakistani Foreign Ministry, police, and army commanders.

But lower-level Pakistani officials didn't budge, and Zia just wouldn't take the calls. Even President Carter, awakened by Secretary Vance at 4:13 a.m. with the news of the embassy siege, couldn't get ahold of the Pakistani leader on the first attempt. As many American diplomats in Islamabad concluded afterward, Zia—reluctant to alienate Islamic radicals among his supporters—had deliberately decided to let the embassy burn. The Pakistani army and police troops, who kept arriving in the diplomatic area throughout the day, behaved—in the words of an eyewitness report in Pakistan's *Dawn* newspaper the next morning—as "silent spectators."

Energized by the government's reluctance to protect Westerners in the country, rioters flooded the streets across Pakistan. In Rawalpindi, just as Zia visited town, mobs incinerated the Christian Convent of Jesus and Mary and burned down the U.S. information center, a British library, and offices of American Express. The American cultural center was set ablaze in Lahore, and the American consulate and Pan-American Airlines offices attacked in Karachi. A Bank of America branch was gutted in Islamabad. Everywhere, there was the same explanation. American institutions, declared a student leader in Lahore, had to be burned because "the Holy Kaaba has been occupied by Americans and the Jews."

Showing considerable personal courage, the West German ambassador Ulrich Schesker approached the blazing American embassy at about three p.m., trying to persuade the protesters to disperse. Nobody listened to him, and the crowds continued to grow, augmented by new buses arriving from Rawalpindi.

The besieged diplomats' spirits were momentarily lifted once a Pakistani army helicopter appeared in the sky. The Americans first heard about its approach by radio; Hagerty even asked for snipers to be aboard. Soon the engine and the rotation of blades became audible inside the vault. For several long minutes, the chopper hovered low above the compound. Everyone expected it to land on the roof, if only to evacuate the wounded marine.

But, after having a close look at the mayhem below, the Pakistani pilot banked to one side and just flew away. Protesters cheered. In the vault, a mood of depression set in. The trapped Americans realized that they were on their own, and that they might not live until the end of the day.

Minutes later, Corporal Crowley bled to death. Afraid of further undermining morale, Hagerty kept this depressing piece of news secret.

Via internal embassy phone, he was contacted by the three Pakistani employees and the Spaniard who remained on the second floor. Choking in the thick smoke, they said they could no longer hold out. Hagerty suggested they jump out the windows and into the crowd below. Because the embassy was set on a slope, that window was not too far from the ground. The four wore Pakistani *shalwar kameez* dress. If they were lucky, Hagerty reckoned, they could be mistaken for rioters.

The Spaniard and one of the Pakistani employees listened to the advice and got away with a few bruises and a twisted ankle. The two other Pakistanis were too scared to jump. They succumbed to the smoke and died of asphyxiation under their desks.

Just before four p.m., attackers climbed onto the embassy roof and started banging on the hatch, trying to pry it open with crowbars. Language specialists among the diplomats noted that, according to the shouting that could be heard from the roof, these assailants were Urdu-speaking Pakistanis and Arabic-speaking foreigners; no Farsi-speaking Iranians appeared to be present. Angered by the sturdiness of the hatch, intruders began to unload volleys of fire into the ventilation shafts. As bullets zinged around the vault, the marines finally received permission to use live ammunition if needed.

The part of the vault under the hatch was a separate room, and the air there seared the lungs, filled as it was with a particularly toxic combination of smoke and tear gas. Placed under Master-Sergeant Miller's command, all Americans with weapons rotated on short stints to that spot, gun barrels pointed upward and ready to fire should the hatch give in. The marine was surprised, and somewhat alarmed, by how many people in the embassy, unbeknownst to him, turned out to possess firearms because of their various undercover jobs. His biggest worry was that the attackers would pour gas down the air-conditioning vents and then torch it, turning the vault into a crematorium oven. Trying to electrocute the Pakistanis on the roof, one enterprising CIA agent hooked up a live four-hundred-volt cable to the vault's exposed metal; this, however, didn't work.

"Do you have any hope for us?" a diplomat manning the radio, the vault's only connection with the outside world, shouted in despair.

Because of the scorching heat, everyone now had to breathe through wet paper towels. As the fire ravaged lower floors of the embassy, the vault's steel floor turned into a giant frying pan. Only a wall-to-wall carpet provided a semblance of insulation. And, at about five-thirty p.m., one corner of that carpet suddenly burst in flames. A scream of "Fire in the vault!" broke the tense silence. Two blasts from a fire extinguisher were enough to put it out, for now. But the temperature just kept climbing, with tiles on the vault's inner surface loudly cracking from overheating. The trapped diplomats would be cooked alive if they remained in the vault much longer.

Master-Sergeant Miller, other armed Americans, and one Pakistani employee decided to make a run to the roof. Darkness had already fallen on Islamabad, and Canadian diplomats—who observed the drama from their compound across the road—radioed in to say that the crowds of protesters had begun to thin out. Groping their way through clouds of smoke in smoldering corridors, the marines' advance party finally reached fresh air, weapons drawn and ready to fire. As Master-Sergeant Miller stepped onto the roof, he saw the last of the Pakistani assailants climbing down a ladder. The rioters had had enough fun for the day and were now almost all gone.

It took several more minutes to open the hatch, which the attackers had tried to jam. One by one, the sooty, sweaty diplomats emerged under the resplendent starry skies. Then, protected by the marines, they went down improvised ladders and onto the lawn. With everyone safely escorted out, Master-Sergeant Miller climbed back to the vault. He returned carrying over his shoulder the lifeless, blood-soaked body of Corporal Crowley.

The young marine was not the only American serviceman to die in Islamabad that Wednesday. As protesters rampaged through the embassy compound, they also ransacked staff apartments. In one of them, they found U.S. Army warrant officer Brian Ellis, a pilot for the American military mission in Pakistan. Ellis had a day off and was having a nap. They gunned him down and then set his body on fire.

Two protesters were reported dead: Asif, the student shot by police early in the attack, and an employee of the local health department, identified by local newspapers as Mr. Ashiq.

Late at night, once Hagerty reached his home, in another part of the diplomatic area, his son Devin, a high school senior, lurked behind the door. In his hands, the teenager clutched a baseball bat, ready to hit whatever Islamic revolutionaries would appear on the doorstep.

The Pakistani government's monumental failure to help people trapped in the American embassy—all 137 of whom could have died in that vault—did not seem to cause any offense in Washington. To the contrary, President Carter and Secretary of State Vance rushed to publicly praise General Zia for his troops' supposedly stellar behavior. "President Mohammed Zia immediately dispatched Pakistani troops to protect our personnel and property, called to extend his personal apologies to me and to the American people, and insisted that his government would pay for all the damages," Carter later wrote in his memoirs.

Americans personally involved in the ordeal had a different opinion: "Shit. They didn't do shit," U.S. Navy Commander Charles W. Monaghan told a *Washington Post* reporter about the Pakistani government after emerging from the burning compound. Carter's praise for Zia, in particular, produced cold fury among the survivors. From then on, every time the marines in Islamabad had a beer, they made a point to curse their president and commander in chief.

Immediately after Wednesday's attack, hundreds of nonessential U.S. personnel and diplomats' dependents were evacuated from Pakistan. This put a freeze on all but the most pressing business between the two countries. The few remaining American officials relocated to an unscathed USAID compound a quarter mile from the embassy's ruins, continuing their work with grim dedication. "We were still pissed, but we were professionals" is how Hagerty felt.

The Pakistani government protested the evacuation as unnecessary. General Zia went on CBS TV, assuring his interviewer that there was no anti-American sentiment in Pakistan and that U.S. citizens in his country were "quite safe" and "in good shape." As for the small incident at the embassy, he was deeply sorry.

While General Zia made these tepid apologies on CBS, his government adopted a wholly different tone when addressing the Islamic world. "The stand of the Muslims in Pakistan was magnificent, historic, and unique," the Pakistani state radio boasted in its Arabic-language broadcast. "The people's emotions were moved and were uncontrollable. The people took to the streets throughout Pakistan. They believed that this aggression against the holy of holies truly warranted the opposition of Muslims around the world."

Far from feeling regret about bloodshed at the embassy, Quaid-i-Azam student leaders pressed on with anti-American demonstrations. They considered themselves the injured party, claiming that the two rioters who died in the attack had been felled by American bullets. Student leaders at the university demanded that the Pakistani government detain and indict the U.S. ambassador, Arthur Hummel, and—instead of reimbursing Washington for damage at the embassy—force the U.S. government to pay compensation, at $30,000 per dead protester.

FOURTEEN

While mobs rampaged in Pakistan, Saudi Crown Prince Fahd found himself that Wednesday, November 21, in a highly uncomfortable position: under klieg lights at the Arab summit in Tunis. Used to dispersing money and advice as he basked in the fawning of favor seekers, the Saudi royal now had to explain to the world the embarrassing reports of trouble at home.

The international journalistic contingent that gathered in Tunis for the summit buzzed with excitement. Everyone bayed for details on the uprising that foreign correspondents, kept out by Saudi Arabia's draconian visa policies, were not allowed to witness firsthand.

While Fahd didn't deign meeting the lowly newsmen and -women in person, his Saudi aides made a valiant attempt to quash the entire story. Statements coming out of Washington were ill-informed exaggeration, they assured; in any case, total calm had now been restored to Mecca. The violence in the Grand Mosque—dismissed by one Saudi spokesman in Tunis as "a domestic incident"—was pronounced over.

Fellow Arab leaders, well versed in the art of lying, didn't believe a word of these denials. Early Wednesday morning, they surrounded Fahd at an informal closed-doors briefing, peppering the Saudi with pointed questions. Then, in a purported show of sympathy—tinged by political calculations about how the summit's resolutions might be affected by a Saudi absence—they advised the crown prince to head home. "The brothers, leaders of the Arab countries, told me . . . that there was nothing at the conference that required my presence," Fahd recalled later. "But I realized that by remaining there I would prove the fallaciousness of the speculations. The atmosphere was filled with rumors. What would have been the situation had I gone back immediately?"

So Fahd stayed put, flashing a smile whenever he happened within sight of the cameras. His manner was persuasive. Jordan's King Hussein relayed to his own crown prince that day just how "very calmly" Fahd seemed to be taking the terrible news from Mecca. For two more days, Fahd was bogged down in interminable debates over Lebanon's request to bar Palestinian commandos from the southern part of that country. The plenary meeting of Arab heads of state, initially scheduled for five p.m. Wednesday, was postponed until nine p.m., and then until Thursday morning. Unlike Fahd, Prince Abdullah, the commander of the National Guard, cut short his Moroccan vacation on Wednesday and headed back home.

The senior princes already in Saudi Arabia—Sultan, Nayef, and the just-returned GID chief, Turki al Faisal—were so involved in the unfolding battle for Mecca that they had no time for American diplomats. In his telegrams, Ambassador West relied mostly on official statements and the reports of Hambley's chopper pilot relative, who continued flying sorties above the holy shrine. "We had a virtual blackout of news and adequate intelligence reports," the frustrated ambassador jotted down in his diary that day. He was desperate to provide Washington with more information about events that now directly affected American interests.

On Wednesday at lunch time, he finally managed to meet Ahmed Zaki Yamani, the Saudi oil minister whose forty-five relatives were among Juhayman's hostages. A native of Mecca, the U.S.-educated sheikh Yamani—the face of Saudi Arabia during the 1970s oil crises—was probably the best-known Saudi commoner at the time. His Van Dyke beard and enigmatic smile mesmerized oil traders worldwide; his every word was able to move markets in New York, London, or Tokyo.

Though excluded from direct management of the crisis in Mecca, Yamani possessed a treasure trove of information, both through his government role and through the reports of Meccan relatives that reached him every fifteen minutes by phone from observation points in houses around the Grand Mosque. Two of Yamani's relatives had now succeeded in fleeing the mosque. They were sheltered in the minister's Jeddah home; one sat in silence during the minister's conversation with Ambassador West.

From Yamani, the American government heard for the first time about the existence of one Mohammed Abdullah. Ambassador West listened with awe as the Saudi minister outlined Muslim beliefs about the Mahdi; he took down copious notes about obtuse theological issues surrounding "the second coming of Jesus," "the false Jesus preceding the real Jesus," and the general religious significance of the first day of the Muslim new century. The Mahdi, he wrote in his diary, is "a sort of John the Baptist type."

The Saudi government already seemed to know a lot about the identity of the rebels. Yamani relayed to Ambassador West crucial pieces of information: that Mohammed Abdullah, a "man of imposing appearance and personality," was a former Riyadh student in his mid-twenties who had been imprisoned for four months for "activities inimical to the government" and who had absolutely nothing to do with Iran.

"What would be the results of this takeover?" the American ambassador wondered. Exuding calm, Yamani predicted that the uprising in

Mecca would have few political repercussions. As for the rebels them-selves, he said matter of factly, "Sooner or later they will be captured and beheaded."

As Ambassador West conversed with Yamani and the American em-bassy burned in Islamabad, outpourings of anger at the desecration of the Kaaba began to reverberate across the Muslim world. Under pres-sure from Washington, on Wednesday afternoon Prince Nayef's Inte-rior Ministry issued a new statement that, for the first time, seemed to exculpate the Americans. "There are no indications that lead us to be-lieve that foreign nationalities were involved in the incident," the min-istry announced. "It has been confirmed that the attack has been carried out by a gang that deviated from the path of Islam."

Such tepid Saudi denials failed to discredit Khomeini's conspiracy theory of American and/or Israeli involvement in the Grand Mosque takeover. The ayatollah's outlandish hypothesis continued to gain ac-ceptance among Sunnis and Shiites alike. Syria's national radio and TV repeated the same allegations, as did the Sunni mufti of Lebanon, Sheikh Hassan Khaled. "According to our religion, in the Mecca enclo-sure, not even a bird could be killed, or a tree uprooted," the Lebanese mufti explained. "We estimate that this operation is a Zionist-imperialist attempt to torpedo the Arab summit."

In Egypt, the chief Sunni Muslim religious authority, Mohammed Abdelrahman Bissar, grand sheikh of al Azhar, turned his wrath in an-other direction: he took the Saudi ulema to task for maintaining a dis-tressing public silence about the grave events at the shrine.

In a telegram sent on Wednesday to Bin Baz and other Saudi ulema, Bissar urged "quick decisive action to save the holy House of God" and called on the world's most important Muslim scholars, Saudi and for-eign, to meet near Mecca to determine a joint Islamic response. Be-tween the lines of this telegram, from the most influential Sunni cleric outside Saudi Arabia, loomed a terrifying message for al Saud and the Wahhabi establishment. Having failed to protect the Grand Mosque from "brutal aggression," the Saudis were now being asked to share their lucrative monopoly over managing the sacred shrines with the rest of the Muslim world. The perpetrators of this outrage, Bissar suggested helpfully, could be put to death by crucifixion.

Bin Baz was able to receive the Egyptian message because by Wednesday night phone and telegraph links between Saudi Arabia and the rest of the world had been restored. This allowed the first independent news on the situation in the kingdom to filter out. After more than a day of frustration, James Buchan, a future British novelist then living in Jeddah and working as a "stringer"—a part time correspondent—for London's *Financial Times*, finally managed to get his editors on the line. Though unable to visit Mecca, he pieced together information obtained from Western diplomats and Saudi eyewitnesses. Once Buchan started dictating the dispatch, an angry Saudi operator cut in, disconnecting the line. "Mecca, *la!*" he shouted ("Mecca, no!").

Buchan still got into print crucial pieces of the puzzle: that the rebels were somehow associated with Juhayman's Uteybi tribe, that they did not appear to be linked with Khomeini, and that the fighting so far had caused "several dozen, possibly several hundred deaths."

These nuggets of truth drowned in the wild speculation the information blackout had provoked around the world. The Grand Mosque's imam, Ibn Subeil, current Mecca governor Prince Fawwaz, former Mecca governor Prince Mishaal, and other senior members of the House of Saud were erroneously reported dead. Lebanon's former president Camille Chamoun, who suggested in these chaotic hours that the Mecca uprising had been inspired by his enemy Syria, made the ultimate faux pas of issuing public condolences. Prince Mishaal, Chamoun announced solemnly, "was a friend of Lebanon and a personal friend."

This declaration wasn't the only episode of comic relief. Taking literally the Saudi designation of Juhayman's group as "kharijites," the French news agency reported that the attackers inside the Grand Mosque belonged to "the 600,000-strong Kharijite Muslim sect, generally considered fanatical and . . . mainly represented in Tunisia, Algeria, Oman and Tanzania."

Sami Angawi, the director of the hajj research center in Jeddah, was determined to find out for himself the identity of the mysterious "deviators" in the Grand Mosque. If the Mahdi had really appeared, this was an event of planetary importance, he thought after leaving the office of the water and sewage director. And, as a direct descendant of the Prophet, Angawi felt that he was duty-bound to be present in Mecca for the historic occasion.

Clearing several rings of checkpoints that now slowed to a grind all traffic in and out of the city, Angawi returned to his hometown. There, he called on Islamic luminaries among Mecca's prominent families. Shunning established Wahhabi ulema who had been imported by al Saud from the Nejd, he sought advice from fellow Sufi sheikhs and from other elders of Mecca's own, more tolerant tradition of Islam. Many of them had been inside the Grand Mosque the previous morning, and they held nothing but scorn for Juhayman and the alleged Mahdi.

A true Mahdi wouldn't have to discharge firearms, attack worshippers, and lock the mosque's gates, these scholars noted with distaste. The rebels' uncouth speech, one turbaned elder mused, was all too similar to the pronouncements that the dreaded Ikhwan had been making in Mecca five decades earlier. "Same Wahhabis, same talk," he scoffed. "Same thing."

This was a consensus that coalesced in Mecca by the second day of the crisis. Juhayman's austere, violent movement may have appealed to many in the Wahhabi heartland of the Nejd, but here in Mecca, a cosmopolitan city whose residents hailed from the four corners of the world and often resented Wahhabi domination, it elicited little sympathy.

Whatever grudges Meccans still held about being subjects of al Saud, they saw these wild, bearded rebels who now held their sacred shrine hostage as a far worse evil. Spontaneously, many locals offered food and shelter to the Saudi troops that started to converge on the city. After much reflection, Angawi, too, came to the conclusion that he must assist the government in liberating the mosque.

He had something to offer. As head of the hajj research center, Angawi had conducted detailed studies of the Grand Mosque compound; he possessed floor plans and large sheets of aerial photography. In his professional capacity, Angawi also dealt with Prince Ahmed, the king's brother and deputy minister of the interior. He called the prince's office and asked whether these documents might be of use.

"Yes, come quickly, quickly," the prince's secretary shouted into the phone.

It wasn't clear, though, where the prince was located. Angawi rolled the maps and aerial photographs into a long tube and headed toward the Grand Mosque. Talking his way past checkpoints, he suddenly found himself by one of the main gates of the enclosure.

A handful of soldiers crouched in the area, taking cover from snipers on the minarets. They were shocked to see Angawi and his tube of maps—the container so similar to a bazooka from a distance—in the middle of the battlefield. Their commanding officer was visibly upset. "You are crazy!" he shouted at Angawi. "What are you doing here?"

Prince Ahmed, the officer said, was to be found in the Shoubra Hotel, the same one where princes Nayef and Sultan, the ministers of interior and defense, had arrived the previous day. To get there, Angawi had to cross the plaza. He finally realized that he was risking his life and that the documents tube in his hands made him a likely target for snipers. He was told to tie up his robe and to make zigzags as he ran toward safety.

The Shoubra by now had turned into a veritable military outpost. Fearing an attack on the hotel's illustrious guests, security forces strung up a booby-trapped trip wire at the entrance. The senior princes and military men were planning the first serious raid of the mosque and were too busy to meet with Angawi. Instead, an aide was dispatched downstairs to meet the academic. Angawi handed him the maps and the photographs and outlined possible ways of organizing the assault.

Abhorring the idea of deploying tanks or artillery on the holy ground, Angawi proposed using bulldozers. These, he said, could knock down gates and protect infantry soldiers entering the enclosure.

Photos and maps brought in by Angawi were snapped up by commanders desperate for hard information about their target. Major Nefai of the Special Security Forces, who was entrusted with drawing up the operations plan for the impending assault, had been expecting some help on this front from Osama Bin Laden's older brother Salem.

Salem had taken over the Bin Laden family's helm after his father's death in a 1967 air crash, and, together with the Bin Laden business empire, inherited close ties to the royal household. The Bin Laden company, which built or renovated almost all the structures surrounding the Kaaba, was the only one to possess detailed blueprints of the shrine. Salem rushed to the Mecca war room right after hearing about Juhayman's intrusion. But he didn't bring these precious blueprints along, and, military officers remarked with scorn, seemed mostly preoccupied with ingratiating himself with the royals. The company was in the middle of moving offices, Salem explained, and it was very difficult to locate the exact boxes that contained these documents.

This meant that until Angawi's documents arrived Major Nefai and fellow planners had to grope in the dark. Nobody told them about the existence of the intricate labyrinth, the Qaboo, in the basement under the mosque. Intelligence about the number of gunmen inside, and about their weaponry, was also scarce. Valuable information could have been gleaned from pilgrims who still continued escaping from the shrine. But most of these were immediately snatched by Mabaheth secret police agents and bundled away for political interrogations in Jeddah or Riyadh—before military intelligence officers had a chance to ask vital questions about the battlefield.

No new reports arrived from the several members of the unarmed police service still holed up inside the Grand Mosque. These men—

whom the imam Ibn Subeil had tried to rouse for action in the first hours of the crisis—remained trapped in their station inside the compound and were in touch via phone after the cleric escaped on Tuesday. The following day, they were discovered. Juhayman's rebels promptly manacled the policemen with metal cuffs taken from the station's cupboards and locked them up in a holding cell in the basement. The duty officer—who had been prudent enough to take off the top of his uniform—managed to pass for a simple trooper and wasn't maltreated.

As Saudi officials discussed their options on Wednesday, some of the royals, remembering displays of paratrooper prowess they had watched at military maneuvers, proposed dropping airborne commandos into the shrine. It took a while for Major Nefai and other military men to deflect this idea. He explained that paratroopers landing into such a confined space would be riddled with bullets before they even reached the ground—and that their choppers would be quite likely shot out of the air.

These arguments were illustrated by the frequent fusillades that the rebels had already unleashed on Saudi aircraft. On almost every sortie, Dan's Chinook was shot at by what appeared to be a 0.50-caliber machine gun placed among the twin minarets. Tracer rounds soared into the sky from several other emplacements. One round narrowly missed the American-piloted chopper, burning out at about eight thousand feet, or more than twice its altitude. Even crews of Saudi F-5 fighter jets, which regularly overflew the shrine, now feared being shot down and adopted a relatively safe flat flight pattern.

Nobody wanted to lose costly aircraft. The senior princes agreed: the operation to recapture the mosque would be carried out from the ground. By late Wednesday, the plans for the attack were finalized.

The House of Saud wanted quick action, and so the shrine had to be liberated without waiting for additional troops. There were also complex considerations of byzantine family politics to be accommodated—at the expense of basic military science. Every senior prince desired a share of the glory. This meant that Prince Nayef's Interior Ministry Special Security commandos, Prince Sultan's Saudi Army, and Prince Abdullah's National Guard all had to participate in the assault, even though the three forces never trained together and didn't even have compatible radios. In a reflection of royal hubris, this hodgepodge attack team lacked armor and—numbering just several hundred men— was not much larger in size than Juhayman's force of well-entrenched zealots.

Unwilling to consider Juhayman's rebels a serious threat, the royal family at the time still regarded the trouble at the Grand Mosque as a law enforcement issue. This meant that Prince Nayef's Interior Ministry rather than the regular military took charge of the joint force. Major General Mohammed Bin Hilal, chief of the Riyadh region police and head of the Special Security, became its commander.

Stuck between the two sides once the battle lines were drawn, several pilgrims spent these harrowing hours cloistered in the Africa Hotel, the windows of which overlooked the sacred enclosure. All the shops in the area had long closed, and the deserted streets were patrolled by the troops—some of whom were already making unauthorized with-drawals from the nearby gold market. The hotel's mostly foreign guests were afraid to venture out into frequent crossfire, and stayed hungry throughout the day.

One of these inhabitants of the Africa Hotel was Abdelazim al Matani, an Egyptian professor of Arabic who had prayed by the Kaaba at the time of Juhayman's takeover, separated by just one row of men from the imam Ibn Subeil, and who managed to flee the Grand Mosque in the first hour of the siege. Once a journalist for an Egyptian newspaper, Matani realized that he had become a rare eyewitness to history, with a panoramic view of the battlefield. His tiny room did not have a desk. So, placing an attaché case on his lap, he began taking notes on the momentous developments just across the street from his hotel.

Through most of Wednesday, he noted, fighting was very light. But, late at night, Matani was awoken by terrifying flashes and the sound of explosions. The hotel's building shook, window panes started to break, and Matani jumped from his bed. Saudi artillery, deployed on hills overlooking the city, had just started shelling the mosque.

FIFTEEN

Concerned with the ulema's sensibilities, and still lacking a formal fatwa from the learned clerics, the Saudi government was very careful not to damage the Grand Mosque in the initial attack. The shells that started to rain on the sacred compound were mostly flash-bang charges that did not produce lethal fragments. These fireworks were supposed to disorient Juhayman's men with deafening noise and a blinding, brilliant light.

Once the shelling began, at about three-thirty a.m., groups of ground commandos raced toward the gates of the enclosure. Major Suleyman al Shaaman led a unit of thirty men to the eastern side of the Marwa-Safa gallery. This two-story arcade stretching some 450 meters (about 490 yards) in length replicates the route that the biblical Hagar had followed as she searched for water for her son Ishmael. Running south toward the main body of the mosque, the Marwa-Safa gallery—lined with carpets, tiled with precious marble, and lit with gilded chandeliers—was a key part of the pilgrimage ritual and contained eleven gates on its sides.

Hoping to take advantage of the confusion, Major Shaaman's men aimed to break through the Bab al Salam, or the Peace Gate, at the midpoint in the gallery and seize a foothold for the next wave of troops. Nobody knew for sure exactly how many militants were holed up inside—officers had been told about dozens, not hundreds.

Very soon, it became obvious that all this cacophony of explosions and flashes of light didn't much impress Juhayman's men: their training in National Guard camps in the desert was paying off. Rebel snipers atop the minarets instantly spotted advancing government soldiers and unloaded volleys of fire on them. Major Shaaman's troops, like the unlucky police team on the first day of the standoff, found themselves in a killing field. Bullets cracked the marble around the unit, sending into the air little fountains of chipped stone and dust. Fire no longer came just from the minarets; gunmen also opened fire from top-floor windows of the mosque itself.

Soldiers desperately sought cover. But the massive gate wouldn't give in, and there was nowhere to hide. Then, suddenly, one of the halves of the gate was pulled from inside, just enough to allow rebel guns to unload at the soldiers point-blank from the pitch-black darkness beyond.

With a thud, one of the officers in the unit, a captain, fell dead. Minutes later, a corporal was riddled by high-velocity lead. And then a mist of pink spray burst from Major Shaaman's face. His khaki uniform turning carmine from spurting blood, the major slumped and then also tumbled to the ground.

Within minutes of starting, this offensive unraveled at the Peace Gate, as it did at other approaches to the mosque. With senior officers out of commission, the remaining soldiers did what anyone would in such a meat grinder: they crammed their bodies behind any semblance of cover, focused on staying alive. Some glued themselves to the wall behind curves that obscured the rebels' line of fire; others curled up in crevices of the structure.

One of Major Shaaman's men, Staff Sergeant Mohammed Ayed, had been hit in the knee. Bleeding, he and a fellow soldier sat in a blind spot, waiting for a lull in the fighting and praying for deliverance. An hour later, searchlights belatedly illuminated the minarets, denying rebel snipers the cover of darkness. The smoke had cleared. The guns had been silent for a while. It seemed like the right moment to try an escape.

The first line of houses that could offer refuge from this carnage seemed tantalizingly close. Juhayman's snipers—many of them expert hunters—patiently waited for just this moment. Once the two bedraggled survivors started to move, they squeezed the triggers. Another bullet tore through Ayed's thigh. Fire once again seemed to erupt from every direction. Crawling back, Ayed saw that what had been Major Shaaman was now a messy pulp of charred flesh. One of the latest rebel volleys had hit an explosive or a grenade that had been attached to the major's belt. The munition went off in a radiant ball of fire, shredding the officer's torso.

Dazed, Ayed abandoned whatever remained of the killed major and managed to pull himself into a nearby hideout next to a surviving comrade. There he remained, holding his leg and attempting to stanch the blood loss, for twelve hours. The two had no food, no medication, and no way of communicating with the outside world. Fellow soldiers seemed in no haste to rescue them. At the end, it was only Juhayman's reluctance to shoot at civilians that saved the men's lives.

Though Ayed and his comrade were not visible to rebels inside the mosque, they sat in plain sight of ordinary Meccans who lived across the street from the Peace Gate. During a pause in the fighting, three of these neighbors dared to venture outdoors. They took pity on the wounded troops and brought out some of their own clothes. Once the injured soldiers donned these robes, pretending to be ordinary civilians, the three neighbors returned with a stretcher. An ambulance was parked behind a nearby house, safely outside the rebel line of fire, ready to take the men to the hospital.

In Ayed's recollection, a total of six members of his massacred unit had been saved this way.

The Grand Mosque remained firmly in Juhayman's hands. Conspirators inside celebrated with prayers: because of God's protection afforded to the faithful, the Saudi army, while not quite swallowed into the ground, had been unable to harm the Mahdi's defenders. From the minarets, rebel snipers surveyed a landscape of soot-coated body parts, burned shells, and pockmarked marble that emerged from under acrid smoke.

Though disturbed by the rebels' battlefield prowess, the House of Saud was in no mood to let up. The senior princes' war council decided to press on with the offensive, sending into the Grand Mosque's death trap freshly arrived rangers of the Saudi Army's Sixth Paratroop Battalion.

The battalion, normally based in the northern city of Tabuk, was commanded by Colonel Nasser al Homaid. Many of his rangers had been trained in France, and, unlike National Guard troopers, they were itching for action, unhindered by the lack of a fatwa from the clerics.

One of these French-trained officers, a twenty-eight-year-old captain who went by the name Abu Sultan, felt a personal injury from Juhayman's outrage: in the times before al Saud's conquest of the holy city, Abu Sultan's grandfather had served as chief of the Grand Mosque police.

A wiry, intense man with a cropped mustache, Captain Abu Sultan spent the first hours of the uprising frantically dialing Meccan acquaintances, collecting every tidbit of news from the shrine. On Wednesday, the second day of the standoff, his battalion was called up on alert, and, following the late-morning prayer, herded onto C-130 transport planes. Abu Sultan was in the first aircraft, arriving in the Grand Mosque's vicinity by the afternoon.

Soldiers already on the ground welcomed the newcomers with awed advice: the Grand Mosque rebels, they noted, shot well, and whenever a trigger was pulled on one of the minarets, a uniformed man was usually felled.

The Tabuk rangers' mission—like that of the late Major Shaaman's unit—was to penetrate the opulent gallery that enclosed the path between Marwa and Safa hills. Major Shaaman's men had been bludgeoned as they tried to enter the Peace Gate on the eastern side of that gallery. The Sixth Battalion would try a different route, breaking into the structure from its northernmost tip at Marwa and then proceeding southward, paying special attention to dangers that lurked around the ill-fated Peace Gate.

As Colonel Homaid outlined this action plan early Thursday morning, one senior prince—most likely Prince Nayef—listened impatiently and then demanded an immediate attack. The colonel, aware of the horrendous casualty rate among other units attempting to storm the Grand Mosque, suggested that it would be better to wait for the night. Blinded by the floodlights, he argued, the rebels might not be able to see the attack force.

Prince Nayef, a portly, mercurial man used to unquestioning obedience, exploded with fury. By one account, he yelled at Colonel Homaid, "You are not a man!" and dismissed the officer's objections as a show of cowardice. Loss of life was not important, the prince declared: in such a noble mission, soldiers killed in battle would be considered martyrs for Islam and win for themselves a ticket to Paradise.

Humbled, Colonel Homaid could only salute and order an immediate attack.

Sixth Battalion rangers managed to sneak undetected by the Marwa Gate, and they affixed TNT charges on its perimeter, running a wire from the detonator to the nearest army outpost. On Abu Sultan's signal, the explosives went off, blowing the massive gate off its hinges. The gate—so heavy that some fifty troopers would be unable to make it budge in following days—fell flat on the ground, dispersing a cloud of dust, ash, and stone fragments.

To prove his courage, Colonel Homaid stepped first into the opening, followed by the battalion's S-3 operations officer, Major Turki al Useimi. Behind them advanced a few dozen men, most of them from a platoon commanded by Lieutenant Abdulaziz Qudheibi.

Amid choking smoke inside the gallery, everything seemed unnaturally quiet. Shoes, prayer books, shawls, and bags left behind by escaping worshippers littered the ground. Not a single rebel was in sight; not a gunshot could be heard. The unit moved ahead step by step, fingers on the trigger.

The gallery, a multilane pedestrian highway that left the unit exposed in its large empty bowels, contained plenty of hideouts. There, Juhayman's men waited patiently for just the right moment to strike. Mohammed Abdullah, the supposed Mahdi himself, was among dozens of conspirators who lurked in this passageway. His chest crossed in the shape of an X by two bandoliers packed with bullets, he trained the sights of his rifle on the advancing troopers. So did Faisal Mohammed Faisal, one of Juhayman's most senior commanders.

By the time the paratroopers realized they were in an ambush, it was too late. The soldiers were almost halfway into the gallery when rebels popped up four at a time from the windows on the sides and from raised platforms, unleashing a hailstorm of lead. Colonel Homaid was killed by the first volley. Seconds later, his deputy, Major Useimi, fell on the ground, wounded in the leg.

As he tried to press with the offensive and rescue the two senior officers, the mustachioed, baby-faced Lieutenant Qudheibi felt a rebel bullet graze his arm. Seeking cover behind columns and crawling on the ground, he and the few surviving members of the decimated assault team radioed for help from the outside.

It took hours for the rescue party to arrive—and it, too, came under heavy fire as soon as it penetrated the gallery. Shell-shocked, these reinforcements were too scared to approach Major Useimi, who now lay in a puddle of his own blood. Instead, they threw him a rope and yelled, "Hold on." Clenching his teeth, the major grabbed the rope, and the rescuers started to pull. As soon as Major Useimi was yanked out of his hideout and onto a stretch of open floor, a new salvo burrowed into his body. Slammed by bullets, his body jerked for a second or two and then went unnaturally limp. He was now obviously dead.

Lieutenant Qudheibi, meanwhile, tried to keep moving forward. He didn't get far before a second bullet skewered his forearm, tearing apart a muscle and causing blood to squirt out. Minutes later, as the young lieutenant lost consciousness, he was hit once again—by a spray of bird pellets shot from a hunting rifle.

When Lieutenant Qudheibi reopened his eyes, the offensive had fallen apart and the gallery was filled with the moans of the dying. As in a dream, he saw two bearded gunmen standing above him. They pulled him up and carted him away to a room on the upper level of the mosque. The lieutenant's vision was blurred, and he no longer felt his arm. Inside the dark room, Lieutenant Qudheibi noticed another soldier from his unit by the wall. The second prisoner, injured in the same engagement, struggled with a nasty chest wound.

There were no medics among the rebels. Still, one of the gunmen tried to help. He brought a piece of cloth soaked in holy Zam Zam water—the closest thing to disinfectant available in the shrine—and tightly bandaged it around Lieutenant Qudheibi's forearm. According to the hadith, he explained, Zam Zam water was the best cure for all ailments. Once the militants slowed the blood loss, they tried to convert the two prisoners to Juhayman's cause. They earnestly explained to their captives that the Mahdi had come and that television, radio, khaki uniforms, and salaries paid by the Ministry of Defense were all deemed *haram*—prohibited by the Almighty.

SIXTEEN

The world did not know about this bloodbath. As the surviving soldiers trickled out of the Grand Mosque neighborhood, leaving dead and severely injured comrades behind, the Saudi government decided to announce a victory. At eleven a.m. on Thursday, November 22, state-run Riyadh Radio broadcast a long speech by the information minister, Mohammed Abduh Yamani. These were the first official comments on the Mecca crisis since the two terse Interior Ministry statements the previous day.

The information minister, theoretically in charge of determining what the country's newspapers could and couldn't write, did not have much actual power. A relative liberal, he—like the oil minister Ahmed Zaki Yamani—hailed from a Meccan family of Yemeni origin and didn't possess the tribal clout of a Nejdi bloodline, let alone the authority that royal descent could confer. In sensitive matters—and few were as sensitive as the one now at hand—he took his cue from senior royals, especially Prince Nayef.

The royal policy was simple: save face and insist that all is well. Defeat is victory. Ignorance is strength.

"Matters, thanks be to God, are now under total control," Yamani proclaimed with a sigh of relief on the radio this Thursday morning, shortly after Colonel Homaid was killed and the platoon commander taken hostage. "This group, which is deviating from the Islamic religion, is under the control of security authorities."

Like other Saudi officials, Yamani was defensive: he felt the need to explain why this "minor incident" had taken so long to bring "under total control." Juhayman's rebels, Yamani assured, "could have been ousted by force at any moment, but the competent security authorities were anxious to handle this matter with all the wisdom and with consideration for the lives of Muslims inside the Holy Mosque, who are innocent and helpless in this matter."

Then, contradicting everything he had said so far, the minister indicated that the total control was not yet quite totally total: "The state will continue tackling this issue in order to end it, God willing, in the next few hours."

This nuance went unnoticed by foreign leaders dependent on Saudi largesse and eager to help al Saud maintain the fiction of having resolved the crisis. They rushed to fire off congratulatory telegrams to Riyadh. "We have learned with a deep sense of relief and thanksgiving that by the grace of Almighty Allah Your Majesty's forces have been able to clear the holy precincts from the benighted elements," the Pakistani president Zia wrote King Khaled that Thursday. "The devotees of Islam who are once again free to offer worship in the Grand Mosque owe to Your Majesty a debt of gratitude."

The Saudi announcement of victory was also taken at face value by the Riyadh-based U.S. Military Training Mission, which coordinated American defense cooperation with the kingdom. Citing its contacts in the Saudi Ministry of Defense, USMTM quickly reported that Saudi forces "gained entry to the first floor of the mosque by means of their M-113 armored personnel carriers, which provided adequate cover against the occupiers' fire."

Dan, the American Chinook pilot debriefed the same day by Hambley and Ryer, provided a completely different assessment. Once the assault on the Marwa-Safa gallery withered, he said, the pilots could see no "activity whatsoever either in the mosque or in the surrounding area, which continue[d] to be cordoned off for a three to five block area." No APCs or track traces could be sighted in the area. On the way back to Jeddah on Thursday afternoon, his chopper carried some fifteen wounded soldiers from the Sixth Paratroop Battalion. Judging from direct observations, Dan reported, it was "implausible" that Saudi forces had managed to seize any part of the mosque.

In composing his Thursday cable to Washington, a perplexed Ambassador West was at a loss over whom to believe. "We have no explanation for the inconsistency between the [pilot's] observations and the various reports we have received regarding the alleged slow but methodical recapture of the mosque from the Islamic dissidents," he wrote. It was highly frustrating that nobody from the embassy had been able to look at the battlefield with his own eyes. Something had to be done.

Abroad, as the continuing absence of reliable news spurred rumormongering, the Mecca affair took on a life of its own. For the U.S. government, the crisis's main repercussion so far was the lethal attack on the American diplomats in Pakistan. State Department officials were shocked by the intensity of anti-American feelings there and the ease with which the wildest accusations against the United States seemed to be believed nowadays. Brzezinski's advice to Carter earlier that year now seemed patently wrong: the Iranian revolution was not isolated. The fervent anti-American propaganda coming out of Tehran was making Muslims worldwide see America as the enemy of their faith.

That Thursday, demonstrators infuriated by the mayhem in Mecca stoned the residence of the U.S. consul in Izmir, Turkey, and attempted to storm the building. The same happened in the Bangladeshi capital,

Dhaka, where Islamist protesters—held at bay by police—tried to burn down the American embassy. In Pakistan, as the evacuation of U.S. personnel continued, schools and bazaars remained closed for the second day in a row.

Secretary of State Vance and other U.S. officials grew increasingly concerned that Wednesday's Saudi denial of involvement by "foreign nationalities" in the Mecca uprising just wasn't explicit enough to quash conspiracy theories propagated by Tehran. So, Thursday morning, Vance set in motion a crescendo of diplomatic activity.

In Jeddah, Ambassador West once again called on the oil minister Ahmed Zaki Yamani. Reading aloud Khomeini's statement, West explained to Yamani that Iranian accusations were "putting in jeopardy the lives of American citizens as well as American diplomats throughout the Islamic world," and that the United States felt it had the right to demand a stronger refutation. Examining the previous day's Interior Ministry statement, Yamani agreed with Ambassador West that the text might indeed be insufficient. He explained that the Saudis were concerned that a more explicit denial of foreign involvement in the uprising might be construed as speculative if it came before the mosque was liberated and an investigation of the affair was completed.

America wasn't prepared to wait so long. Surely, Ambassador West retorted, the Saudi government knew even without an investigation that Washington had nothing to do with the Mecca events! Impressed by the vigor of American protests, Yamani promised to take up the matter directly with Prince Sultan in the afternoon.

At the Arab summit in Tunis, meanwhile, American diplomats sought out the Saudi delegation and passed an urgent personal message from Vance to the Saudi foreign minister, Prince Saud al Faisal. It was "a matter of great importance," Vance wrote sternly, that the Saudis make an unequivocal statement on the crisis in Mecca, "dealing with the allegations that Americans engineered this behind the scenes." A few hours later, Saud al Faisal discussed the request with Crown Prince Fahd and wrote back promising action: "The Saudi Arabian Government has the deepest faith in the non-existence of any relationship of the U.S. to the incident under discussion."

Speaking in unison with the Great Satan, revolutionaries in Tehran were making similar demands; they requested that the Saudis rule out any suggestion of *their* involvement in the Mecca uprising. Early Thursday afternoon, Prince Nayef obliged, finally releasing a new declaration that pleased everyone.

"Neither the United States, Iran, nor any other countries have had anything to do with the attack on the Holy Kaaba," he announced. "News reports alleging U.S. involvement in the incident were absolutely untrue and baseless."

There is a reason it took so long for Saudi officials—and especially the conspiratorially minded Prince Nayef—to clear up the blood libel against their American ally.

In their heart of hearts, Saudi royals just couldn't forgive Washington for leaking the news of "a disturbance" in Mecca on the first day of the crisis. This PR blunder caused al Saud a humiliating loss of face just as the kingdom was expecting to revel in its oil-fueled influence at the summit in Tunis. For years to come, opponents of the Saudi regime held up this disclosure by Washington as proof positive of the royal family's subservience to the United States.

Prince Nayef himself outlined his frustrations in an interview with a Lebanese newspaper a few weeks later. The Americans, he complained, had publicized the "incident" in Mecca so quickly that it seemed that they had known about it in advance! Such inexplicable haste, in the prince's opinion, justified anti-American violence. "We have the right to speculate about the reason why the Americans announced the report the way they did," he pronounced. "Thus, we understand why the demonstrations that were staged in several Islamic cities against the U.S. embassies and other symbols of U.S. presence took place, for everyone thought the United States was associated with this issue."

Nayef's explicit denial of U.S. involvement in the Mecca affair, extracted by such an intense diplomatic effort, failed to impress Tehran's revolutionary propagandists. The Iranian media and pro-Iranian radicals worldwide kept up denunciations of a "criminal deed perpetrated by gangs of Zionists and imperialists, and masterminded by U.S. intelligence." Khomeini personally notched up the rhetoric on Thursday evening as he welcomed in the Iranian holy city of Qom a delegation of some 120 senior Pakistani military officers who transited Iran on their way home from the hajj in Mecca.

In this televised encounter, Khomeini warmly praised the Pakistanis for the previous day's destruction of the American embassy in Islamabad. "It is a cause of joy that . . . all Pakistan has risen against the United States," the ayatollah told the politely listening Pakistani officers.

All Muslim armies and law enforcement agencies, Khomeini continued, should now join Iran in this battle, for the confrontation was not between America and Iran but between "the entire world of disbelief and the world of Islam." Victory was close, the ayatollah assured, because America's own society was about to implode: "There is, in fact, discord and disunity among blacks in America, who have been oppressed by the United States and who are now behind us and supporting us," Khomeini explained. "It is possible that they may start an uprising, too."

The Pakistani officers, many of whom had graduated from Western military academies, seemed swayed by the ayatollah's intoxicating words.

"Inshallah"—"God willing"—they shouted at the end of Khomeini's speech.

"May God give strength to Muslim armies," Khomeini cried.

"Amen," the officers roared back.

SEVENTEEN

Fridays, of which the following day was one, have special significance in the lands of Islam. Usually a holiday for everyone except
barbers, who busily groom and perfume their festively dressed clients,
Friday is known in Arabic as *yawm al-jumaa*—the day of the gathering.
The gathering happens on Friday noons in the mosque, where the imam,
in addition to usual prayers, delivers his weekly sermon. Even those who
skip the prayers during the week tend to show up on Fridays, if only to
trade gossip with acquaintances and follow up with a lazy meal.

The Friday sermon, which can last as long as an hour, often delves
into current events, explaining to the flock the nuances of national politics and the affairs of the world. In the centuries before radio, TV,
and newspapers, these gatherings in the mosque provided the Muslim
ummah with a crucial source of news and official announcements. In the
1970s, thanks to radio and television, Muslims around the world could
tune in every Friday to the most important of these sermons—the one
delivered from the Grand Mosque in Mecca itself.

Saudi radio and TV traditionally broadcast the Mecca speech live. On this Friday, November 23, 1979, Muslims worldwide held their breath as they waited for noon. After all, hadn't the Saudi government announced the day before that the holy shrine was now secure? Surely one of the learned ulema—maybe Bin Baz himself—could offer a thanks to the Almighty and explain the ghastly occurrences of recent days.

But this time there was no broadcast from Mecca. The Friday prayer did not occur in the city's Grand Mosque, for the first time in centuries. As an alternative, Saudi radio transmitted a sermon by the imam of the Prophet's Mosque in Medina, Sheikh Abdelaziz Bin Saleh. The imam, while respected, was not one of the thirty topmost ulema, whose continued silence became increasingly puzzling.

Men occupying the Grand Mosque, Bin Saleh shrieked, were "criminals exploiting the sanctity of the shrine . . . to slaughter innocent people performing their devotions." A penalty was clear: "Those who fight God and his Prophet and endeavor to spread corruption on earth deserve to be killed or crucified or have their hands and legs cut off!"

The imam of the Grand Mosque of Riyadh and one of the descendants of Ibn Abdel Wahhab, Abdulaziz al Sheikh, took an equally stern line: Juhayman's men, he bellowed in his noon sermon, had earned themselves the curse of God and man.

To millions of Muslims worldwide, the absence of a Friday sermon from Mecca came as a shock. It meant that Saudi assurances of having restored control to the sacred precinct had been a blatant lie. And if this was a falsehood, what about Saudi guarantees of American innocence in the affair?

In sermons that cascaded around the Middle East and Asia, anti-American fury was stoked once again. And, as worshippers dispersed after the prayers, fired up by foamy-mouthed imams who conjured dark conspiracies against God's religion, violent demonstrations resumed with new vigor.

Though Pakistan remained relatively calm, some 10,000 people rampaged that Friday through the streets of the Bangladeshi capital, Dhaka,

Worshippers on the plaza in front of the Grand Mosque. *(Abdullah Y. Al-Dobais/Saudi Aramco World/PADIA)*

The faithful praying by the Kaaba in the courtyard of the Grand Mosque. *(Burnett H. Moody/Saudi Aramco World/PADIA)*

Pilgrims circumambulating the Kaaba with the Zamzam spring in the foreground.

The Fatah Gate of the Grand Mosque in Mecca during the 1979 uprising.

A bird's-eye view of the Grand Mosque in Mecca in 1979, with the Kaaba in the center of the enclosure and the Marwa-Safa gallery at the far side of the compound.

The minarets of the Grand Mosque that were used as firing positions by Juhayman's rebels.
(S. M. Amin/Saudi Aramco World/PADIA)

The pickup trucks used by
Juhayman to smuggle arms
and ammunition into the
Qaboo.

Smoke rising from
the Grand Mosque
during the army
assault on the
Marwa-Safa gallery.

Fan blades in the
Grand Mosque's
underground curled
up because of the
heat during the
battle.

The Mecca Hotel near the Grand Mosque, used as headquarters by senior Saudi princes during the assault on the shrine. The mosque's minarets are in the background.

Prince Abdullah, current king of Saudi Arabia and commander of the National Guard. *(Hulton Archive/Getty Images)*

Prince Turki, chief of Saudi Arabia's General Intelligence Directorate in 1979. *(AP/Wide World Photos)*

Prince Sultan, minister of defense and aviation of Saudi Arabia. *(AP/Wide World Photos)*

Crown Prince Fahd, the day-to-day ruler of Saudi Arabia in 1979. *(AP/Wide World Photos)*

Prince Nayef, interior minister of Saudi Arabia. *(AP/Wide World Photos)*

Ambassador John West at an audience with King Khaled of Saudi Arabia. *(John Carl West Papers, South Carolina Political Collections, University of South Carolina)*

Ambassador John West and President Jimmy Carter. *(John Carl West Papers, South Carolina Political Collections, University of South Carolina)*

National Security Advisor Zbigniew Brzezinski, President Jimmy Carter, and Secretary of State Cyrus Vance. *(Courtesy of the Jimmy Carter Presidential Library)*

Two views of the Shiite city of Qatif in Saudi Arabia's Eastern Province in the late 1970s. *(Tom Eigeland/Saudi Aramco World/PADIA)*

The U.S. embassy in Islamabad on fire during the assault on November 21, 1979.
(Courtesy of Loyd Miller)

A Pakistani military helicopter flies above the U.S. embassy in Islamabad, but fails to provide help. *(Courtesy of Loyd Miller)*

Rioters at the U.S. embassy in Islamabad during the attack. *(Courtesy of Loyd Miller)*

French commandos Ignace Wodecki, Christian Lambert, and Captain Paul Barril (far right) with a Saudi officer in Taef during the Mecca uprising.

A Saudi trooper in a gas mask shortly after the seizure of the Qaboo, showing a basket of dates taken from rebel stocks.

Saudi troopers in the final hours of battle, in the Qaboo underground of the Grand Mosque.

Saudi troopers in the Qaboo.

A close-up of what the Saudi government said was the cadaver of Mohammed Abdullah, Juhayman's brother-in-law and the alleged Mahdi in the Mecca uprising.

Juhayman al Uteybi, leader of the Mecca uprising.

Detained members of Juhayman's group, hours after the clearing of the Qaboo underground.

Saudi army officers in the Marwa part of the Marwa-Safa gallery shortly after rebels were driven out of the area.

chanting, "Death to America." The mob's intention was to break into the American embassy and to finally set it alight. The Saudi ambassador to Bangladesh, who himself knelt for prayers in Dhaka's main mosque that noon, saved the day by addressing the crowd. The robed envoy managed to convince at least some of the faithful that neither America nor Iran had anything to do with the Mecca upheaval.

Things didn't go as smoothly in the nearby capital of Indian Bengal, Calcutta. There, the opposition Indian National Congress faction of the former premier Indira Gandhi was actively courting the Muslim minority in an upcoming election. Joining the anti-American chorus seemed a guaranteed vote getter, and so the faction helped organize a Friday protest outside the U.S. consulate. At the rally, eloquent speeches about an American-Zionist plot to destroy the shrines of Islam electrified the mob. Protesters rushed toward the consulate, pelting with rocks a protective ring of police. Unlike Pakistani troopers two days earlier, Indian security men held forth, firing tear gas into the crowd; eight policemen and scores of demonstrators were injured in the scuffles. Driven away from the consulate, the mob vented its anger by vandalizing Calcutta's storefronts and torching parked cars and buses. An unlucky Frenchman happened to be driving by. Attacked by the mob, he was dragged out of his vehicle just before it became a fireball.

Unlike in Calcutta, there were no Westerners to attack in the southern Indian city of Hyderabad. So, following the Friday sermon there, Muslim radicals turned on their Hindu neighbors. Hyderabad's Muslim merchants, following the Pakistani example, had shuttered their stores in the old city and proclaimed a strike to protest the profanation of Mecca. The Hindu stores stayed open—at least, until outraged Muslim mobs tried to loot and burn them. Dozens of people were injured on Friday and a curfew was proclaimed; communal violence continued for days. The mayhem ended only after security forces deployed en masse, making more than a thousand arrests.

A different kind of violence germinated in Turkey. A new Catholic pope, John Paul II, was about to arrive there for a visit with his Orthodox counterpart, Istanbul-based Patriarch Dimitrios. The trip, planned well in advance, aimed to bridge a schism that had begun almost a millennium earlier, when the Catholic pope and the Orthodox patriarch excommunicated each other, dividing the Christian world into two hostile halves. Muslim-Christian relations were not supposed to be an issue, but the recent outbreak of Islamic fervor across the region frightened Turkish authorities. "This is not the right time for the Pope to be visiting Turkey: this visit puts Turkey into a difficult situation with the rest of the Muslim world," the Islamist-leaning *Yanki* magazine warned its readers. Fearing street protests, the government tried its best to keep the pope's trip as low-key as possible.

The planned visit still infuriated many Turkish radicals, including one who was kept behind bars in Istanbul's maximum-security Kartal-Maltepe military prison. A nationalist and an Islamist, Mehmet Ali Agca had been imprisoned earlier that year for killing the editor of *Milliyet*, a popular left-leaning newspaper. The night of November 24, Agca—apparently helped by an accomplice among the guards, and disguised in a military uniform—managed to escape. Then, he tauntingly dispatched to *Milliyet* a handwritten letter that explained his motives.

Parroting Khomeini's conspiracy theories, Agca lamented in the note the desecration of Mecca's Grand Mosque as an American and Zionist outrage against Islam. "The U.S. and Israel are responsible, and they will pay for this," Agca scribbled. A visit to Muslim Turkey by the pope was part and parcel of the same infidel plot, he wrote: "The Western imperialists are afraid that Turkey's brotherly Islamic countries in the Middle East will create a new political, military and economic superpower, and are sending the Pope—a leader of the Crusaders who is masquerading as a man of faith—to Turkey at a very wrong time." To redeem Muslim honor and wash off the stain of humiliation in Mecca, Agca pledged in the letter—which *Milliyet* duly printed on its front page—to personally assassinate the Catholic pontiff: "If the visit is not called off, I will definitely kill him."

A year and a half later, on the cobbled Piazza San Pietro in Rome, Agca would attempt to make good on this threat. Firing point-blank as John Paul II's vehicle passed nearby, he discharged three bullets from his nine-millimeter Browning pistol. Just narrowly skirting vital organs, one of these bullets burst through the pontiff's abdomen, almost killing him.

Amid all this fury, Mark Hambley, the young Arabic-speaking political officer at the American embassy in Jeddah, embarked on a mission that was hazardous in the extreme. Ambassador West, still puzzled by the contradictions between various reports on the fighting in Mecca, felt that he badly needed to know what exactly was going on inside the holy shrine.

Mecca, because of the natural attraction that forbidden fruits always exert, has long captured the imaginations of adventurous Westerners. From Sir Richard Burton to T. E. Lawrence, the more entrepreneurial ones have managed to penetrate the city's sacred boundaries in Arab disguise. A collector of carved Arabian doors and an avid student of Islamic culture, Hambley believed that his Yemeni accent and knowledge of local ways put him, too, in a unique position to sneak into the holy city undetected. Colonel Ryer, his partner in debriefing the American chopper pilot, could come along for backup as long as he remained silent.

This kind of covert operation was extremely risky. The last thing the United States could afford in those days, as outlandish conspiracy theories provoked American deaths, was for an infidel American diplomat to be caught red-handed as he defiled Mecca's sacred soil with his presence.

But ignorance of the truth about Saudi Arabia's worst security crisis in decades also presented dangers. The recent collapse of Iran illustrated to everyone the perils of overestimating an allied regime's stability. And, as had been the case with Iran, CIA spooks in Saudi Arabia provided frustratingly little information. "Details of the incident are still sparse, in part because of Saudi reluctance to discuss the problem openly and in part because Mecca is off-limits to non-Muslims," one agency memorandum confessed at the time. "The situation in Mecca remains unclear," admitted another. Ambassador West, safe in his friendship with Carter, decided in the end that he could—and should—authorize a quick trip to Mecca for an embassy employee or two without necessarily informing the jittery State Department brass back in Washington.

Soon thereafter, Hambley and Ryer, sporting Arab dress, melted into an influx of worshippers who—encouraged by reports of a government victory—clogged the roads toward the holy city. The ruse worked. The two managed to approach the Grand Mosque's vicinity, driving past outlying Mecca neighborhoods that bustled with unexpectedly normal activity. Extracting a camera, Hambley snapped graphic pictures of the fighting that obviously still continued around the shrine, and then hurried back. The mission was a success; their cover wasn't blown.

Because the embassy's communications equipment took forever to transmit photographs, this pictorial evidence never reached State Department officials. Hours later, it became irrelevant: reliable photo intelligence began to arrive from SR-71 high-altitude strategic reconnaissance planes that had been dispatched to circle above Mecca.

Hambley and Ryer pondered in following days whether they should make a fortune by selling these exclusive photographs of the fighting in Mecca to *Time* or *Newsweek*. They decided against such a move: their close friends and colleagues still remained captive in Tehran, and the release of such highly sensitive photographs by an American magazine could have rekindled Khomeini's conspiracy theories, jeopardizing the hostages' safety.

The American hostages' fate, as well as the ramifications of Islamist violence that now infected Saudi Arabia and Pakistan, monopolized President Carter's attention. At eight a.m. Eastern time on Friday, November 23, the morning after Thanksgiving, the president greeted his senior advisers—Brzezinski, Vice President Mondale, Secretary of State Vance, Defense Secretary Brown, and the CIA director, Stansfield Turner—at the Camp David helipad. Then they all retreated to the red-brick Laurel Lodge for a two-hour debate.

Just as at the National Security Council gathering three days earlier, the continuing standoff in Mecca was still seen by top administration officials as a "data point" in America's escalating confrontation with Iran. Despite well-informed cables from Ambassador West in Jeddah, the assumption that Shiite militants were involved one way or another still held. The CIA added to this mistaken perception, warning in a memo that Khomeini was "seeking to exploit the situation at the expense of the U.S." and that Iran had started broadcasting the ayatollah's inflammatory speeches in Arabic to Saudi Arabia's Shiite minority.

From Tehran, the American chargé d'affaires, Bruce Laingen—who continued to hide in the Iranian Foreign Ministry building—had managed to pass a confidential message to Vance the previous night. Laingen's language betrayed the stress of recent days. "The public atmosphere here is one of dangerous emotional frenzy," Laingen reported. "Khomeini and his entourage of clerics have skillfully used the seizure of our embassy . . . to develop a mass psychology of hate that may have few parallels in history."

With American lives now lost to Khomeini-sponsored hysteria over the Mecca upheaval in Pakistan, and with American hostages in Tehran facing trials and possible execution, President Carter asked administration officials gathered in Camp David to explore America's options. "The violence in Saudi Arabia and Pakistan, on the heels of Khomeini's statements about trials and punishment for our hostages, were grave threats to world peace," the president later described his thoughts.

Hawks, led by Brzezinski, believed it was time to prepare for action—blockading Iranian trade, bombing the Abadan oil terminals, or maybe even seizing an Iranian island. They brought along aerial photographs of Iranian refineries and other strategic targets. Carter, a retired U.S. Navy lieutenant, pored over these pictures, scrutinized maps and charts of coastal waters, and suggested mining the entrances to all Iranian seaports. Mondale and Vance disagreed, insisting on a softer approach. The secretary of state—who believed that it was still possible to reason with Khomeini—opposed any public threats to Iran and even objected to Carter's suggestion to expel Iranian diplomats.

Carter, as he usually did in the early stages of the Tehran hostage crisis, followed Vance's advice. Later that day, the president sent to Iran a stern—but confidential—message via several allied governments. He warned Khomeini that the United States would blockade Iran if American hostages were put on trial, and retaliate militarily if they were harmed. Iranian diplomats were allowed to remain undisturbed in the United States.

Traumatized by the loss of embassies in Tehran and Islamabad, Vance appeared to his administration colleagues as increasingly gloomy in these hours, succumbing to what one of them described as a "grim and fatalistic attitude." Above all, the secretary of state was determined to protect the lives of American diplomats still remaining in the region. The persistence of the myth of American involvement in Mecca—as shown by the rioting that had now spread to Turkey, India, and Bangladesh—made him realize that American embassies had become sitting ducks all over the region. He didn't want to receive another nighttime call about yet another American mission overrun overseas to the chants of "Allahu Akbar."

So, on this Thanksgiving weekend, Vance followed the pullout of American personnel from Pakistan with a move to evacuate the bulk of American diplomatic presence elsewhere in the Muslim world. This, he explained, would "forestall other hostage situations from developing" and "make it easier for local authorities to protect remaining Americans." Several hundred nonessential personnel and dependents were flown home from across the Middle East. American embassies in the region—with the notable exception of the one in Saudi Arabia—became isolated empty shells.

The move didn't go unnoticed among Muslim radicals. A chain of events unleashed by the takeover in Mecca had put America on the run from the lands of Islam. America's foes drew a conclusion that Osama Bin Laden would often repeat: when hit hard, America flees, "dragging its tail in failure, defeat, and ruin, caring for nothing."

Precisely these feelings caused considerable dismay about Vance's decision among the staff of Brzezinski's National Security Council. Paul Henze, a Middle East scholar and former CIA Turkey station chief who served as one of Brzezinski's top advisers, fired off a perplexed—and, in many ways, prophetic—memo to his boss. "Rather than demonstrating to the world that we break and run under pressure, we would serve our own interests better if we displayed a stubborn insistence on staying in place, asserting ourselves and being ready to fight (let the Marines shoot!) to defend our installations and our principles when challenged," he wrote. "We are well on our way to being cast as anti-Islamic . . . in most of the Muslim world. Local demagogues find such tactics expedient, and their appetites are whetted every time we look weak."

Henze found it appalling that the Soviets, who had been "viciously oppressing Islam in their own territories for 60 years," and who now sponsored a Communist regime battling Islamist insurgents in Afghanistan, had managed to capitalize on America's predicament to such an extent that they began to emerge "with an enhanced image as protectors of Islamic nationalism" in the Middle East: "What has been happening in Iran, Pakistan and Saudi Arabia has pushed Afghanistan far into the background."

By showing vacillation and weakness, Henze warned, the administration's response so far was dangerous: "[It] contributes exactly to what our enemies most want to see: we isolate ourselves from the Muslims, mutual suspicions grow, and permanent alienation sets in . . . If we do not stem this process, the Carter administration will have left its successors a legacy that will require many years to eliminate."

EIGHTEEN

By the end of Friday, November 23, the thirty senior Saudi ulema finally agreed on the text of the long-awaited fatwa, authorizing the government to act. The untenable silence was broken, and not a minute too soon. Islamic clerics worldwide had already shown unanimity in condemning Juhayman's reckless usurpation of the shrine. And it looked as though the Saudi state, chastened by the battering its soldiers received at the Grand Mosque the previous day, needed all the help it could get.

Unlike government statements and pronouncements by Muslim clerics abroad, the ruling by the Saudi ulema eschewed flowery language. It didn't even describe Juhayman's men occupying the Grand Mosque as renegades or deviants. Instead, the ulema employed the strikingly mild appellation of "an armed group."

First of all, the document said, the rebels inside the shrine "must be asked to surrender and lay down their arms." Should the militants agree, "they must be imprisoned until their case is considered in accordance with the Islamic Sharia." But if the rebels resisted, the ulema determined, "all measures could be taken to arrest them, even if it led to a fight and the killing of those who were not arrested and had not surrendered."

To justify this binding legal decision, the ulema cited a Quranic verse that waives the traditional ban on using weapons in the holy precinct: "Do not fight with them at the Sacred Mosque until they fight with you in it, but if they do fight you, then slay them; such is the recompense of the unbelievers."

This last clause caused something of a theological conundrum, for the ulema knew that Juhayman and his men were Muslim, manifestly not "unbelievers." So, alongside the fatwa, the learned scholars felt the need to issue a nonbinding explanatory statement. "Although this verse has been revealed in connection with the infidels, its connotations include them and those who acted like them. The ulema, therefore, unanimously agree that fighting inside the Sacred Mosque has become permissible," the statement said. It was a lesson that future generations of radicals would never forget. If Muslims like Juhayman could be branded as infidels because of their actions, so too could American allies across the Islamic world, the Saudi royal family included.

The fatwa's publication meant that the gloves were now off. Up until then, the government's paramount concern was not to damage the Grand Mosque, something that could inflame religious sensibilities and even undermine support from the clerics. Now the Saudi state no longer had to worry about theological cover. It could finally unleash on Juhayman's rebels the full might of the latest American and European weaponry, purchased by the kingdom with billions of dollars in oil proceeds.

The bloody battles of recent days made it clear: this was open warfare, not a policing action. The regular army had to be in command. General Dhaheri was placed at the helm of the task force and his King Abdelaziz Armored Brigade called into action. The army's fleet of U.S.-

built M-113 armored personnel carriers and artillery support finally rumbled into the Grand Mosque's vicinity. Recognizing that numerous casualties would be unavoidable, Saudi officials ordered all Muslim doctors and staff at Jeddah's military hospital to travel to Mecca with an overnight bag.

Matani, the stranded Egyptian professor, was awakened in the Africa Hotel by the noise of the APCs, trucks, and ambulances that poured into the area. Once he looked outside, he noticed that the mosque was no longer in the dark: military floodlights turned night into day. Troops lay in the prone position on the ground, weapons pointed at the sacred enclosure.

For several hours, a military jeep with mounted loudspeakers circled around the Grand Mosque's compound, broadcasting a surrender message that had been requested by the ulema. "To all those who are underground and inside the mosque. We warn you so that you can save your souls. Surrender or we shall force you to do so. You have to surrender and head to the central part of the courtyard. Those who surrender will not be harmed. Surrender."

Matani wrote in his notebook that he saw no one answering this call.

The new forces' first mission was to suppress Juhayman's snipers, who continued to inflict unacceptable casualties from the minaret tops. The best shots—such as Ridan al Homeidan, a relative of Juhayman's from Sajir, and Egab al Mahia, another Sajir native—by now had achieved legendary status among fellow rebels. These snipers even nearly killed General Dhaheri himself, firing a bullet that grazed the general's cheek just as he peeked out of a top-floor window in the Imarat al Ashraf tower that faced the minarets.

Solidly built and each containing two cuplike balconies that shielded their occupants from fire from below, the minarets also provided the gunmen with embrasure-style windows halfway upstairs. This protection posed a military problem that couldn't be resolved without heavy weaponry. The only way to drive down the snipers, military commanders decided, was by lobbing into the minarets American-made missiles known as TOWs, an acronym for tube launched, optically tracked, wire-command-link guided.

Designed to be used against tanks, the TOWs packed a powerful payload that went off with a deafening bang upon hitting the marble of the balconies. On impact, a spray of jagged shrapnel and bright orange fire engulfed rebel snipers as plumes of thick smoke began to obscure the minaret tops. No one remained alive in the gun nests. The sturdy minarets themselves withstood this rocketing, with only balcony balustrades caving in.

Below, in the streets around the mosque, M-113s—boxy, threaded vehicles with 0.50-caliber machine guns mounted on the roofs— prepared for the ground invasion. The plan was to drive these nimble APCs into the mosque's wide passageways, blasting out the gates and securing the inner courtyard around the Kaaba.

As in the early days of the operation, the attack was to be carried out by three different forces—the Saudi Army, the National Guard, and the Interior Ministry Special Security Forces—all of whom reported to different masters despite theoretically unified command. Prince Sultan, the defense minister, remained in the Shoubra Hotel, while Prince Nayef, the minister of the interior, set up alternative headquarters in the Mecca Hotel west of the mosque. Prince Abdullah, the National Guard commander, ran the operation from Riyadh without actually coming to the holy city. Crown Prince Fahd, who had returned from Tunis, also stayed away, barking down orders from his coastal palace in Jeddah. By then, Salem Bin Laden had finally come up with the maps and blueprints of the mosque, giving the planners more clarity about the shrine's internal structure.

As military commanders scrutinized these documents, General Dhaheri decided that his armored troops would keep on pushing into the Marwa-Safa gallery, advancing from there into the depths of the mosque. The National Guard and the Interior Ministry Special Security Force were to move toward each other in an interlocking ring through the main perimeter of the compound that encircled the Kaaba.

As the new offensive began, F-5 fighter jets roared atop the compound, flying just above ground in a show of intimidation that made the buildings vibrate. Shelling made part of the gallery's side wall collapse, exposing its interior. The initial attack concentrated on the gallery's upper level, with M-113 carriers pouring in from the blasted-out gates and through the new side opening.

Infantry troops crouched behind the slowly moving APCs, the armor of which shielded the men from rebel bullets, and unloaded their guns into the darkness inside. It was almost like fighting ghosts, some soldiers felt. The rebels, who smeared black soot over their faces, were invisible; only muzzle flashes indicated their positions. The floor was slippery because of blood and human entrails, leftovers of earlier fighting. Rebels hid behind the ancient rocks of Safa and behind the brand-new columns and parapets built by Bin Laden. Some rolled themselves into thick woolen carpets that abounded in the area, and fired upward as troops passed nearby. Because of this unusual angle of fire, a disproportionate number of troops sustained wounds in their lower body.

Mohammed Abdullah, the supposed Mahdi, was at the forefront of this battle. He fully believed himself to be more than just a mere mortal and therefore behaved as if he were impervious to bullets. And indeed, he seemed to be charmed, emerging unscathed from salvos of gunfire again and again.

The introduction of armored vehicles into the gallery changed the rules of the battle, for the first time providing an edge to government forces. While the Interior Ministry commandos and the National Guard faced stiff resistance elsewhere in the compound, here rebels began to retreat. Bullets from their rifles bounced harmlessly off the APCs' armor. The gunmen didn't possess anything like the TOW missiles that had just pulverized the snipers' nests atop the minarets.

The M-113s had to be stopped at all costs. Mohammed Abdullah decided he would be the one to destroy them. As others tried to discourage him, he smiled back calmly: "I am the Mahdi, and I do not fear anything. I cannot die." With a canister of petrol and a flaming piece of cloth in his hands, he dodged the bullets and sprinted toward the nearest APC. Miraculously, once again he received nary a scratch, pouring petrol on the vehicle and setting the liquid ablaze. The fire, however, failed to disable the APC. The carrier turned back and roared away to safety outside the gallery.

Juhayman, undeterred, proposed a different plan. Some rooms inside the shrine's basement, the Qaboo, had been used as living quarters by staff and students of the Grand Mosque academy. They were equipped with rudimentary kitchens and had stoves powered by metallic cooking gas cylinders. On Juhayman's orders, fellow rebels rolled these cylinders into the Marwa-Safa gallery, planning to thrust them under the threads of the APCs and trigger an explosion.

But, as more and more APCs entered the gallery, their machine guns clattering without stop, the rebels found it impossible to shove these cylinders close enough to their targets. The plan didn't work.

Rebels were more lucky in the lower level of the gallery. There, an APC tried to drive in through one of the blasted-out gates. The clearing was just tall enough for the APC's main body to squeeze through, but not for the antenna tower at the back of the vehicle. With its nose already indoors, the vehicle stalled and then got stuck, held back by the antenna. Threads started excavating the ground as the nervous driver hit the gas.

Rebels who lurked nearby seized their opportunity. Thrusting rolled carpets into the threads of the APC, they locked the vehicle in place. Then they tried a new tactic, taught by an African American convert who remembered recipes from *The Anarchist Cookbook*. Pilgrims had abandoned hundreds of glass bottles by the holy source of Zam Zam under the mosque. Filled with gasoline and stuffed with a piece of cloth that served as a fuse, these became fearsome Molotov cocktails. Though rudimentary, such firebombs could disable sophisticated American-made fighting machines.

As the hapless M-113 remained stuck at the gate, one of the rebels jumped on the roof, lit the fuse, opened the hatch and threw a flaming Molotov cocktail inside. Seconds later, the insides of the APC turned into a blazing oven; the unlucky crew was carbonized in a flash of fire. Rebels rejoiced with a powerful cry of *"Allahu Akbar."*

Molotov cocktails now also started to rain on the M-113s in the upper gallery. Some went up in flames; panicked crews turned their vehicles to escape the kill zone. The APC drivers' field of vision is by necessity limited: in this rush to safety, they trampled several of their own men. Unfortunate soldiers who happened to be in the way were mashed up by the carriers' threads.

At the lower-level gate, the carbonized APC still blocked the way, hampering the offensive. It was Captain Abu Sultan's job to try to remove the burned-out hulk. On the streets of Mecca, he rounded up a Pakistani construction worker with a bulldozer and got him to drive toward the Grand Mosque. Near the shrine, rebel bullets began to whiz by. The frightened Pakistani jumped out and ran. Cursing, Abu Sultan climbed into the driver's seat, steering the bulldozer toward the back of the APC. Once his men attached a towing chain to the armored vehicle, the captain put the bulldozer in reverse, pulling out the wreck and unclogging the gate.

The soldiers pressed on. As they penetrated deeper and deeper into the mosque, they discovered a terrifying scene. Body parts coated the ground. Some of the rebel dead appeared to be deliberately defaced, their heads doused in gasoline and torched by fellow conspirators in order to make identification impossible. After days in the heat, some of the cadavers had now turned into sludgy mounds of rotten flesh. The sweet, putrid stench of death mixed in the air with the smell of cordite, urine, and stifling smoke from the fires.

Government troops had been given orders not to shoot in the direction of the sacred Kaaba and to avoid hitting children, women, and civilians. This was the order of priorities: protecting the House of God came before human lives. General Dhaheri's biggest fear, as he recounted it later, was that Juhayman's men would use as a fortified stronghold the Kaaba itself, a windowless stone structure that would be impossible to conquer without major damage. But Juhayman shared most Muslims' belief about the sacredness of the site, and, with some exceptions, his men concentrated on fighting Saudi forces in more modern parts of the mosque.

In the confusion of battle, where every moving shadow meant likely death, orders to spare the civilians were not easy to follow. With scores of comrades now dead, Saudi troopers squeezed the trigger whenever they spotted any motion in the darkness. This led to predictable tragedies. Once the offensive began to overwhelm the rebels, scores of hostages tried to run out and toward the advancing troops, only to be mistaken for militants and mowed down.

Lethal firefights also erupted between the Saudi Army, the Special Security Force, and the National Guard, who all operated with separate radio systems and mistook one another's men for rebels. No matter: as Prince Nayef had said, any Muslim killed while liberating the mosque was an envied martyr who had now earned a fast-track promotion to Paradise.

By mid-Saturday, the armored offensive finally cleared out the Marwa-Safa gallery, opening the way to the main courtyard. Abu Sultan returned to the shrine in a new APC. He made it all the way to the center of the plaza, near the Kaaba. Though minarets were now secure, Juhayman's snipers still operated on the upper floors of the mosque that ringed the courtyard. As he crossed the plaza, leaving thread marks on the marble, a staccato of bullets—unable to penetrate the APC's armor—tapped the vehicle's surface like heavy rain. Three Egyptian militants were shooting at the approaching vehicle from behind the C-shaped wall, the *Rukn,* that contained the holy remains of Hagar and Ishmael.

The heavy machine gun of Abu Sultan's APC fired back, killing two of the Egyptians. As Abu Sultan's vehicle inched closer, he noticed that the third Egyptian militant was still alive, his legs shredded by 0.50-caliber bullets and soaked in blood. Like some of the rebels, the Egyptian wore the *ihram*, the pilgrims' outfit made of two white strips of cloth. "Help me, help me," the man cried as Abu Sultan opened the hatch. "Don't shoot, don't shoot. I am just a pilgrim."

Abu Sultan had his doubts: he spotted a Kalashnikov rifle next to the man's hands.

"Come down, please help me," the Egyptian continued to cry. "Please help me."

The captain thought better: leaving the APC's armor would be clearly suicidal. He threw a rope from the hatch, shouting, "Hold this." The Egyptian grasped at the rope and the APC slowly drove back, dragging the prisoner behind and leaving a trail of dark red blood from his hemorrhaging legs on the marble.

American pilots ferrying GID officers on a reconnaissance sortie above the Grand Mosque's courtyard witnessed the final hours of this assault firsthand. Two more Saudi APCs, Dan reported to American diplomats, rumbled onto the plaza around the Kaaba at three-thirty p.m., spraying the outer ring of buildings with rapid fire. This hailstorm of bullets riddled the walls, causing severe damage. Plumes of black smoke rose from the ramparts as a result of this fusillade, and a giant fire began to swallow the Marwa-Safa gallery area and the Fatah Gate zone between the twin minarets. From outside the mosque compound, civilian fire trucks tried to prevent this inferno from spreading into adjoining neighborhoods, dousing the gallery with water.

Journalists at Mecca's local newspaper, *al Nadwa,* had a perfect view of the fireworks from their desks. While other reporters were barred from the area, *al Nadwa*'s photographers rushed to snap the dramatic pictures. The photos were splashed the next morning across the front page. The Saudi government, angry about such adverse publicity, had most outstanding copies of the newspaper recalled.

As this battle raged on Saturday, Ambassador West and much of the top American embassy brass flew to Riyadh, accompanying visiting treasury secretary G. William Miller. Their initial meetings with oil minister Yamani and other midlevel officials were businesslike, but a late-night appointment with King Khaled and Prince Abdullah turned into a disaster. At the ambassador's suggestion, Miller started out by expressing regret about the desecration of the Grand Mosque. "That set the king off," West wrote in his diary. "He started chattering to Abdullah and they started going back and forth" in Arabic. A junior American diplomat tried to interpret, but the monarch cut him off every time he opened his mouth. The two Saudi royals kept arguing about the Grand Mosque for a half hour, with Ambassador West and Secretary Miller unable to understand a single word. "We got one thing out of the meeting . . . namely the king was terribly upset at what had happened in Mecca," the ambassador jotted down afterwards.

NINETEEN

Between Saturday and Sunday, most of the rebels retreated from the mosque's surface and into the Qaboo underground. Only a small group of zealots made a last stand in the shrine's burning corridors. Defying death, once again, was the supposed Mahdi, Mohammed Abdullah.

His long hair matted and speckled with blood, the young man chose a new way of demonstrating his immortality. Government soldiers now tossed one hand grenade after another to clear passageways on their path. Whenever Mohammed Abdullah heard the unmistakable *clink* of a metal grenade hitting the marble, he ran to pick up the munition. Then, in the fraction of seconds that remained before the explosion, he hurled it back at the soldiers.

Time after time, he succeeded in returning these lethal devices to their senders. Finally, he ran out of luck. Just as Mohammed Abdullah prepared to scoop up yet another grenade, it exploded, turning parts of his lower torso and legs into carbonized goo.

Cowering under barrages of fire, fellow rebels were unable to rescue their Mahdi, who writhed in agony amid the toxic haze. He was left behind on the battlefield—if not already dead, fellow fighters concluded, then most likely mortally wounded.

The fire that blazed in the Grand Mosque was mostly extinguished by Sunday morning, as Dan flew his Chinook once again above the compound. Five of the shrine's seven minarets, he observed, had been shelled; most of the gates lay on the floor, blown off hinges. Almost all windows facing the mosque's inner courtyard had been smashed. In spooky silence, some sixty Saudi soldiers milled in a corner of the courtyard; another seventy-five or so could be seen on a roof. Aboveground resistance seemed crushed.

The capture of the mosque's surface momentarily buoyed morale among Saudi soldiers. Major Nefai of the Special Security Force, the man who had drawn up the assault plans, finally felt he could steal a few hours of sleep after staying awake for five days in a row. The handful of rebels who remained isolated in the mosque's corridors, cut off from staircases that led to the Qaboo, had been taken prisoner and began providing valuable intelligence. In his hotel room, Professor Matani watched two gunmen jump from the mosque's upper windows, to be immediately surrounded by troops and spirited away. Twelve other suspects—including three women—were spotted in chains in a holding area of Jeddah's military airport, awaiting a transport flight to Riyadh.

For the first time since the assault began, senior Saudi princes ventured in person into the sacred compound. Donning military fatigues, the intelligence chief Prince Turki, his brother the foreign minister, Prince Saud al Faisal, General Dhaheri, and the indomitable Salem Bin Laden penetrated the mosque, keeping their heads low in case more rebel gunmen remained undetected.

As he surveyed the damage, Prince Turki noticed dead bodies sprawled in the corridors. But these didn't disturb him as much as the eerie, unnatural quiet in the usually crowded shrine. Never before had he seen the Grand Mosque so empty of people. It was not so much the visual evidence of fighting that struck him, Prince Turki later recalled, as a lingering aura of the evil that he knew had occurred there.

It was clear to him and other senior Saudi officials that more bloody battles loomed ahead. As military commanders examined Bin Laden's blueprints, they realized that the basement labyrinth, a veritable underground city, would be a much harder target to conquer than the shrine's surface structures. Since the first hours of the siege, Juhayman had been using this underground as his headquarters, and it was there that he had stockpiled ammunition, weapons, and food.

Prince Bandar bin Sultan, the defense minister's son and future Saudi envoy to Washington, told Ambassador West in those hours that Bin Laden "ought to be given a medal—and then shot" because of the construction work's superior quality: even TOW missiles couldn't break the sturdy gates that led into the Grand Mosque's basement, and the structure's maze of caverns and pillars made it ideal for hand-to-hand fighting.

Saudi rulers were particularly concerned that the Qaboo's network of cisterns, caves, and storage rooms might be connected via secret passageways with mountainsides on the outskirts of the city. On Sunday, the government deployed a fleet of helicopter gunships to patrol the desert around Mecca, seeking out anyone attempting to escape the compound or to smuggle in reinforcements.

Busy defending approaches into the Qaboo and battered by the government offensive, Juhayman's rebels no longer had the time or manpower to watch over their prisoners of war: shackled members of the Grand Mosque police and officers like Lieutenant Qudheibi, the paratroop platoon commander captured during Thursday's ambush in the Marwa-Safa tunnel. Locked in a small basement cell, Lieutenant Qudheibi and a fellow captive paratrooper, whose chest wound kept deteriorating, were left alone with a bottle of water. They didn't see their guards for three days.

Only four meters (about 13 feet) of corridor separated the cell's door from a staircase that led to freedom aboveground. On Sunday, as fighting raged just outside, soldiers' shouts were clearly audible to the two captives.

Trying to smoke out the rebels, Saudi forces now began to fire round after round of tear gas canisters into the basement. The gas didn't spread deep into the Qaboo, however, and the rebels quickly learned to filter it out by dipping their headdresses in water and breathing through the wet cotton. Lieutenant Qudheibi and his comrade, caught in the middle of the tear gas cloud that wafted into the cell, had no such protection. The lieutenant was already feeling sick as his infected wounds resumed bleeding. Now he was overwhelmed by an intense burning in the eyes, nostrils, and mouth, panting for breath.

The two officers reckoned they would die in this cell if they didn't try to escape. Later on Sunday, they found a metal rod among the debris and managed to pry open the door. "We are fellow soldiers, come bring us out," Lieutenant Qudheibi shouted toward invisible troops up the staircase. "Come here with stretchers."

Juhayman's men were not far away. Hearing these pleas, they started firing again. As bullets zinged in the corridor, Lieutenant Qudheibi managed to limp the short distance toward the staircase and turned the corner toward safety. His comrade was not as quick. He was seized halfway by a dagger-wielding rebel. "Your friend who tried to escape, we killed him," he growled. "If you try again, we'll kill you too."

Then he shoved the captive officer further underground.

Such prisoners were not the only noncombatants in the dark, fetid Qaboo. Several women, including Mohammed Abdullah's wife and two sisters, had also fled downstairs and now tried to comfort their hungry, scared children. Dozens of pilgrims, some too sick or too old to move around, sat listlessly on the carpeted floor. One, an eighty-year-old, quietly expired.

One area of the basement became an improvised field hospital. Dripping feverish sweat, injured rebels and hostages slowly died there of infections that could have been cured with simple antibiotics. The rebels had no medication except for the holy waters of Zam Zam.

Samir, the teenage brother of two senior conspirators, was entrusted with applying generous quantities of this miraculous liquid to the ward's patients.

While sufficient food was still available for the gunmen, those who didn't bear arms now had to survive on minimal rations: a dried date in the morning, another date in the evening, and some water in between.

These physical privations, however, didn't distress the rebels and their supporters as much as the puzzling and worrying absence of Mohammed Abdullah, the Mahdi. The handful of gunmen who had witnessed the grenade explosion upstairs, and who managed to reach the Qaboo alive, shared this disturbing piece of news with some of the most senior conspirators.

Faisal Mohammed Faisal was shaken by the report. His belief in Juhayman's cause—weak even before the operation began—now evaporated completely. Why had he let himself be talked into joining this venture? Why hadn't he insisted on saying no to Juhayman during that cursed encounter at the farm in Amar?

Seething, Faisal confronted Juhayman. "I think the Mahdi is dead," he began.

Juhayman flew into a rage. These words were pure blasphemy. "You know well that the Mahdi cannot be killed," he shouted back. "He is not dead. He may have been captured. But he is not dead!"

Faisal stared back. Realizing that he could no longer convince his old comrade of the righteousness of their cause, Juhayman relented after a minute. He changed tack, speaking in a soft, complicit voice. "Whatever you do, don't tell the others," the rebel leader begged. Faisal nodded, put down his gun, and remained cloistered in a remote basement cell, praying for Allah's mercy. This was no longer his war.

Despite Faisal's silence, glum rumors started to swirl among the ragtag band of rebels. If the Mahdi was not here among the believers, wasn't this whole operation now without a purpose? And if, God forbid, he was dead, didn't this mean that their glorious venture had turned out to be a terrible, terrible mistake? Hadn't it been promised in the hadith that the Mahdi would be impervious to bullets and bombs?

The faithful peppered Mohammed Abdullah's older brother, Sayid, with questions. Were the death rumors correct? If so, what should be done with the Mahdi's body, if it was found? The Muslim faith, after all, calls for an immediate burial. Sayid responded that he did not know the answer to the first question. But he did not dither on the second count. "If you see him, don't bury him," he replied. "If my brother is the Mahdi, then Allah will take care of him. If he is not the Mahdi, we don't care about him anymore."

This reply wasn't sufficient to reassure the besieged gunmen. Juhayman, the master himself, had to speak up.

Sensing a potential revolt on his hands, the rebel leader finally left his room and stood up to face the believers. In this hour of reckoning, he deployed his best powers of persuasion. His eyes sparkled with anger; his loud, roaring voice echoed in the confined space. How did the doubters' faith become so weak! he bellowed. How could anyone question God's clear commands? And what proof did anyone have of the Mahdi's death? The battle for justice on Earth must go on!

"If you want to leave, leave," Juhayman cried. "But I will stay here to fight until the end, even if I'm the only one who remains!"

Shamed, and impressed by Juhayman's ardor, the potential dissidents lowered their eyes and withdrew to their posts. Indeed, it was no time to surrender, some mused. The Mahdi's defenders still had battles to fight. They were still inside the holy shrine; the war was not yet lost. And, if their faith remained strong, God might still grant them victory.

The Saudi government in these hours was just as puzzled as Juhayman's rebels about the precise fate of the man who proclaimed himself Mahdi. On Monday, November 26, the *al Medina* newspaper reported his arrest. But, the next day, another Saudi newspaper, *al Jazira,* cited officials as denying that claim and saying that Mohammed Abdullah was not in government custody. "As far as we know, he remains at large, doubtless in the basement of the mosque," the British ambassador, Sir James Craig, informed London in a confidential telegram.

Reliable information was especially hard to come by because Saudi troopers, infuriated by massive casualties, shot on sight anyone who tried to surrender. In one incident that week, Prince Bandar told Ambassador West, the National Guard gunned down six of the seven unarmed men who emerged from the depths of the mosque, their hands raised above their heads.

The few rebels captured alive confused matters further: every male prisoner claimed under interrogation that his name was Mohammed Abdullah.

According to a rumor widely shared in Saudi Arabia, the real Mohammed Abdullah's mother was flown to Riyadh at the time for a meeting with King Khaled, who desired to find out in person about the royal family's most serious challenger in decades. Introduced to the monarch, the veiled woman allegedly spoke with Bedouin bluntness. "If my son is the Mahdi, he will kill you," she purportedly said. "If he is not, you will kill him."

TWENTY

As Saudi forces attempted to advance into the Qaboo on Monday and Tuesday, they discovered that the rebels, shielded by darkness, were as lethal as ever. Trying to spare lives, shell-shocked military commanders decided to rely once again on the protection of M-113 armored vehicles. These carriers could be driven underground through the accessway that had been used by Bin Laden's construction crews.

Corporal Abdu Ali al Jizani, a tall, black-skinned man, was among a dozen soldiers packed into the lead APC that headed down this ramp. Barring their way was a GMC pickup truck that Juhayman's rebels had used to smuggle ammunition and supplies. The APC's driver hit the gas as he tried to ram the GMC and sweep it aside.

Seconds later, the murky passageway was illuminated by a flash. The rebel pickup had been booby-trapped, and it burst into hissing flames that quickly engulfed the troop carrier. Smothering smoke filled the APC's inside compartments. Struggling for breath, coughing soldiers opened the rear armored door and began jumping out.

Every single one was hit by well-aimed rebel bullets.

Corporal Jizani, among the last men to hit the ground, felt the high-velocity lead rip his left leg in three different places. Lobbing two grenades toward the muzzle flashes, he managed to jump up and hobble away.

The success of this ambush encouraged Juhayman's conspirators. Unlike the broad expanse of the Marwa-Safa gallery, the Qaboo's narrow passageways severely limited the mobility of armored vehicles. This wasn't lost on Abdullah Mubarak Qahtani, one of Juhayman's senior aides. A former military man, Qahtani once served in the armored corps himself. He knew how to operate the M-113s. Wouldn't it be great, Qahtani excitedly told Juhayman, if we captured one of these machines and turned its guns against apostate forces! Qahtani even knew how to do it: the APCs could be immobilized in a narrow corridor by thrusting rolled-up carpets into the threads and by throwing another layer of smoldering carpets onto the roof, to asphyxiate the crew.

That was what the rebels tried to do as soon as another group of M-113s rumbled deeper into the bowels of the Qaboo. The ambush seemed to be working at first. Immobilized and covered by burning carpets, two or three armored troop carriers stalled in the pitch-black corridors, their crews struggling against noxious fumes. But, as Qahtani lunged toward the hatch, attempting to seize control of the lead vehicle, a bullet fired by one of the soldiers perforated his throat. Choking on his own blood and unable to speak, Qahtani fell back, carmine foam gurgling out of the wound. Fellow rebels dragged him back to the improvised hospital, where he barely managed to scribble a short testament before passing away. No one else among the conspirators knew how to drive an APC. The tactic was abandoned.

Though heavy fighting raged underground, the mosque's surface now was misleadingly tranquil. With bullets no longer flying from the minarets, cleanup work began. Traffic police hauled cranes to the neighborhood and started to remove abandoned cars, including the carbonized hulks of military vehicles. Sanitation teams sprayed disinfectant onto the sidewalks. Municipal workers in yellow uniforms collected the rotting garbage that had piled up everywhere.

By Wednesday, November 28, a handful of Saudi officers felt secure enough to finally pose for the cameras in an authorized photo op, offering prayers by the Black Stone of the Kaaba. These images were broadcast on TV. After more than a week of government lies about their being in control, the footage provided the world with the first undisputable proof that the Saudi regime had truly regained the shrine's holiest part. Any evidence of harm to the mosque was carefully cropped out.

Foreign leaders—from the Italian premier Francesco Cossiga to the Togolese dictator Gnassingbe Eyadema—responded by flooding Riyadh with congratulatory telegrams that lauded King Khaled for a successful end of the siege.

But this pretense could hold up for only so long. With the rebels remaining in control of the Qaboo—and potentially able to break out—the Grand Mosque remained a war zone, closed to ordinary worshippers. Every hour that such an interruption continued chipped away the prestige of the House of Saud, encouraging further dissent. The royal family knew that it sat atop a volcano. Waiting for Juhayman to run out of food and surrender was not an option.

After a week of horrendously bloody combat, it was clear: the Saudi military needed help from abroad. Ministry of Defense hospitals around the country overflowed with the wounded. The number of injured and killed began to climb up to a dangerous percentage of the kingdom's entire armed forces   then numbering a total of just about 30,000 Saudi Army soldiers and 20,000 members of the National Guard. Something had to be done, fast.

Any foreign assistance, of course, had to be as secret as possible. With astute timing, Tehran radio had notched up its revolutionary rhetoric that week, filling the airwaves with denunciations of the Saudi kingdom and pro-Western regimes in Morocco and Bahrain for a dependence on "foreigners to protect their hollow monarchies." The Soviet news agency, Tass, had already transmitted a report—flatly denied by the Saudis—about the landing of American commandos at the military base in the eastern Saudi city of Dhahran. (Though it was true that American personnel were present in Dhahran, this was part of an ongoing military cooperation unrelated to the Mecca crisis.)

Of all the potential military allies, nearby Jordan seemed the most natural choice for riding to al Saud's rescue. A fellow conservative monarchy, the Hashemite Kingdom of Jordan—while much smaller and poorer than Saudi Arabia—boasted a top-notch military that had been extensively trained by Britain. Just a few years earlier, Jordanian troops had fought in a bloody civil war, ousting Yasser Arafat's Palestinian guerrillas, who had tried to take over the country. Already, Jordanian instructors worked with the Saudi National Guard under the auspices of the U.S. Military Training Mission. Battle-tested Jordanian soldiers were fellow Arabs and Muslims, which meant that they could easily enter Mecca unnoticed by outsiders.

The Jordanians, wedged uncomfortably between Israel and Iraq, had gone into near panic at the first reports that their only pro-Western Arab neighbor was in trouble. Unable to get any hard information from within Saudi Arabia, senior Jordanian officials peppered the U.S. government with requests for intelligence. Lieutenant General Zaid Bin Shaker, commander general of the Jordanian military forces, told American diplomats in those days that he had engaged in "almost frantic" efforts to activate a link with Prince Turki's GID and that he was unable to reach any senior Saudi prince.

Once King Hussein finally managed to speak to the Saudi monarch, he offered any help needed, including the use of the Jordanian military. Elite Jordanian commandos led by Tahsin Shordom, an officer of Circassian origin, were gathered at the Marka military airport near Amman, ready to fly to Mecca on a moment's notice.

But the commandos remained on hold. King Hussein and General Bin Shaker were invited to Riyadh only a week into the crisis. The Jordanian king badly wanted to meet there with the key Saudi decision makers, Crown Prince Fahd and defense minister Prince Sultan, but the two were still away from Riyadh, too busy to talk with foreigners. Dressed in a bespoke suit and a tie, the Jordanian ruler had to make do with meeting King Khaled and the Saudi National Guard commander, Prince Abdullah.

The Saudi monarch greeted his guest in a traditional Arab headdress and dark shawl, and, as King Hussein later remarked, was "unfailing in his courtesies." But the Saudis balked at accepting Jordanian assistance, for a very obvious reason. As the two kings exchanged pleasantries and rejoiced in mutual sympathy, they were acutely aware of just how the Saudis had come to rule Mecca in the first place. Back in 1924, King Khaled's father had unleashed a war of aggression against King Hussein's great-grandfather and namesake, the Hashemite sharif of Mecca and king of Hejaz.

For Riyadh, it would have been an unacceptable loss of face to rely on—of all people—the defeated Hashemites to win back Islam's holiest shrine. King Khaled proved to be surprisingly frank in discussing with King Hussein the persistent differences between the Hejaz and al Saud's heartland of the Nejd. The Saudi king confided he was thankful that Juhayman's rebels—most of whom hailed from the Nejd—had chosen to strike in the Hashemites' former domain, where the Nejdi brand of Islamic radicalism enjoyed little sympathy. Had they attacked in the Nejd itself, he said, "it would have been much more dangerous."

Viewed from this perspective, any Jordanian military operation in the Hejaz was equally fraught with perils. The Saudis suspected—not altogether without reason—that the Hashemites had never really accepted their loss of Mecca and still nurtured dreams of a revanche. King Hussein made such feelings painfully clear after returning to Amman. The Hejazis, he complained ruefully to the American ambassador, were "considered second-class citizens by the ruling authorities," and the feelings of Hejazi resentment were bound to be exacerbated by the Mecca affair.

The last thing the House of Saud wanted to see was an upsurge in Hejazi separatism—which would be inevitable should the Hashemites cover themselves with glory as liberators of the Grand Mosque. As one Saudi officer put it: "The fear was: if the Jordanians come to Mecca, they will never leave!"

Such concerns obviously didn't arise with Riyadh's Western allies, which—by virtue of being Western—could not challenge Saudi Arabia's status as the sole custodian of Islamic orthodoxy and of Islam's holy sites.

Of these allies, the United States was by far the most important. The CIA already ran an assistance program in Taef and would have been a partner of choice in different times. But Prince Turki, the Saudi intelligence chief, was ambivalent. He felt that the American spy agency had been "emasculated" by strict congressional restrictions and that its operational capacity had been largely destroyed under the Carter administration.

Unnervingly, the CIA also couldn't keep secrets secret. Earlier in 1979, its Saudi station chief, George Cave, had been personally expelled by Prince Turki. Because of infighting within the Carter administration, Cave's classified report to Langley that laid bare internal divisions within the Saudi royal family had been leaked to the American press, causing much embarrassment to the House of Saud. Given the drumbeat of anti-American propaganda streaming from Tehran, leaks of CIA involvement in Mecca would have produced far more disastrous consequences.

While Prince Turki demurred from involving the CIA mission, the Saudi Ministry of Defense on Tuesday, November 27, made an urgent request to the U.S. government: it wanted potent tear gas and smoke equipment that could be used by assault teams in the Qaboo catacombs. According to American officials, this request was forwarded to the CIA station, which had stockpiled precisely this kind of gas and equipment for the training of Saudi forces at the Taef facility; the Americans also supplied blood, which had begun to run out in Saudi military hospitals.

Not being Muslim, CIA operatives theoretically could not enter

Mecca. A quick conversion of the kind that had been administered to American helicopter pilots appears to have remedied this problem. The agency's spooks made a rapid tour of the battlefield. The tear gas—in nonlethal concentrations—was hauled to Mecca and put into action. Because any active involvement by the CIA in combat required a presidential finding, the agency's role was limited to what could reasonably be passed for liaison and advice.

This resort to chemical warfare, by the account of Saudi soldiers inside the Grand Mosque, proved a complete fiasco. Hardened rebels shielded themselves with old mattresses and pieces of cardboard and cloth, blocking the passageways and preventing the gas's spread through narrow underground corridors. Water-soaked headdresses effectively protected their breathing. Hiding in the darkness below, the rebels also easily made out the silhouettes of soldiers who approached the openings above and skewered the troops with well-aimed salvos.

Laws of nature were on Juhayman's side, too. The operation's planners didn't foresee that the American-provided gas had a natural tendency to rise. When fired into the basement, it quickly wafted back to the surface floors and to the mosque's courtyard.

There, only the better-trained troops knew how to properly use their gas masks. Many among ordinary Saudi soldiers wore bushy beards, and their abundant facial hair prevented the masks from sealing on the skin. Gas filtered in through the beards, and it was the Saudi soldiers—not Juhayman's zealots—who became most incapacitated by the chemicals, collapsing in bouts of vomiting and gasping for air.

The gas also rapidly drifted to nearby neighborhoods. In the Africa Hotel, where Professor Matani was trapped, the wind blew in such a strong dose that the manager fell on the floor, unable to move. People on several street blocks—including, to their relief, Matani and other residents of the hotel—had to be evacuated for days because of the toxic cloud that continued to hang over the area.

Prince Turki came to a realization: he had to seek more competent help.

TWENTY-ONE

Just two months before the siege started in Mecca, the unsuspecting Emperor Bokassa the First had arrived on a state visit to the Libyan capital, Tripoli. An on-and-off convert to Islam, the emperor, born Jean Bedel, ruled a dirt-poor and landlocked African country on the right bank of the Congo. His Central African Empire, known in French colonial times as Oubangui-Chari, was desperately strapped for cash. Libya's erratic dictator Moammar Ghadhafi had already developed a habit of doling out Libya's oil money to fawning African rulers. Bokassa figured he'd get his share by parroting Ghadhafi's anti-Western rhetoric.

A despot unusually cruel even by African standards, Bokassa, a former French army captain, had lived off French subsidies for years. As long as he remained pliant to French wishes, nobody in Paris specially minded about his reputed proclivity for cooking and eating political opponents. But now, in the fall of 1979, with Libya on the brink of an open war with French-backed forces in nearby Chad, French patience snapped.

Under cover of darkness, two planeloads of French special forces landed in the empire's ramshackle capital, Bangui. Using loudspeakers, French soldiers stunned Central African soldiers in the airport by addressing them in their local dialect. Then they hauled out boxloads of fresh cash for the troops. The capital was seized without a single bullet being fired.

The man who organized this daring operation—kept secret even from France's own Foreign Ministry—was Count Alexandre de Marenches, the balding, mustachioed boss of France's intelligence agency called Service de Documentation Extérieure et de Contre-Espionnage, or SDECE. Born to an American socialite mother and a French general who had served as General Pershing's aide-de-camp in World War I, de Marenches was a devoted cold warrior. An early volunteer with anti-Nazi French forces in World War II, he had served as French liaison to the U.S. Chief of Staff General George Marshall. For him, the Atlantic alliance with America was sacrosanct.

In a reversal of their familiar positions in the early twenty-first century, France's elite at the time firmly believed in using military force and protecting national interests, as the ousted Emperor Bokassa could testify. The conservative government of President Valéry Giscard d'Estaing looked with disdain at Carter's moralistic endeavors and was aghast at American impotence in Iran. America's bizarre new inclination to turn the other cheek, in de Marenches's view, was little short of a betrayal of Western ideals. The French count, who would greatly admire Ronald Reagan, scornfully referred to Carter as "that baby-faced Boy Scout."

As head of SDECE, de Marenches had long paid great attention to Saudi Arabia, traveling there throughout the years and nurturing a friendship with King Faisal and his successors. In the early days of that outreach, Saudi Arabia was fully dependent on the United States—so much so that communications between the French spy and the Saudi royals had to be handled by American telecommunications officers attached to Aramco, the oil company.

De Marenches doggedly worked on rectifying this imbalance. He employed as an SDECE station chief in the kingdom a certain Colonel C. A camel-corps officer who had spent years in the Sahara and was fluent in Arabic, the colonel—according to de Marenches—had developed profound relationships with senior Saudi princes "through long evenings spent sipping tea in a tent around a campfire fueled with camel dung."

All this tea sipping paid off. Toward the end of the 1970s, France flanked America as a major provider of weaponry to the kingdom, selling the Saudis its AMX tanks and providing training to scores of Saudi officers and special-force troops near Toulon.

Prince Turki first met the French spymaster when de Marenches visited with his father, King Faisal, in 1974. An enormous man whose bulging belly could never be contained by a belt, de Marenches was hilariously funny and charming when he needed to make friends. Turki thought him "extraordinary." And, after becoming head of Saudi intelligence in 1977, Turki established with de Marenches's SDECE a powerful covert-action alliance, filling a vacuum that the CIA's incapacitation had left in the region.

This alliance, which also included spy agencies of pro-Western Egypt, Morocco, and, until the Islamic revolution, Iran, called itself the Safari Club. As CIA officers enviously watched its exploits, the Safari Club busied itself with cloak-and-dagger operations from Somalia to Zaire. Though the first, nonlethal CIA aid for Afghan guerrillas began to trickle in only in July 1979, it was the Safari Club that began pouring money and weapons into a fledgling Islamic insurgency there soon after the Communist takeover of April 1978.

Because of these tight connections with Paris, as well as a genuine admiration for the French count, it was only natural for Prince Turki to pick up the phone and call de Marenches for advice a few days into the Grand Mosque crisis. What kind of assistance, the Saudi prince wanted to know, could be offered by Paris?

"We are at your service," the French spymaster replied. "What can we do?"

Discreet professional help would be much appreciated, Prince Turki replied.

De Marenches had already given some thought to the upheaval in Mecca, and he realized the immense religious importance of the shrine. He watched American interests attacked in previous days all over the Muslim world because of mere rumors of U.S. involvement in the affair. Was it really necessary to commit non-Muslim French soldiers to such a sensitive mission? Only a purely Islamic force, he suggested to Turki, could intervene in a precinct as sacred as the Kaaba.

As it happened, another of Saudi Arabia's traditional Safari Club partners was eager to help. Morocco's royal protocol chief, General Moulay al Alaoui, had just flown to Jeddah with a proposal to dispatch to Mecca several hundred French-trained commandos of Morocco's Gendarmerie Royale.

But the Saudis had no desire to become indebted to fellow Arabs. If they wanted to solicit the Jordanians or the Moroccans, they could have asked them directly. What Saudi Arabia required in these dangerous times was the high expertise and absolute discretion that, senior princes believed, only the French could provide.

Shortly after this conversation, President Giscard d'Estaing followed up with a formal overture. He passed a personal message to King Khaled: France was outraged by the desecration of the holy shrine, and, should His Majesty so request, was ready to provide assistance, having some experience in the matter. The response from Riyadh was almost immediate: "How soon can you come?"

To preserve utmost secrecy, top French and Saudi officials from then on talked directly to each other, bypassing normal diplomatic channels. The French embassy in Jeddah, and even the country's foreign minister, were kept out of the loop, with communications entrusted to the head of the French military cooperation mission in Riyadh, General Hervé Navereau.

Having read the desperate-sounding Saudi reply, General Navereau boarded a plane that same day and rushed to Paris for an emergency meeting in the Elysée presidential palace.

The crisis he was leaving behind was about to get dramatically more complicated.

TWENTY-TWO

S ome seven hundred miles east of Mecca, in the palm-fringed oases
sandwiched between the gravelly desert and the Persian Gulf, another uprising was starting in these hours, fueled by decades of resentment at Saudi government policies and ignited by revolutionary fires
that raged across the water, in Iran.

Coastal towns such as Qatif, Safwa, and Sayhat were the bastions of
the kingdom's 350,000-strong Shiite minority. Though a fraction of
the overall Saudi population, these embittered Shiites constituted a majority in the kingdom's vast Eastern Province—home to almost all
Saudi oil. At the time, they also accounted for more than a third of the
workers at the company that extracted this oil, Aramco.

Ever since conquering Arabia's eastern coast in 1913, the Saudi state
had relegated the Shiite community to impoverished ghettos. Though
Shiite towns and villages literally sat atop the oil fields that provided
Saudi Arabia with newfound wealth, they remained excluded from the
ambitious development projects that transformed the rest of the king-

dom. It was not just that the area's oil brought few benefits to the locals. Aramco's practice of filling oil wells with water pumped from the Shiite oases' underground aquifers had led to an ecological disaster. The lowering of the water table made irrigation canals go dry, replacing with dusty shrub much of the region's once luscious vegetation.

Discrimination against the Shiites wasn't limited to distributing oil funds. Deemed heretics if not outright infidels, they were excluded from senior Saudi government jobs and the military. In government-run schools, Shiite children were taught that their sect of Islam was a devilish Jewish invention that aimed to undermine the true faith. Shiite-cooked food was deemed unclean. And, crucially, their custom of mourning processions during the main Shiite religious festival, the Ashura, was prohibited by the state.

Ashura, which falls on the tenth day of the month of Muharram, commemorates the martyrdom of Hussain, the son of Ali and grandson of Prophet Mohammed. The tragedy of Hussain's death, in the battle of Karbala against vastly larger Sunni forces, defines the Shiites' millennial sense of having been wronged by the Sunni majority of the Muslim world. In traditional, blood-soaked Shiite processions, worshippers mourn Hussain on Ashura by beating their chests, flagellating themselves with iron chains, and even cutting their foreheads open with knives.

Although Juhayman was a Sunni, his takeover in Mecca—which began on the First of Muharram, precisely ten days before Ashura—reinforced the convulsions of religious fervor that usually seize Shiite lands at this time of the year. Shiites in the Eastern Province—unlike Wahhabi radicals in Riyadh or Medina—knew very little about Juhayman's program or ideology; few realized that the gunmen in Mecca happened to be much more hostile to the Shiite freedoms and aspirations than the Saudi state ever was.

As exciting rumors about Mecca events swept Shiite towns that week, hotheaded young radicals were awed by Juhayman's uprising, which they imagined to be an Iranian-style revolution against the

House of Saud. The weakness that Saudi forces displayed in the Grand Mosque emboldened these radicals to act in their own hometowns, opening a second front of the war against the hated regime. "Mujahed Juhayman," the foe of their foes, emerged for years to come as the Shiite revolutionaries' unlikely idol.

Saudi security services had been fearing for months that Shiite Iran might use its religious affinity with local inhabitants to foment unrest in the Eastern Province. The warnings about Iranian agitation that the American consul-general in Dhahran, Ralph Lindstrom, cabled to Washington on the first day of the Mecca crisis were not without foundation: the Iranians indeed ran a large network of intelligence operatives and clerics intent on destabilizing the Saudi regime. In recent days, as the Mecca crisis escalated, the tone of Iranian radio broadcasts in Arabic had become more and more shrill, urging the Saudi Shiites to rise up and overthrow the "tyranny."

America—whose companies still played a crucial role in operating Aramco—was portrayed in these broadcasts as the community's enemy. For the first time, visible anti-American feeling swept the oil-producing areas of the Eastern Province, home to most of the 40,000 Americans living in Saudi Arabia. On the first day of the Mecca crisis, Aramco's security chief had already relayed to Lindstrom that Shiite activists in the area near the critical Ras Tanura terminal had been agitating for a campaign to "chase" Americans from the region.

Days later, at least fifty American employees of Aramco at Ras Tanura, Abqaiq, and other key Saudi oil installations received threatening letters from these Shiite revolutionaries. "You are to know that all facilities and properties for all the Americans will be destroyed," the letters promised in stilted and ungrammatical English. "We are serious and very eager to distroy [sic] you all."

Corroborating these threats, the CIA picked up and passed to Crown Prince Fahd an alarming intelligence report: Shiite revolutionaries intended to blow up a major refinery in the Eastern Province, and to score propaganda points by blaming the explosion on American mischief.

The Iranians' point man coordinating subversion on the Arab side of the Gulf was Hadi Modarresi, the Iraqi-born cleric who had tried to barge into the Arab League summit in the Tunis Hilton, and whose fiery sermons had already sparked Shiite unrest in the nearby island-state of Bahrain. Just a few weeks before heading to Tunis, Modarresi preached in person the gospel of Islamic revolution in the Shiite prayer houses of Safwa and Qatif.

Among Saudi Arabia's native Shiites, the mantle of the most senior Islamic revolutionary belonged to a Qatif-born sheikh, Hassan al Saffar. For years, Saffar and other radical Saudi Shiites refined their theological acumen and political conspiracy skills at the al Rasoul al Azam religious academy, in the relative safety of nearby Kuwait. It was in Kuwait that, just like Juhayman, they printed their propaganda leaflets and insurrectionary tracts.

Saffar, who remains the Saudi Shiites' main religious leader today, masterfully urged his people to abandon their deference to the Wahhabi regime. Like Juhayman, he blasted older clerics and notables for being unduly accommodating to the House of Saud. "The excessive fear which handicaps the mind, exhausts the body, impedes the progression . . . of energies is the illness from which the overwhelming majority of our society suffers," he proclaimed. "Waiting for the danger to occur is worse than the danger itself, and thus it is better to attack the danger."

Just before Muharram 1400, as Juhayman was putting in motion the takeover in Mecca, Saffar sneaked back into Saudi Arabia and went on a clandestine lecture tour in the *husseinias*—Shiite temples dedicated to the mourning of Hussain—across the Eastern Province. In these lectures, Saffar and his aides compared the Shiite community's current predicament with the battle of Karbala. Such a parallel inevitably turned the celebration of Ashura, a religious holiday, into an outpouring of anger against the House of Saud—seen as the modern-day incarnation of the Sunni caliphs who had martyred the beloved Hussain.

It was after one of these lectures, in the Sinnan *husseinia* of Qatif on the evening of November 25, 1979, that one emotional youth jumped up from the mat and shouted *"Allahu Akbar"* at the top of his lungs. As eyewitnesses remember it, hundreds of fellow young men, dressed in traditional gowns and checkered headdresses, thundered with an *"Allahu Akbar"* in return. Then, they all filed out of the building, waving clenched fists and shouting revolutionary slogans.

This burgeoning crowd marched to the center of Qatif, where nervous police lined up. Military presence was thin, as on this day Saudi troops were still engaged in an all-out assault on Mecca's Grand Mosque, sustaining heavy casualties. Using loudspeakers, the police declared the demonstration illegal and urged Shiite protesters to disperse. The reply was a defiant *"Allahu Akbar."* Some prominent merchants and tribal leaders, fearful that such demonstrations would backfire against the community, tried to call for calm, but they were haughtily brushed aside by the young zealots.

After a tense standoff, policemen ran into the crowd, beating back the protesters with clubs. Some of the demonstrators tried to resist, hurling rocks, but had to retreat once the officers started firing volleys of tear gas canisters. Soon the clouds of gas became so thick that the rioters could no longer see one another.

For that evening, the protests were over.

Nevertheless, Saudi officials were badly shaken by this display of Shiite discontent. A mass-scale uprising here in the heart of the Saudi oil industry could hurt the House of Saud even more than the already unbearable trauma in Mecca. A rattled Major General Hussein Malki, the General Intelligence Directorate (GID) boss for the Eastern Province, fretted about Iranian subversion, speculating in a meeting with Consul-General Lindstrom the following morning that the seizure of the Grand Mosque "might have been an operation intended to divert attention from the major objective of those who might have sponsored it."

· · · ·

Violence resumed hours later in the town of Sayhat, the Shiite community closest to Dammam-Dhahran-al Khobar, the modern, predominantly Sunni conurbation that housed provincial authorities, the American consulate, and the Aramco headquarters. Demonstrators who poured out of the Sayhat *husseinia* after the evening prayer were ready for battle: they carried iron bars, sticks, and stones. These presented only limited danger for government troops. Unlike Juhayman's Bedouins occupying Mecca's Grand Mosque, the urban Shiites of the Saudi east coast possessed no military training and rarely owned firearms.

Which is why, once tear gas was fired into the crowds at Sayhat, some of the protesters tried to rectify the imbalance of force by grabbing weapons from the police. One of several youngsters involved in this melee was Hassan al Qalaf, a recent graduate of Aramco's industrial training center. By one account, he lunged toward a policeman's handgun. The officer proved alert and shot at Qalaf. The first among many martyrs of the Shiite uprising fell dead. His body was snatched away by fellow rioters and paraded through the streets of Sayhat as a rousing symbol of the crimes perpetrated by al Saud.

That night, the Saudi government grew so alarmed by the metastasizing of domestic upheaval that it began to withdraw National Guard units from Mecca, where the surface of the mosque had just been secured. Entire battalions of the Guard were rushed to the rebellious Shiite province. Scarred by the ferocity of rebel fire in Mecca, many of these Bedouin troopers had been reluctant to fight their kin among Juhayman's men. But they felt no such compunctions about battling the "infidel" Shiites of the east. Rebels of Qatif or Sayhat would see no mercy.

An ancient center of Gulf commerce, fishing, and the pearl trade, Qatif was a maze of narrow alleys that zigzagged among elaborate fortress-like houses made of coral and mud. It was here that the Karmatian heretics had taken the magic Black Stone from Mecca more than a millennium ago. Almost completely Shiite, the town was not the kind of place that government troops would find easy to control as the uprising expanded.

The morning of Wednesday, November 28, the young men of Qatif were determined to avenge the death in Sayhat. They were further inflamed by reports that some of the prominent locals had been arrested the previous night. Senior leaders of the uprising, such as Sheikh Saffar, had to go into hiding, eventually fleeing across the desert to Syria.

Freshly arrived National Guard troops were already deployed in large numbers, their machine guns mounted on flatbed trucks and ominously facing the city. Protesters concentrated at first on a local government headquarters, showering the building in a hail of rocks. As a ragtag column of demonstrators approached Guard lines, waving portraits of Khomeini, some in the crowd tried to counter anti-Shiite prejudice among the troops with a catchy slogan favored by the ayatollah himself. *"La Sunniya la Shiiya—Wahda wahda islamiyya,"* the demonstrators chanted. "There is no Sunni or Shiite—just Islamic unity."

The troops were not swayed. As demonstrators ignored orders to stop, machine guns opened fire at chest level. The first volley was greeted with something close to disbelief. Then, amid cries of horror and the gurgling of the dying, the crowd broke up in chaos. Some ran away; others tried to pick up the wounded from the pools of blood. With government hospitals refusing to accept the casualties, feverish, often delusional victims were housed in *husseinias*, where a few Shiite doctors and nurses provided basic first aid.

The unwashed corpses of the dead—and there were at least five of those—were also dragged into the *husseinias* and then carried through the streets. The martyrs' blood, which smeared marchers' robes, was meant to convince those not yet demonstrating that staying home was no longer an option.

As the Guard closed in, troopers were given orders to arrest any man walking alone. This became a high-risk mission: the narrow lanes of old Qatif made for perfect ambush opportunities against soldiers unfamiliar with the terrain. One by one, Guard patrols who wandered too deep into town were attacked by squads of youths armed with knives and iron bars. As troopers were killed, their captured weapons were turned against other Guard units.

Fearing that the Shiite rebellion would spread across the entire Eastern Province, disrupting the country's oil output, the Saudi government that day sealed all roads into the Shiite heartland around Qatif and severed phone lines. And—just as was the case with the seizure of the Grand Mosque a week earlier—it allowed no hint about these disturbing events in the tightly censored media. Instead, aiming to appease Khomeini, King Khaled sent the ayatollah a telegram expressing gratitude for Iran's "Islamic, brotherly position" in the Grand Mosque affair.

TWENTY-THREE

In the refined splendor of the Elysée Palace in Paris, President Valéry Giscard d'Estaing assembled his senior military aides for a confidential late-morning meeting. Though the operation he would discuss concerned a foreign land, the French foreign minister was not invited, in the interests of maintaining strict secrecy. The stuffed chairs were occupied by the minister of defense, Yvon Bourges, the commander of the Gendarmerie Nationale—and by General Navereau, fresh from Riyadh.

Though spreading unrest in the Shiite towns of the Eastern Province had not yet been reported to the general public, French intelligence—just like the CIA—already knew about new troubles facing al Saud. General Navereau painted a somber picture of the kingdom's state of affairs. The Saudi monarchy, he announced, tottered on the brink of collapse. Saudi officials had severely misjudged the extent of resistance that Juhayman's men could offer in Mecca, and as a result Saudi troops had been mauled in a veritable massacre. The Saudi National Guard no longer wanted to fight in the Grand Mosque. The Americans had tried to help on the ground—and failed. France was the only hope left. It had become the French Republic's responsibility to rescue a monarchy that guaranteed the Free World's oil supplies.

It was obvious that regular French army troops—even the famed Foreign Legion—were ill suited for this job. There was no chance of keeping French aid under wraps should they deploy to the vicinity of Mecca. And, at such a sensitive moment, any leak about French involvement would inevitably fuel Khomeini's propaganda against the Saudi regime, making the kingdom's position even more precarious.

These objections, it was understood, did not apply to a very special unit: the nimble and secretive Groupe d'Intervention de la Gendarmerie Nationale. Created after the 1972 debacle at the Munich Olympics, where Palestinian terrorists took hostage and then murdered Israeli athletes, the GIGN was reputed at the time to be Europe's—if not the world's—best-trained special force.

Part of the Gendarmerie, a branch of the French military that carries out law enforcement duties, the GIGN had already shown its mettle. In Djibouti, across the Red Sea from Saudi shores, a group of terrorists had seized a bus full of French schoolchildren in 1976. GIGN commandos flown from Paris first persuaded the militants to eat food spiked with tranquilizers, and then—applying the lessons of the Munich fiasco—opened up with a simultaneous barrage of fire that allowed almost all the children to escape unscathed.

Senior Saudi princes knew all of this well. Prince Nayef himself had watched the GIGN commandos in action in the spring of 1979 at a military exhibition in the French town of Satory.

The GIGN's officer in charge of the show for the Saudis was the unit's deputy commander, Lieutenant Paul Barril, then thirty-three. A blue-eyed combat diver with a shock of blond hair and a deceptive babyish smile, he was a third-generation gendarme, raised in an Alpine outpost on the Italian frontier. A rising star in the murky world of antiterrorism, Barril had joined the GIGN after stints in West Berlin, where he commanded an AMX-13 battle tank, took part in guarding the Nazi war criminal Rudolf Hess, and instructed American soldiers at an inter-allied training center.

In West Berlin, Barril also began dabbling with spywork, making forays across the Berlin Wall to snap pictures of the Soviet zone and helping Count de Marenches's SDECE collect and debrief East German defectors who had managed to sneak into the city's French sector. These intelligence ties meant that, despite his lowly rank, the young officer had plenty of friends in the corridors of French power.

As a GIGN commando, he had already been sent on top-secret assignments all over the world—from El Salvador to Tahiti. When not on a mission, Barril experimented with the newest weapons and gadgets of his tradecraft at the unit's base in Maisons-Alfort near Paris. He dedicated particular energy to a piece of equipment that was still considered exotic at the time: a Kevlar bulletproof jacket.

For Prince Nayef's benefit, Barril's commandos rappelled down from a helicopter, guns blazing. Then the lieutenant unloaded his Magnum 357 into the chest of a fellow trooper who wore a clay saucer on a necklace. The saucer shattered into a thousand pieces, and an awed Prince Nayef was invited to pick out the hot bullets lodged in the grinning trooper's Kevlar vest.

The conversation after the show, however, quickly turned sour. Nayef asked Barril whether the French could train Saudi combat divers and commandos to protect the kingdom's oil installations from possible Iranian sabotage.

"How well trained are these men already?" Barril inquired.

"They are Bedouins. They don't even know how to swim," Prince Nayef replied honestly.

"Then it's just impossible. It won't work," the Frenchman scoffed with disdain.

Offended by such impudence, Prince Nayef gave the lieutenant a blistering look. But the impressive display of firepower at Satory remained stuck in his mind. Months later, once Prince Turki's phone call to Count de Marenches opened contacts on possible French help in the Mecca affair, the Saudis specifically requested the GIGN.

· · · ·

The unit—then numbering just a few dozen gendarmes—was commanded by Captain Christian Prouteau. A tall thirty-five-year-old graduate of the elite Saint Cyr military academy, Prouteau combined a commando's dedication to martial arts with a more bookish passion for antique watches. To unwind, he played guitar in the GIGN rock band.

Prouteau was training with his men at Maisons-Alfort when he received a summons to the Gendarmerie Nationale headquarters. Barril, promoted to captain since the Satory show, immediately guessed the reason. It must be something to do with the trouble in Mecca, he told fellow commandos. He was right. A few hours later, Prouteau was whisked into the Elysée Palace by the Gendarmerie chief and now sat in the august presence of the president of the republic himself.

Formal and impeccably courteous, President Giscard d'Estaing exuded all the inborn confidence of an aristocrat—even though the noble title of d'Estaing, extinct since the French Revolution, had been purchased by the president's bourgeois father only in 1922 in order to improve the provincial family's social standing. A lanky, balding man with an oblong, finely featured face, Giscard d'Estaing didn't say much during the meeting. But when he opened his mouth, his instructions were clear. "Do the maximum possible," he ordered Prouteau.

The captain responded that his men were ready for action. He had only one concern: how to exfiltrate his team from Saudi Arabia once the operation was over. The need for discretion meant that no French aircraft could be on standby in Mecca. And the nearest French base in the area, in Djibouti, was several hundred kilometers away. These details, he was told, were to be worked out through the chain of command.

Back on base in Maisons-Alfort, Prouteau assembled the unit that would be sent to Saudi Arabia. Though Prouteau usually participated himself in most GIGN operations, this time he chose to stay behind. This, he reckoned, would ensure that the commandos wouldn't get abandoned by France should unforeseen complications arise. Barril would be the one actually heading to Arabia.

Men of great ambition who now held equal rank, captains Prouteau and Barril maintained an uneasy relationship that would implode in following years. In 1979, however, the hierarchy was clear. Prouteau was called by his men "le grand." Barril's nickname was "le petit."

Two more men were assigned to go to Saudi Arabia with Barril. Warrant officer Ignace Wodecki, then thirty-nine, was a career gendarme who had supervised Barril's fitness test when the young officer had first joined the GIGN—and, much to Barril's annoyance, made him run a few extra miles. Unlike the dreamy, multilingual Barril, Wodecki, the son of a Polish coal miner, was a stickler for the rules. This was precisely the reason Prouteau wanted him in Saudi Arabia: to provide independent feedback, and to keep Barril's impulsiveness in check. The third member of the team was Christian Lambert, a thirty-two-year-old explosives specialist and another veteran of the GIGN.

Before his departure for Saudi Arabia, Barril was summoned by Bourges, the minister of defense. The minister didn't consider the mission ahead all that difficult. "You have to eject a couple of imbeciles from some grotto," he dismissively told Barril. "All you'll have to do is throw a couple of grenades at them. Child's play."

But the commandos prepared for the worst. They simply didn't know what to expect. Intelligence support was so scarce that Prouteau had to rip a picture of the Grand Mosque from a news magazine to familiarize himself with the geography of the shrine. Later that day, he called a journalist friend for a quick lecture on Islam. As Prouteau brainstormed with Barril, the two officers hit on the same idea of using chemical weapons that—unbeknownst to them—had already been tried by the CIA.

"We'll gas them in the basement like rats," Prouteau mused.

Instead of good old tear gas, the French went for a potent, concentrated fine-powder variety of a chemical called dichlorobenzylidenemalononitrile. Known simply as CB to the soldiers, this chemical had already been used by the GIGN in hostage situations in France and abroad. During training at Maisons-Alfort, Barril even experimented with the stuff on himself, almost going blind in the process.

Similar to the gas used by Russian troops to free hostages seized by Chechen rebels in a Moscow theater in 2002, in a debacle that caused over 170 deaths, CB is an irritant that blocks respiration and inhibits aggressiveness. Nonlethal if the subject is removed quickly, the concoction, by Barril's calculations, could kill within five minutes if only 0.3 milligrams are present per cubic meter of confined space. The French powder had an active-agent concentration of nearly 100 percent—compared with the 30 percent or less for tear gas usually used in riot control.

The three Frenchmen packed a small amount of CB and dispersers, gas masks, and flak jackets. Carrying this gear, they arrived before dawn of Thursday, November 29, at the Villacoublay military airport near Paris. There, at six a.m., they boarded a Mystère-20 executive jet that was usually used by senior government officials. General Navereau traveled with the GIGN men, explaining during the flight the intricacies of al Saud's current predicament.

The word "Mecca" never appeared in the government's paperwork. Instead, the Gendarmerie Nationale travel order number 3016 dispatched Barril, Wodecki, and Lambert on a "provost mission" to Saudi Arabia, destination Riyadh.

The jet stopped for refueling in Larnaca, Cyprus, and landed in the Saudi capital at about six p.m. There, French commandos were driven straight from the airport to a meeting of the Saudi general staff. The city looked tense and deserted. Inside the palace that housed Saudi generals, everything suggested revolutionary times. Edgy troops with large machine guns facing in all directions camped on garish carpets, in a mood of deepening gloom and suspicion. As he walked through, Barril whispered to a colleague that should someone discharge a weapon by accident the Saudi military command would most likely be instantly decimated in jittery crossfire.

Once he presented himself to the potbellied Saudi generals, Barril asked who these rebels in Mecca actually were. To his surprise, the Saudis told him that they didn't know. Then it was their turn to gasp. The Saudis had been expecting a somewhat larger force and appeared shocked once Barril explained to them that the French mission consisted just of him and two other men.

The French commandos, accompanied by a military attaché, were assured that a senior Saudi general—possibly even the Mecca governor, Prince Fawwaz—would meet them on the ground. Then they were driven back to the airport, where a large transport plane had already started the engines. From this point, the mission went under deep cover. To maintain the secret of their true identities, Barril and his men had to surrender their passports and military papers to the French embassy staff. Dressed in civilian clothes—Barril sported bell-bottom jeans with a cowboy belt—they no longer had weapons for personal protection, and had no way of communicating with their superiors except for the unreliable Saudi telephone system. To the outsiders, they were supposed to be three French businessmen, albeit a bit too muscular and broad-shouldered to make the story entirely convincing.

Reassuringly, the plane taking them from Riyadh had an American crew, who exchanged friendly banter with the French during the flight. It was near midnight when the commandos finally arrived at the Taef military airport. There were no generals and no princes to greet them. After a while, a low-level Saudi officer emerged to welcome the French commandos. He drove them to their rooms—not in the Saudi barracks, but in Taef's marble and glass Intercontinental Hotel.

The following morning, the GIGN commandos were assigned a guide, a major of the Saudi armored corps who had studied in France and spoke fluent French. They retrieved their gear from the airfield and, in a white Peugeot GL provided by their Saudi hosts, headed to a secluded villa where training sessions for Saudi troops would begin.

The first of these meetings was in a bare classroom, with a blackboard, battered chairs, and a framed picture of the Grand Mosque on the wall. The French were stunned by just how demoralized the Saudi officers seemed to be. Some were bandaged after sustaining light wounds. Others shared stories of how their comrades had fallen under rebel fire. Everyone appeared reluctant to return to the battlefield. Barril realized it would be extremely hard to persuade these men to head down the mosque's dark, dank staircases into the basement where Juhayman's men—invisible from above—shot without missing.

One officer's helmet, pierced by a bullet, was a vivid reminder of the dangers. The man had worn this helmet on the hip when it was struck, at the staircase to the mosque's basement. The very same bullet had burst through the chests of two other Saudi troopers. They didn't survive.

To raise morale, Barril and the two other commandos started teaching the Saudis about flak jackets. While these were initially designed to protect against flak—fragments of an exploding shell or hand grenade—newer versions used by the French at the time were also supposed to stop bullets. To make his point, Barril hung one of these jackets on the wall and unloaded a gun into the chest plate area. Unlike at the demonstration for Saudi princes at the arms show, he didn't risk performing this experiment with one of his own men actually wearing the gear.

This was wise. Though they shielded their wearers from Magnum pistol shots, the French vests, it turned out, provided only limited protection against high-velocity 7.62- and 5.56-millimeter assault rifle bullets of the kind fired by the rebels in Mecca. Employed in action in following days, the vests would come back riddled with bloodstained holes.

The Saudis briefed the French about what had been attempted in Mecca in previous days. They told the GIGN's men about the carbonized APCs, about the failure of tear gas attacks, and about the dogged determination of Juhayman's rebels. The very topography of the Qaboo labyrinths seemed to be protecting the militants, limiting the damage inflicted by government attacks to just a few rooms.

Now it appeared that the Saudis had run out of options and simply didn't know what to do.

In this atmosphere of chaotic improvisation, not even a map of the area was on hand. Trying to understand the layout of the shrine, Barril plucked the framed picture of the Grand Mosque from the wall. Without a second thought, he then started to mark on it possible approaches to the basement. A groan of shock went through the room: Saudi troopers were aghast at such a blasphemous use of sacred imagery. For the next session, they fetched more detailed plans that Salem Bin Laden and Angawi had provided in the initial days of the siege.

At lunch, Barril examined his Saudi-issued food ration. Unlike the mostly illiterate Saudi troopers, he noticed that the ration pack was long expired—as one could expect in a country where defense contracts were designed to provide maximum kickback opportunities for senior princes.

It became clear to the French gendarmes that day that the Saudis lacked basic concepts of military planning: attacks in Mecca so far were mostly frontal, without any concern for casualties. Saudi officers became visibly animated, exchanging excited murmurs, once Barril suggested making a diversionary strike in one part of the basement and sending the main thrust of the troops through a different area. Such concepts—part of Tactics 101 in any war college—seemed a total novelty, French commandos concluded with unease.

Barril expected that he would soon be heading to the Grand Mosque himself, to supervise the planned operation firsthand. Some of the Saudi officers seemed to think so, too. "You know, you have to convert to Islam if you want to go to Mecca," one of the officers in charge told him. Barril, raised a Catholic in a village of regular churchgoers, knew very little about Islam at the time. But he didn't think long before replying: he was ready to convert if this was necessary to get the job done. After all, Barril figured, it was common for the GIGN commandos to assume other identities during operations. They posed as stewards in plane rescues, or as prison guards while quelling jailhouse riots.

What would be the difference between wearing a steward's uniform and pledging allegiance to Islam?

After the first day in Taef, Barril grew convinced that the material he had brought from France was insufficient. GIGN commandos needed to equip and train several hundred men, and quickly.

Back in his room in the Taef Intercontinental, the captain wrote a long wish list and then called Prouteau. Barril told his commander that he wanted more flak jackets, grenades, sniper rifles, field radios, night-vision goggles, and gas masks. And, most important, he needed CB. A ton of it. Literally.

Prouteau thought he misheard when Barril first named this stagger-ing amount. One ton of CB was, after all, enough to poison an entire city. But Barril wasn't joking: the precariousness of the Saudi regime, he insisted, should not be underestimated by Paris.

Prouteau immediately went to work putting together this mammoth shipment. In the French military bureaucracy, the sheer size of Barril's request prompted snickering suggestions that the captain must have suc-cumbed to panic. Some of his demands, after all, exceeded the French military's entire stockpile!

Barril, who understood the difference of perceptions between Taef and Paris, remained glued to a phone in a parallel effort to convince key French officials that this equipment was really needed. His army friend from common service in West Berlin now commanded the presi-dential guard in the Elysée Palace. Barril used this friendship to make sure that President Giscard d'Estaing was personally briefed about the gravity of the situation in Mecca.

Shortly after this phone call, the French were driven to a military compound where they were supposed to train a different batch of sol-diers. When their Peugeot rolled into the base, the French-speaking Saudi major who accompanied the GIGN men grew inexplicably tense. He parked the car in an isolated area, far away from the main barracks, and then told the French to remain seated.

Half an hour later, the major returned, turned the ignition key, and hurriedly drove his charges away. It was too dangerous to stay there, he explained. Considering the rotten morale in the Saudi forces and the doubtful loyalty of some units, it was anyone's guess what reaction a presence of Western personnel might provoke. The French realized that they might be in grave danger—and that they had no way of protecting themselves. "Who are our friends here?" warrant officer Wodecki wondered. "Who are our enemies?"

TWENTY-FOUR

The French were working on plans for seizing the Grand Mosque's basement-level galleries just as violence in the Shiite Eastern Province reached a fever pitch. The situation had gotten so desperate that Secretary of State Vance sent Ambassador West a long cable on November 29, instructing him to begin preparations for a possible evacuation of American citizens from the kingdom. Appalled, Ambassador West replied that, if the Americans indeed evacuated from Saudi Arabia, "it would wreck the armed forces, oil production, transportation, etc. and . . . would lead to the overthrow of the Saud regime." In any case, he informed the State Department, Prince Bandar had assured him that the Saudis were confident of crushing the Shiite uprising "as long as [Washington] didn't complain too much about human rights violations." The Iranian lesson had been learned, and no such complaints were forthcoming.

On Thursday, November 29, the eve of the Ashura holiday, the final battle erupted in the Shiite hub of Qatif. The National Guard, harassed since the previous night in the downtown maze, initially withdrew to the town's outskirts. Several military vehicles were set ablaze overnight: Shiite rioters, just like Juhayman's men in Mecca, had discovered the art of Molotov cocktails, hurling them at passing military vehicles from rooftops and upstairs windows.

The morning began with the burials of youngsters who had been gunned down the previous day. Angry sermons at the cemetery sent crowds of men, armed with sticks, rocks, and crowbars, to the town's main square. Like Juhayman in Mecca, these demonstrators, no longer satisfied with simply affirming Shiite rights, now openly demanded an end to the monarchy. Entranced by the apparent strength of their numbers, they chanted "Death to Saud" and "With our spirit and our blood, we'll redeem you, Islam." Then they turned their rage on the symbols of the Saudi state and its Western allies.

The first targets were the local branches of the Riyadh Bank and the Saudi British Bank. The police guards there tried to offer resistance, but they were quickly overpowered by the crowd; one man was shot in the attack. Having ransacked the two banks, the crowds surged to another building housing the Arab Bank, which was also looted. Then the tumbledown amusement park of the city was set alight, condemned by Islamic revolutionaries for supposedly undermining public morals and distracting the townsfolk from their noble struggle. The mobs, demolishing everything in their way, continued to the local courthouse and the offices of Saudi Airlines.

In the midmorning, National Guard troopers returned. Dispersing death from mounted machine guns, they drove back the rioters, recapturing sections of the downtown. Some revolutionaries attempted a last-ditch resistance from the Qatif water tower, which—like the minarets in Mecca—provided a high-ground position for snipers. But the Shiites had only limited military training and were quickly dislodged. By the afternoon, helicopter gunships hovered in the sky, strafing anyone seen moving in the streets of Qatif. Electricity and water were cut off, in addition to the severing of telephone links the previous day. Frightening the locals, heavy artillery was deployed around the town in the afternoon, ready to pulverize Qatif if need be.

The day was just as dramatic in the town of Safwa, separated from Qatif by a patch of desert crisscrossed by thick Aramco pipelines. A native of the town had been killed in the previous day's demonstrations in Qatif. Following the funeral, the morning of November 29, a discussion broke out among younger revolutionaries and the town elders. The hotheads wanted to march toward the police station. "Let's go ask them—why did they kill our man!" they urged. The elders warned against any rash moves. "They will not hesitate to kill you too if you give them a chance," one argued.

But passions were too inflamed for such caution. By the late morning, a burgeoning human mass spilled from the cemetery into Safwa's main street and then blocked the coastal highway connecting the Dammam-Dhahran-al Khobar conurbation with the giant oil refinery complex and oil export terminal at Ras Tanura farther up the coast.

The town's police station stood on that road, named after Prophet Mohammed's son-in-law Ali, so revered by the Shiites. That was where the demonstrators now headed. As they approached within a few blocks, the National Guard suddenly opened fire, prompting a chaotic retreat by hundreds of frightened demonstrators. Once again, bodies fell on the ground, in the final convulsions of death. The wounded, often delirious, were brought into *husseinias*, and helicopter gunships appeared in the sky. Advancing into town behind armored cars, Guardsmen shot at anything that moved as frightened residents shivered indoors.

By the time Ashura arrived on Friday, November 30, it was clear that—though sporadic violence in the area would continue for years—the Saudi Shiite uprising was by and large suppressed. Nearly twenty Shiite demonstrators and several government troops had been killed, and Shiite towns were wrecked by the violence. Lacking weapons or training, the young Shiite revolutionaries realized that they were no match for the National Guard. "What are you going to fight them with—your sandals?" an eighteen-year-old protester who had agitated for a march toward Safwa's police station, Hamza Hassan, was scolded by his grandfather that night.

Police and the National Guard blocked all the roads, isolating the Shiite heartland from key oil industry installations. Police even seized in this security sweep an Aramco oil company bus with some forty employees that happened to be driving near Qatif. It took a high-level intervention by the oil company to have its workers released.

The older-generation Shiite community leaders, ostracized as sellouts in the first days of the uprising, now felt able to sue for peace with authorities. The king's brother and the Saudi deputy minister of interior, Prince Ahmed, flew to the Eastern Province in these hours and received in the Dammam governor's building a delegation of Shiite sheikhs, prominent merchants, and moderate clerics.

Prince Ahmed began the meeting by demanding the return of five large-caliber weapons that had been captured by rebels from government forces. But he wasn't interested in escalating the confrontation. Minutes later, Prince Ahmed listened with concern as prominent Shiite businessman Abdullah Matrood and other notables voiced their grievances at the lack of job opportunities and social services in towns like Qatif. Somewhat apologetically, the prince replied with a promise to take up the matter with King Khaled as soon as he returned to Riyadh. The government wouldn't just direct money to relieve Shiite poverty, Prince Ahmed said. Should calm be restored, some restrictions on Shiite religious practices would also be lifted. The House of Saud couldn't afford to be vengeful. After all, the royal family still had to deal with another security nightmare: Juhayman's gunmen, who remained holed up in the basement of the Grand Mosque.

In the wider Muslim world, meanwhile, the ripples of anti-American anger unleashed by the holy shrine's seizure ten days earlier continued to spread.

A major Kuwaiti newspaper, *al Siyassa*, relayed for the first time to the general Arab public the details of Juhayman's ideology. The newspaper obtained a copy of "The Seven Epistles" and in the November 29 edition dedicated prime space to key extracts, including the Saudi rebel's denunciation of the presence of embassies of Christian states.

This touched a raw nerve among American diplomats. "Of most obvious and immediate concern is the 'teaching' against 'embassies in our lands,' " the U.S. ambassador in Kuwait commented in an "immediate" telegram to the State Department that outlined *al Siyassa*'s article. "The extent to which propaganda of this kind have been propagated in Kuwait is unknown to us."

The answer came the following day, November 30. Inspired by the destruction of the U.S. embassy in Pakistan and assaults on American interests in Turkey, India, and Bangladesh, a mob of Kuwaiti radicals converged near the U.S. embassy there and tried to break in. Kuwaiti troops had to use tear gas and flash-bang grenades to disperse the rioters.

Two days later it was the turn of the Libyan capital, Tripoli.

The American embassy there, on a quiet side street in the central part of the city, was already operating with skeleton staff, a result of growing hostility between the Carter administration and Libya's firebrand military dictator, Colonel Moammar Ghadhafi. Following a downgrading of ties, the United States no longer had a full ambassador in Libya and was represented by a chargé d'affaires, William Eagleton.

State Department officials didn't seem unduly worried by Ghadhafi's refusal to let a customary U.S. Marine unit deploy on embassy grounds. Attack wasn't deemed imminent: after all, President Carter's brother, Billy, had just spent a month touring Libya and would soon become its paid lobbyist. Responding to a letter sent by President Carter the previous week, Ghadhafi assured the United States that its mission in Tripoli was safe from any harm.

In the absence of marines, security duties fell on the CIA station chief in Tripoli, Jack McCavitt. He wasn't as sanguine: after the hostage taking in Tehran, the Mecca uprising, and the bloodshed in Islamabad, the spy grew convinced that it was just a matter of time before a similar assault was made on Americans in Libya. First, he destroyed or pouched to Tunis sensitive documents, lest they fall into the wrong hands, as had happened in Tehran. Then, late at night, McCavitt drove to a cliff and threw into the sea his cameras and other incriminating tools of spycraft.

He searched for ways to defend the embassy from an attack that he now expected anytime. In the embassy basement, McCavitt and one of the diplomats, a former marine, found a treasure trove: canisters containing a mixture of tear gas and a potent nauseating agent, and coils of razor wire. The wire was immediately used to bar access to the embassy roof. The gas canisters were brought up to prepare an unpleasant surprise for the anticipated invaders.

Early in the morning of Sunday, December 2, a working day on the Islamic calendar, a Libyan contact approached McCavitt with a warning. The man's children, students in a high school, had told him to stay away from the American embassy that day because it was going to be burned down, on orders from above. McCavitt ran to inform the chargé, Eagleton, and the embassy staff braced for the attack. The visa section was closed and all female employees except one were sent home. Only about a dozen Americans remained indoors, tear gas grenades and gas masks at the ready.

Dressed in suits and ties, McCavitt and an embassy political officer, Jim Hooper, went outdoors for a look at around nine a.m. Students, clad in paramilitary attire, already thronged the streets. The two Americans followed one such group all the way to Tripoli's huge al Saha al Khadra square. There, their jaws dropped: the square was teeming with thousands of youngsters. Many waved banners proclaiming solidarity with Iranian students who had occupied the U.S. embassy in Tehran and calling for the downfall of "American imperialism."

At that moment, McCavitt realized that there was only one place for all these youngsters to go: the American embassy. It also suddenly dawned on him just how conspicuous he and Hooper were, with their ties and suits, on this square—"like FBI agents at a peace march."

Back at the embassy, everything still seemed surprisingly calm. An elderly Libyan policeman slept in his chair near the building, caressed by the morning sun. The mob arrived twenty minutes later.

Diplomats trapped inside first heard the roaring sound of chanting: "Death to America! Death to America!" Then, the battering ram started working on the front gate. Students outside also started burning effigies of the Iranian Shah and of the Egyptian president, Sadat, who, as the official radio helpfully explained during the protest, was "in collusion with the butchers and executioners of peoples"—the United States. Then the turn came to set ablaze the American flag and an effigy of Carter himself.

As the battering continued, McCavitt instructed all Americans to don their gas masks, pulled the safety pin of the tear gas grenade, and threw it into the main entryway. The grenade fell down clanking. Then, nothing happened.

Now McCavitt was seriously worried. Nobody knew just how long these grenades had been lying in the embassy basement. What if none of them worked? He pulled another safety pin and threw down a second grenade. This one went off, emitting a cloud of gas. Encouraged, McCavitt lobbed the rest of the grenades one by one, saturating the lower floor, and retreated to higher ground. As planned beforehand, embassy employees then poured motor oil on the marble staircases.

It was time to escape. Unlike the isolated embassy in Pakistan, the one in Libya had the benefit of being part of an O-shaped block of apartment buildings. The embassy's back door led to the courtyard inside the O. Across this courtyard was the back door of an apartment that had long been rented by the embassy and that allowed an exit to a busy street around the corner from the main entrance. Coincidentally, it was Mark Hambley—the political officer now in Saudi Arabia—who had prepared this escape plan while previously posted in Libya.

Hurrying safely across the courtyard, the Americans opened the escape door—and were shocked to see that the main thoroughfare was clogged with green-clad teenagers, the overflow of the main column now busily breaking into the embassy. At that moment, a Libyan janitor—who knew the diplomats' affiliation—walked through the building's hallway, smiling enigmatically, and headed outside, toward the crowd of demonstrators. McCavitt briefly considered capturing the man and keeping him in the apartment, but then thought it too complicated.

Without wasting time, he decided to divide the trapped Americans into smaller groups. Men were told to remove jackets and ties and to walk through the crowd casually, without running or displaying anxiety. They were all to avoid eye contact with rioters and to gather in the British embassy. McCavitt himself left in the last group, with Hooper and the one woman, a secretary.

As he walked through hostile stares, he heard some of the youngsters on the street exchanging puzzled comments and wondering aloud whether these three foreigners in the middle of a riot could be American. But none of the mob leaders were here, around the corner from the main action. And, without orders from above, the suspicious students didn't dare take the initiative. McCavitt and his two companions were allowed to walk away undisturbed.

Once Libyan students overran the embassy, they were in for a shock. Thick clouds of tear gas they encountered in the lobby prompted spells of retching and pain. Overwhelmed by the chemicals, some students tried to run up the stairs. Inevitably, they slipped on the motor oil that had been generously poured around, and they tumbled down the marble steps and the banisters, rolling onto the heads of fellow protesters. As some of the more excited ones ran outside, screaming that they had been gassed, the crowd rushed away, trampling some of the teenagers.

Libya's official Jamahiriya News Agency that afternoon issued a whining report about American perfidy. "Upon the students' breaking into the embassy, the staff fired toxic gases believed to be used only by the military, confirming that the embassy employees are military personnel," the Libyan mouthpiece complained. "The use of toxic gases by U.S. embassy personnel resulted in the injury of several Libyan students who were carried to the hospital in serious condition."

Of course, not just students entered the embassy. Libyan military intelligence officers also arrived in the building and were spotted carting away boxloads of documents. None of these contained classified information: riches pillaged by Libyan intelligence included all eleven volumes of the State Department's publicly accessible Foreign Service Regulations, the embassy's "Learn a Foreign Language" tapes in Italian, and the cashier's records documenting petty cash foreign currency exchanges by the staff.

The following day, just after embassy personnel managed to reattach the dislodged front door, a young Libyan man arrived and started pounding at the entrance. One of the rioters who attacked the building the previous day, he surveyed the damage with glee, proud of a job well done. Then he told McCavitt he needed a visa to return to a college he was attending in upstate New York. Once McCavitt slammed the door with a curse, the flustered Libyan started screaming in English: "You can't do this to me!"

TWENTY-FIVE

As rioters rampaged in the American embassy in Tripoli on Sunday, December 2, a French Caravelle jet landed in Saudi Arabia.

The aircraft, which once ferried President Charles De Gaulle, had had its seats stripped out to make more room for seven tons of cargo. La Société Nationale des Poudres et des Explosifs, which manufactured CB, had not been able to satisfy Barril's request for the toxic concoction in full. Only three hundred kilograms of the chemical, the entire available stock, were aboard the Caravelle, along with gas masks, hand grenades, gas dispersers, and 150 flak jackets.

Captain Prouteau, the GIGN commander who had supervised the loading of this gear in France, chose not to tell the pilots exactly what they transported: the airmen, he figured, might have balked at flying potentially lethal chemicals.

In a small breach of the rules, Prouteau also placed onboard a small gift that his men would greatly appreciate in dry Saudi Arabia: a box of Sauvignon. This particular wine had been bottled in 1974—the year of the GIGN's creation. "Good luck," Prouteau scribbled in an enclosed note to Barril, Wodecki, and Lambert. "But be careful: remember, this is not your war."

In a mishap that could have caused a major problem, one of these bottles broke during unloading, leaking its precious liquid all over the tarmac of the Taef airbase. Saudi officers who supervised the operation either didn't realize this was wine, or, being pragmatic, pretended not to notice such a flagrant violation of Saudi Arabia's prohibition on alcohol.

In addition to the Sauvignon, the three French commandos managed to pilfer from the plane and bring to their Intercontinental rooms a few hand grenades, as extra insurance should events spin out of control.

Once the French supplies were transferred down the road to Mecca, Barril rehearsed with Saudi officers the final details of the planned assault. The French captain desperately wanted to travel to Mecca himself to help direct this carefully choreographed operation firsthand.

Some of the Saudi officers also wanted him there: the Grand Mosque, after all, was just a few minutes' ride by helicopter from Taef. But penetrating the holy city—thus violating a taboo on visits by infidels—was against instructions given by Paris. Worrying that Barril might disobey these orders, Lambert phoned Prouteau in Paris. "The captain is having all these wild ideas," he warned the GIGN commander.

Prouteau was furious. He gave Barril a tongue-lashing over the phone and then spoke to Lambert again. The two other commandos, he said, should keep a close eye on their captain. Prouteau left Lambert with an instruction should Barril persist in attempting to enter Mecca: "Go ahead and lock him up in the room."

In spite of this prohibition, Barril, by his own account, briefly sneaked into the holy city and into the Grand Mosque itself before the attack on the compound began. Some U.S. officials concur with his version.

Barril's two comrades in arms and Prouteau, however, are adamant that this never happened. The French role in the Mecca affair, they insist, was strictly limited to providing equipment and training in Taef and its vicinity. According to them, neither Barril nor any other French soldier set foot on Mecca's sacred ground during the siege.

Even if the French captain did visit Mecca during the crisis, it was in a strictly advisory capacity. No French commandos engaged in actual combat on Saudi soil. When the final push into the Qaboo began the morning of December 3, the GIGN troopers were holed up in their Taef hotel rooms. It would be hours before they received the first news from the battlefield.

Implementing the French-drafted plan on Monday morning, crews of workers—many of them civilian Pakistanis or Turks—started to drill perforations in the thick floor of the mosque. Soon an O-shaped ring of boreholes around the enclosure connected the surface with the underground labyrinth. These openings were supposed to be broad enough for the CB canisters to pass through but not sufficiently large for the rebels to use as escape hatches.

As soon as the drills were pulled from the holes, Juhayman's rebels—who patiently waited below, unseen in the darkness—obtained a clear line of fire toward the workmen above. Short, well-aimed fountains of bullets from these perforations were as lethal as they were unexpected. Several workmen fell dead, their blood gathering in pools and starting to drip into the boreholes.

Clad in French-supplied gas masks and chemical suits, Saudi soldiers fired through these perforations canisters of CB wired with explosives. Since the radio systems of various units were not compatible, soldiers had been ordered to pull the triggers of CB launchers at the sound of the first detonation. A near simultaneous series of blasts thundered in a circle around the Grand Mosque's courtyard, stunning the rebels trapped underneath in a cloud of powerful toxins. Attempting to saturate the basement, Saudi forces reinforced this initial shower of CB with regular tear gas and grenades.

As expected, the potent chemicals momentarily disabled the rebels, allowing the attack teams to burst through the barricades and barbed-wire fortifications that Juhayman's holdouts had erected on ramps and staircases. The main thrust of this invasion concentrated on the ramp that led down from the Peace Gate area of the Marwa-Safa gallery, the area where so much blood had been spilled in the early days of the fighting.

Pouring into this breach, the bulk of the assault force rushed in a counterclockwise direction toward the Umra Gate on the northwestern side of the compound and then south toward the King Abdelaziz Gate. A smaller part of the force headed the opposite way, moving clockwise to meet up with fellow soldiers after completing the circle under the Safa Gate and Jiyad Gate areas.

As they descended into the Qaboo, about a hundred soldiers with motor-powered CB-spraying devices pumped rising clouds of gas into the narrow passageways. Closely behind them advanced three additional units numbering sixty men each and armed with machine guns and flash-bang grenades.

These soldiers took no chances, riddling the corridors ahead with salvos of bullets and lobbing grenades before turning a corner. Along the way, they searched and secured room after room. Anyone found alive in these rooms was handed over to two arrest teams, which followed behind and numbered more than forty soldiers. Additional interception teams, with about ten men each, were posted at all exits from the basement within three minutes of the operation's beginning, catching any rebel attempting escape.

With a choking chemical mist filling the basement, Juhayman ordered his fighting men to redeploy away from the rooms occupied by the wounded, the hostages, and the women and children. He and his closest aides retreated into the depths of the Qaboo to mount their final battle against the miscreant servants of al Saud.

As the soldiers advanced, they found many hostages still alive, including the wounded paratrooper who had unsuccessfully tried to escape almost a week earlier and members of the Grand Mosque's police force. Emaciated and often knocked down by gas, these captives hadn't eaten anything for days. Some had had to resort to drinking their own urine.

They were lucky to have survived this ordeal. Though standing orders called on Saudi soldiers to give anyone in the mosque, rebel or not, a chance to surrender, in reality the Qaboo was a free-fire zone. Their visibility limited by foggy gas masks, the threat of sudden death lurking behind every corner, jittery Saudi troopers instinctively fired at anything that moved in the forbidding darkness. Uncounted civilians were gunned down by mistake in these final hours of combat.

With passageways between some rooms of the Qaboo only ninety centimeters (three feet) high, soldiers had to crawl in the clammy, foul underground. In some areas they waded knee-deep in putrid stagnant water. Juhayman's men had pulled out all electric wiring, and so lines of cable had to be rolled behind troops to power floodlights and communications equipment. Adding to the gas, thick black smoke from car tires that the rebels had set alight quickly enveloped the cellars, making it hard to see anything even with military flashlights. It had gotten so hot from the fires that the blades of ceiling fans in parts of the Qaboo curled up, taking the shape of giant tulip petals.

As effects of the French chemicals began to wear off, Juhayman's men recovered from the initial shock, putting up ferocious resistance in some parts of the basement. Hiding under false floors, they even managed to ambush a part of the advancing government force. Springing up from trapdoors, these small clusters of rebels unloaded their guns point-blank into the troopers, briefly taking some hostages. Soldiers kept dying in the Qaboo until the last minutes of the fight.

Though Saudi forces regularly used bullhorns to urge Juhayman's gunmen to give up, nobody on the rebel side accepted this call in these hours. "All our prisoners, we captured them," General Dhaheri, the operation's commander, later said. "No one surrendered on his own."

Eighteen hours after the last assault on the Qaboo began, the two main military forces finally sealed the circle under the mosque, meeting up— as planned—in the King Abdelaziz Gate area. It had been precisely two weeks since the start of the Mecca uprising. Just before dawn on Tuesday, December 4, 1979, the official Saudi Press Agency sent around the world a celebratory statement from Prince Nayef. "With God's help," the interior minister announced, "the purge of all members of the corrupt gang of renegades from the basement of the Grand Mosque was completed at 01:30 this morning."

The Saudis, however, were once again getting ahead of themselves. Eugene Bovis, the chief political officer at the American embassy, sought more information in the early afternoon of that Tuesday from a senior Saudi Foreign Ministry official, Abbas Ghazzawi. Despite Prince Nayef's early-morning announcement, Ghazzawi said frankly, there were still two roomfuls of gunmen holding out in the basement. Juhayman, Saudi authorities believed at the time, had escaped.

By nightfall, a paratroops unit led by Captain Abu Sultan, the French-trained grandson of the former chief of the Grand Mosque police, finished the mopping up in its sector of the Qaboo and reached the metal door to the only room not yet secured.

The captain ordered his troops to wire explosives to the door and blow it open. Once the soldiers burst inside, they spotted more than a dozen men hunched by the stone walls, their faces covered by soot, their tattered gowns soiled by blood and vomit. Some shook uncontrollably. But one, while visibly exhausted after days of fighting, retained an unbending, fierce look.

This man, older than the others, had tangled hair and a long, disheveled beard. Nearby were crates of weapons, barrels of *labne* cheese, bowls of dates, and piles of leaflets.

"What is your name?" Abu Sultan asked, pointing his gun at the man.

"Juhayman," he answered softly.

Abu Sultan already knew from interrogations of other detainees that this was the name of the rebel ringleader. He had caught the big prize.

The captain's immediate concern was that Juhayman, whose gunmen had killed so many government soldiers, would be lynched or shot dead before even leaving the mosque. Mobs of triumphant soldiers were already setting on prisoners who emerged from the basement, kicking them down and venting all the frustrations accumulated in the past two weeks of warfare. It was with great difficulty that security squads managed to drag off these bloodied, half-dead detainees.

To spare Juhayman such a fate, Abu Sultan escorted the rebel leader, sandwiched between two officers, to the surface, and then immediately hid him in an ambulance parked nearby. The ambulance then sped out of the mosque and delivered the prisoner to the Mecca Hotel, where senior princes now assembled.

Along the way, one of Abu Sultan's men asked Juhayman with disgust: "How could you do all this? How could you?"

The rebel was unrepentant.

Without showing emotion, he murmured his reply: "This was God's will."

A courtyard outside the Mecca Hotel by now became an open-air detention facility for the captured rebels. Manacled, they were made to sit on the ground, occasionally being slapped or shoved by the troops. Some were bleeding from their wounds. One man's blackened, gangrenous limb exuded a dizzying stench; he was soon taken away by an ambulance.

Samir, the teenage brother of two key rebels, was also brought into this courtyard. He and a dozen other nonfighters had been hiding behind a wall in the Qaboo and had evaded capture when the troops first entered the area; they were caught hours later as they groped their way out of the basement.

A Saudi TV crew and official photographers were brought in to film the trophy shots for the evening news. Some prisoners defiantly looked into the cameras, with one even sticking out his tongue and making a face. Faisal Mohammed Faisal was notable for his air of complete, inconsolable despair and regret.

Juhayman was taken across this courtyard and into an area occupied by Prince Nayef and other senior members of the royal household. A soldier dragged the rebel leader by his beard, Arabia's ultimate gesture of disrespect. Seeing this, one of the princes shouted at the soldier to let go. Then Prince Nayef pulled out an old passport-size picture of Juhayman. The rebel leader now had only a passing likeness to the man in the photograph. "Do you know who this is?" Prince Nayef asked.

"It is me. I am Juhayman" was the reply. "You don't have to be asking the others."

As Juhayman was led away, one of the officers asked him again why he had desecrated the holiest shrine. The reality of utter defeat began to sink in. "If I had known it would turn out this way, I wouldn't have done it," Juhayman muttered in response.

As princes and senior commanders celebrated their costly, bloody victory in Mecca, the only mystery that remained was the fate of the supposed Mahdi, Mohammed Abdullah. Had he managed to escape to fight another day?

This riddle was solved soon. Throughout the siege of the Grand Mosque, killed soldiers had been brought to a hospital morgue near the shrine. Officers from every unit involved in the fighting regularly inspected these rows of stiff, bullet-ridden bodies, identifying their own and taking them away for burial. Now that the fighting was over, one cadaver remained in the morgue, still unclaimed. The dead man wore two bandoliers across his chest, in the fashion of National Guard troopers.

Puzzling over who this might be, some officers noticed the distinctive red birthmark on his right cheek. Wasn't this supposed to be the sign of the Mahdi? Captives shown the body confirmed: this was indeed Mohammed Abdullah. The corpse was only beginning to decompose—which meant that the rebel had survived for days after the grenade explosion shredded his lower extremities.

For the Saudi authorities, a dead Mahdi was the ultimate prize. With this precious cadaver, they held unassailable theological proof that Juhayman's entire enterprise had been based on error, deception, and lies.

TWENTY-SIX

The Saudis never bothered to tell French commandos in Taef about the final push into the mosque. The French realized something was afoot only when their phone lines went dead on December 3. Effectively prisoners in their hotel, they found themselves isolated from their commanders and the outside world, without any way to get out. Throughout the night, at least one of the commandos remained awake on a rotating watch in the corridor, grenades in his pocket.

Wary about the loyalties of Saudi troops and the secretive nature of the kingdom, Barril was preparing himself for the worst. The fact that French infidels had played such a key role in a mission to recapture Islam's holiest shrine—and learned so much about Saudi failures—was deeply embarrassing for the House of Saud. It wouldn't be beyond the Saudis to stage an "accident" that eliminated these inconvenient witnesses, Barril figured. The three Frenchmen were undocumented and on their own in Taef—who would ever know the truth?

The three commandos agreed not to surrender without a fight. "We came here together, we'll leave together," Barril said.

In Paris, Prouteau was even more anguished by this sudden rupture of communications. All his concerns about exfiltrating the team now seemed ominously prescient. The GIGN commander managed to contact General Navereau in Riyadh, but the French general, too, had been unable to get through to Barril and the two other commandos.

"The guys must have been taken captive," Prouteau decided as his imagination ran wild. This blackout, which, to Prouteau, seemed to last an eternity, ended hours later with a frantic phone call from Barril. "You have to get us out of here, right now. It's very dangerous here," Barril implored.

In those hours, the French could infer how the operation had developed in Mecca only from one indirect piece of information: they were contacted by a Saudi medic who wanted to know how to deal with the effects of CB.

Impressed by the worried tone of the usually fearless, cocky Barril, Prouteau got in touch with France's top military officials and de Marenches's intelligence service. Absent an immediate removal of GIGN's men from Taef, he urged, France had to consider an emergency rescue mission for the team. He went as far as suggesting landing choppers with gun-toting commandos at the Taef Intercontinental Hotel.

It never came to this. Once all the rebels were routed from the Grand Mosque, the Saudi major who usually accompanied Barril, Wodecki, and Lambert announced that the French guests would be going home soon. Before heading to the airport, the commandos were allowed a detour to the old Taef market, where women fully shrouded in black sit on the hard-packed ground, selling a bewildering variety of wares and battling pesky flies.

Practical as always, Warrant Officer Wodecki—instead of splurging on Arabian souvenirs—bought a Japanese stereo, which was much cheaper in tax-free Saudi Arabia than at home.

On the way to the airport, the Frenchmen were still riddled with anxiety, worrying that the plane that was taking them to Riyadh might be shot down or sabotaged. They relaxed only after taking their seats and realizing that the aircraft had an American crew. The Saudis, they figured, would never dare play dirty tricks on Americans.

In Riyadh, General Navereau collected the commandos on the tarmac and drove them to a banquet with the staff of the French military cooperation mission. Wodecki carried a cherished possession—three bottles of Sauvignon, to be divided among ten men. Surprised that such an ungodly item could have arrived from the vicinity of Mecca, one of the officers asked Wodecki, "Where did you get this?"

"Oh, we just bought it in the nearby supermarket," the warrant officer replied, straight-faced. "Too bad we couldn't find any champagne."

Their mission completed, the French commandos were sworn to secrecy by the French attaché. Then, to show appreciation, Saudi officials passed along precious gifts: a gold Rolex watch engraved with the portrait of King Khaled for Barril and cheaper silver Rolex Oyster Perpetuals with the logo of the Saudi Air Force for Lambert and Wodecki.

The evening of December 5, the French finally flew home, on a commercial aircraft. Barril kept the hand grenades in his pockets until the last minute, dumping them in the toilets of Riyadh International.

In Washington, the Carter administration spent these days debating how to tackle the dramatic explosion of anti-American anger that had erupted in the two weeks since Juhayman's takeover of the Grand Mosque. That attacks on American embassies in the Muslim world by now were almost routine deeply anguished Carter's national security adviser, Brzezinski. On Monday, December 3, the day the final push in Mecca began and a day after the Libya embassy sacking, Brzezinski wrote the president a memo with several practical suggestions. "I am concerned over . . . the transformation of the conflict from Iran vs. international community into America vs. Islam," Brzezinski began. "Recent attacks on our embassies, as well as various Middle East press comments, point in the direction of transforming the conflict into a wider assault on 'corrupt and impotent' America. This is a dangerous trend."

Brzezinski's suggestion was to shatter this image of impotency by ramping up American military muscle in the Gulf. Saudi Arabia, rocked by the Mecca uprising and assailed every day by Iran as an American stooge, was unlikely to risk openly embracing American troops, Brzezinski realized. As an alternative, he pushed for creating—with Saudi help—a large American military base in the nearby sultanate of Oman. An American military buildup in the region, Brzezinski wrote, should be accompanied by "a public statement (a 'Carter Doctrine') explicitly committing U.S. military power to the defense of countries in the region that are of vital importance to us." Under such a doctrine, the United States was to formally guarantee the security of its Gulf allies—a commitment that would lead Washington into a war over Kuwait eleven years later and eventually bring U.S. Marines to Baghdad.

At a National Security Council meeting on December 4, Carter tentatively agreed with Brzezinski's suggestions. A few days later, U.S. negotiators flew to the Gulf to discuss basing rights with the Omani sultan and reluctant Saudi princes. The process leading to massive U.S. military presence in the Persian Gulf—a presence that would motivate droves of jihadis to join al Qaeda in following decades—was set in motion.

TWENTY-SEVEN

Though the ancient Kaaba—the holiest part of the shrine—
survived the battle for Mecca largely intact, several other parts of
the Grand Mosque had been blown to smithereens. It would take several months to restore the surface structures alone; the gutted Qaboo
never reopened to public access. For days after the end of the siege, the
sickly sweet smell of decomposing bodies combined into a nauseating
cocktail with cordite and the lingering gas, making a large area around
the mosque uninhabitable.

Saudi press—the only media allowed on scene—preferred not to
dwell on the extent of this devastation in Mecca. After all, the royal
family had made much of its care to preserve the shrine and innocent
lives. It wanted this unpleasant "domestic incident" to be forgotten as
soon as possible.

A rare exception was provided by an eyewitness report that appeared
in Jeddah's *Arab News* daily. The paper's journalist, identified only as "a
staff reporter," was allowed to visit the sacred compound with security

forces on Tuesday, December 4—a few hours after the last rebels were routed.

Damage, he noted, was heaviest in the Marwa-Safa gallery, where the paratroopers led by Colonel Homaid had been massacred by rebels and where artillery had to be used to breach Juhayman's defenses. "The wall separating the Marwa from Safa on the eastern side of the mosque was completely destroyed. Traces left by bullets and shells could be seen on walls, doors and in the few fragments of windows left intact. Even lamps, air conditioners and fans were twisted into rubble," the article said.

On the way to the courtyard, the journalist stumbled upon a military jeep, burned out and riddled with bullets. All along the mosque's perimeter, he noticed that some gates were totally blown out and that the staircases and ramps leading to the upper floors "had collapsed under the weight of armored cars and half-trucks which had been run up them during the assault."

Once the reporter walked through the underground gallery and into the basement, he almost fainted because of the smoke. Soldiers there still wore their gas masks, helmets, and white chemical-protection coveralls, automatic rifles ready to fire. He was cautioned about booby traps left behind by the rebels. Small rooms on the sides of the corridor still contained the belongings of the gunmen who had lived there for two weeks: bowls of dates, plastic bottles of water, tattered mattresses.

Underground columns "which were delicately faced with marble were now stripped of that glistening mineral and everywhere bent and pockmarked with bullets," the *Arab News* journalist wrote.

Eager to showcase the hard-won victory in Mecca, on the night of December 4 the House of Saud paraded its prisoners on state television. At first, a grinning Prince Nayef addressed the viewers, boasting that government forces suffered a "surprisingly low number of casualties" given the fierceness of the fight and the fortified positions that had been occupied by the rebels. The Saudi military, he said, lost just 60 men and treated 200 others for injuries. Those killed in battle were "better off than all of us because they died as martyrs in the service of God and the defense of his places," he crowed.

Some 75 rebels had died in the Grand Mosque, Prince Nayef continued, and 170 had been captured. The 23 women and children among these prisoners included Juhayman's wife and the supposed Mahdi's sister; though too young for the role, she initially tried to convince Saudi interrogators that she was Juhayman's mother.

After an appropriate pause, the most important of these detainees appeared on the screen.

A bedraggled, black-faced Juhayman sat upright on a hospital bed. He was barefoot and his hands were tied behind him. It was only a couple of hours after he had been pulled out of the basement of the Grand Mosque. He wore a stained smock, and his curly hair and beard were in complete disarray. The man's eyes burned like little coal fires, staring into the camera with unadulterated hatred. He kept mumbling something, but the audience couldn't hear a word. Instead, the footage—the only publicly seen images of Juhayman—was accompanied by the indignant voice-over of a Saudi TV announcer.

"Before you is Juhayman bin Seif al Uteybi, one of the most evil people of this world in our age," the announcer intoned. "We will not forget him and history will not forget him."

American diplomats who watched the program disagreed on whom Juhayman resembled most: Rasputin, Charles Manson, or John Brown.

Then the camera panned to a large group of prisoners sitting on the floor in the courtyard of the Mecca Hotel. Guards wearing rubber gloves unceremoniously pulled up the faces of those who tried to shy away from the camera. Some of these captives seemed barely past puberty; others had the gaunt look and graying beards of old men. There were men of all backgrounds—plump Egyptians, ebony-skinned Africans, Pakistanis in white skullcaps, fine-featured Saudi Bedouins.

"The terror that they have instilled in the hearts of the faithful, the innocents, the blood that they shed—and thought it was their right to shed—fuel the fire that will burn them in hell," the TV announcer said. "They were combating God and his Prophet, the religion and the Sharia, and so they deserve to receive a just punishment for their horrendous deeds."

The following night, Saudi TV broadcast another trophy shot—the proof of the death of the Mahdi. Rumors were rife that the young Mohammed Abdullah had somehow managed to escape from the mosque. The House of Saud needed to squash such dangerous speculation once and for all. And so it assembled in front of the camera several of Mohammed Abdullah's captured relatives, including his brother Sayid.

A tall, black-skinned interrogator in a crisp white robe approached these captives, holding a photograph. "Who is this?" he asked Sayid.

"It is my brother, Mohammed bin Abdullah Qahtani."

"A full brother?"

"Yes, a full brother. I am older than him."

"Are you sure it's him?"

"Yes, I am sure."

The interrogator then walked to a child, aged eleven, and thrust in his face the same photograph.

"This is Mohammed Abdullah. He is the husband of my sister," the child answered. "I know it's him because of the birthmark on his right cheek."

The next prisoner, a frightened twenty-four-year-old, insisted plaintively that he had only a passing acquaintance with the man in the picture. The first time I saw Mohammed Abdullah, he said, was as he accepted the oath of *baya* as a Mahdi, near the Black Stone.

Following several other such conversations, the camera treated the viewers to a close-up of the picture. It was a headshot of a cadaver: eyes shut, jaw muscles seized by rigor mortis, and crooked front teeth protruding in a rictus of death.

"Here is the false Mahdi," the announcer intoned. "He was with Juhayman, he killed, he violated the faith—and now he is dead."

A couple of days later, Prince Turki visited Juhayman in his cell. The Saudi spymaster was surprised by how small the fearsome militant turned out to be, with his slender fingers and finely chiseled nose. The defiance of previous hours seemed to be gone from his eyes.

Seeing Prince Turki, Juhayman leaped up. "Your Highness, could you ask King Khaled to pardon me?" he asked.

Taken aback, the prince just laughed in response. "You have to ask pardon from God," he said. Sizing up Juhayman with the kind of curiosity usually reserved for caged animals, Turki then noted that the captive still had his unruly long mane. "Why do you have long hair like that?" he wondered.

"What's wrong with that?" Juhayman grunted unhappily.

The death toll announced by Prince Nayef on TV reflected only a fraction of the real casualties. Weeks later, he released new numbers that doubled previous estimates. Juhayman's rebels, according to Nayef's updated figures, had managed to kill 12 Saudi officers and 115 enlisted men and NCOs; some 450 more soldiers had been hospitalized for injuries sustained in battle.

On the rebel side, Prince Nayef reported, total deaths stood at 117, a number that included 75 bodies retrieved during the battle, 15 cadavers found in the rubble and subsequently identified by captured rebels, and 27 captives who died of wounds after their arrest.

The scope of casualties among pilgrims was never updated. The figures released by the Saudi government in early December mentioned the deaths of 26 people of Saudi, Pakistani, Indonesian, Indian, Egyptian, and Burmese nationalities. Not all of these 26 dead could be identified. The 110 wounded, whose origins ranged from Indonesia to Afghanistan to Nigeria, included one American citizen, identified by his Muslim name, Jamal Ameer Khaled Abdullah.

The combined official toll of some 270 fatalities in the Mecca uprising was greeted with skepticism by Western diplomats and independent analysts. Many, including the GIGN commandos, believe that the true scope of casualties, especially among pilgrims, has been hidden by the Saudi government. "Sources at hospitals in Jeddah indicate government casualties much higher than stated," Ambassador West also cabled the State Department at the time. Independent observers and witnesses estimate that the two weeks of warfare in and around the Grand Mosque cost well over 1,000 lives, and possibly significantly more.

Once the Qaboo was secured, cleaning crews in the Grand Mosque worked day and night, scrubbing away the blood and the burn marks and removing crushed marble, twisted metal, and crumbled concrete. The floor perforations through which CB chemicals had been fired into the basement were hastily filled with cement. Disinfectants generously sprayed by sanitation teams overpowered at least part of the stench.

By the afternoon of Thursday, December 6, 1979, the compound was finally deemed ready for a royal visit. Welcomed by Prince Nayef and Sheikh Ibn Rashed at one of the gates that remained intact, King Khaled slowly walked inside at five-fifteen p.m. The mosque's public-address system, destroyed during the fighting, had been replaced with new equipment that now broadcast passionate prayers and thanks to the Almighty. Chants of *"Allahu Akbar"* broke out among the crowd of soldiers and local dignitaries. Aided by his courtiers, the monarch approached the Kaaba and kissed the Black Stone. Surveying the pockmarks on the porticos around him, he made the seven required circumambulations around the Kaaba, prostrated himself twice on the ground, and paused to sip sacred water from the Zam Zam spring.

This prayer in the Grand Mosque was broadcast by Saudi TV all around the world—the first such live transmission since the crisis began. Because of the reek, King Khaled didn't stay long in Mecca, instead driving to his seaside palace in Jeddah for a festive meal. At the banquet, attended by a multitude of princes and notables, the deputy head of the royal advisory council, Sheikh Ahmad al Ghazzawi, recited a laudatory poem he had just composed. The ode reverberated with praises for King Khaled's great wisdom and striking success in defeating the miscreant renegades.

Crown Prince Fahd, meanwhile, was busy responding to a flood of similarly congratulatory messages from all over the world. "The position which was taken by His Majesty's government . . . was based on patience and a great deal of self-restraint," Fahd wrote in a reply to one such telegram, dispatched December 5 by President Carter. "All these qualities," he added modestly, "were bestowed on us by the Great God Almighty whom we owe a great deal of gratitude."

Despite the sycophantic tone of flattering telegrams and official pronouncements, the king and the seniormost Saudi princes didn't delude themselves: they knew full well that the regime had just barely survived a two-pronged assault. It was pure luck that Juhayman had chosen to target a religious symbol. "If he had attacked my palace, he might have met with more success," King Khaled reportedly told foreign visitors in the weeks after the battle. The siege of the Grand Mosque lasted so long because of the weakness of the regime, not because of its self-restraint. Someone had to pay for such a disgrace.

The interior minister, Prince Nayef, who had allowed himself to be swayed by Bin Baz and other senior ulema into releasing Juhayman's supporters in 1978, would have been a natural candidate for punishment under a different government system. After all, it was the security services under Nayef's ministry—especially the dreaded Mabaheth, charged with ferreting out dissidents—that had failed so miserably in anticipating the Mecca conspiracy.

But Saudi Arabia was a family-owned property and as interior minister Nayef was far too valuable to Fahd, the kingdom's de facto ruler. Like Fahd and Prince Sultan, the defense minister, Nayef belonged to the so-called Sudayri Seven cabal of full brothers born to King Abdelaziz and Princess Hussa bint Ahmad al Sudayri. These seven princes long struggled for dominance within the House of Saud against a rival alliance represented by Prince Abdullah, the commander of the National Guard. For Fahd, any step to weaken Nayef, or for that matter Sultan, was simply unthinkable. Lesser officials would have to take responsibility.

Mecca governor Prince Fawwaz, decried for his liberal ways in the rebels' sermon at the Grand Mosque, became the first scapegoat. Relatively neutral in the standoff between the Sudayris and Abdullah, Fawwaz had been a dissident himself, joining the so-called Red Princes in Egyptian exile in the 1960s and demanding at the time secular reforms that would bring democracy to the kingdom. This youthful dalliance with infidel ideas ensured him a lasting hatred of the senior ulema, who rejoiced at Fawwaz's resignation—ostensibly for "health reasons"—in late December 1979. Tainted by the Mecca fiasco and kept outside government ever since, the supposedly unhealthy Fawwaz went on to outlive both King Khaled and Fahd.

A couple of days after the departure of Fawwaz, King Khaled ousted the top brass of the Saudi military and security forces. The head of Mabahcth was replaced by a general who was descended from Ibn Abdel Wahhab and who could count on kinship of blood with the senior clerics. The chief of the Saudi general staff, who had greeted Captain Barril in Riyadh, was retired. So was the commander of the Saudi Air Force. Of course, Saudi spokesmen explained later, with a straight face, all these decisions had absolutely nothing to do with what had happened in Mecca.

TWENTY-EIGHT

While generals were being purged in Riyadh, Prince Nayef's investigators—some of them still nursing wounds they had sustained in the Grand Mosque—questioned their prisoners in the grim concrete basements of Saudi prisons. Juhayman, it is said, refused to cooperate. But many other ex-rebels, their faith undermined by the death of the Mahdi, were overwhelmed by penitence. Old-fashioned torture and injections with sodium pentathol, otherwise known as truth serum, loosened their tongues.

Though insisting to Ambassador West that Saudi investigators refrained from "pulling out fingernails," Prince Bandar felt no qualms about admitting at the time that the captured suspects were subjected to starvation and denied water, to speed up confessions. The few survivors among former rebels recall being beaten to a pulp in the Mabaheth's dungeons.

It didn't take long for the interrogators to determine that Juhayman's movement extended far beyond the group that had actually invaded the shrine. Confirming these concerns, Saudi border guards had intercepted a messenger with a letter to Juhayman from acolytes in nearby Kuwait. The message pledged the Kuwaitis' allegiance to the Mahdi— and expressed regret at being unable to participate in the Mecca operation directly.

Nervous that a second uprising might be in the works, Prince Nayef ordered a wave of follow-up arrests in December. Targets of this dragnet included Juhayman's adepts such as Hozeimi, who hadn't experienced night dreams about the Mahdi and therefore had refused to participate in the takeover in Mecca. Fearing an international conspiracy, Saudi security men were especially ruthless with non-Saudi suspects resident in the kingdom. Scores of Egyptian, Yemeni, and Kuwaiti men were thrown in jail at the slightest sign of connection with Juhayman's group.

Behind bars, many of these detainees—who usually subscribed to Juhayman's virulent hatred of the Shiites—ended up sharing cells with another fresh crop of prisoners: Shiite revolutionaries who had just been captured in the Eastern Province. Despite common hatred of the regime, the two inmate populations didn't get along. Juhayman's followers usually kept to themselves; they refused contact with the Shiite disbelievers, concentrating on loud prayers and such religious duties as scratching pictures of cows from their cartons of milk. When one of the Shiite detainees suggested to a Juhayman follower from Kuwait that he might visit his prison mate once they both were released, the Kuwaiti scowled back: "If you come anywhere near my home, I will shoot you."

As more details emerged from these interrogations, senior Saudi princes began to understand the extent of support for Juhayman's movement among prominent Wahhabi luminaries. Prince Turki, for one, was surprised by just how little the government's intelligence agencies seemed to know about this new threat. He compared it to a new virus maturing within a body. Until November 1979, the Saudi state's internal defenses were all deployed against other, proven dangers: the Arab nationalists, the Communists, the pro-Iranian revolutionaries. The Sunni Islamic radicals of Juhayman's ilk just hadn't seemed to be a grave threat. The virus had been allowed to multiply, up to the point of putting the host's survival in peril.

This, however, wasn't something that Saudi authorities were prepared to admit in public.

Instead, the official propaganda machine went into overdrive trying to convince the world that the kingdom remained a bedrock of peace and stability and that the dramatic events of the past two weeks represented—just as Prince Fahd's courtiers had insisted in the early hours of the crisis—merely an unfortunate "domestic incident" without much consequence.

Spreading this gospel, Prince Fahd himself spent several hours briefing solicitous interviewers from Arab newspapers. In one interview after another, he angrily denied any suggestion that Juhayman's uprising had ever posed a political threat to the regime. "Juhayman was an extremely ordinary person unable to express himself properly in terms of language and ideas. He was not capable of writing books or speaking about the hadith," Fahd said in one such interview. The Mecca incident had "no political dimension," the crown prince proclaimed, and "the popular reaction and resentment of the crime came as a referendum of support" for the House of Saud.

The best parallel with Juhayman's movement, Fahd argued, was not some Middle East revolution but an event that had happened almost exactly one year before the Mecca uprising—the Jonestown massacre in Guyana. In that South American nation, American followers of a religious cult that had flourished in California committed mass suicide by gulping down poison-laced Kool-Aid. Apparently believing that Guyana belongs to California, Fahd told an Arab interviewer who questioned him about Mecca to remember "the great holocaust of California." After all, Fahd explained, "there, some nine hundred people died, with some people killing themselves and others being killed by their leader."

Eager to maintain U.S. support for the regime, Saudi royals tried a wholly different spin when explaining their "domestic incident" to Americans. Though insisting that the Mecca uprising didn't signal any internal tension in the kingdom, they cast the violence of previous weeks in stark Cold War terms, with Juhayman depicted as a Moscow stooge. Prince Bandar assured American officials in those days, without much evidence, that Juhayman's rebels had learned their devastating accuracy of fire in training camps in Marxist South Yemen. "I think it was sponsored by international organizations, probably Russians, to undermine the stability of Saudi Arabia," another senior Saudi told the *New York Times*.

Trying to discredit the rebels and undermine their appeal to Islamic conservatives, the very same Saudi followed up with a ludicrous allegation that Juhayman "was not a fundamentalist, but a government worker who ha[d] been dismissed and publicly flogged for drinking."

This propaganda effort wasn't quite swallowed in the West. "There could hardly be a greater mistake than to dismiss this incident as merely an isolated episode of obscurantist hysteria, which, with the restoration of order, is ended," warned an editorial about the Mecca attack in the *Washington Post*. "If this affair still seems minor in comparison with the events in Iran, it may well turn out to have a comparable impact on the world."

A few weeks later, the *New York Times* translated into English an excerpt from Juhayman's diatribes against the House of Saud and the kingdom's alliances with infidel Christians. These clear, fiery passages certainly didn't sound like pro-Soviet propaganda that had been penned by a drunkard, or the musings of someone "unable to express himself."

Senior Saudi princes, used to being treated with reverence by an Arab press that was largely on the Saudi payroll, were infuriated by this incisive reporting. To the thin-skinned Fahd, such impolite investigations of his kingdom's internal problems could have only one explanation—an anti-Saudi conspiracy by Jews who supposedly dominate the Western media.

"Our enemy is . . . the world Zionism, which is seeking to harm the Saudi Arabian kingdom and to distort its role in every way possible. If we take the [Mecca] incident and assemble everything that has been written about it, we would easily see that the purpose and the objective was to cause harm," Fahd complained to a sympathetic Lebanese editor. "A media war was in the full sense of the word waged against us . . . Psychological rape—this is the right expression." The Saudi royals would use precisely the same language to complain about Western reporting on Saudi affairs after September 11, 2001.

Bitter about the loss of face, and not completely comprehending the First Amendment and the nature of U.S. society, Fahd even warned after the Mecca affair that Riyadh might abandon its historic alliance with Washington if "malicious press campaigns" against the House of Saud were not stopped by the Carter administration, presumably through an instauration of censorship. Profuse apologies by U.S. diplomats didn't defuse his anger. "We are not compelled to be friends of the Americans. There are many doors wide open to us . . . We can easily replace the Americans," the crown prince blustered.

Paranoid about showing signs of weakness to the outside world, the House of Saud didn't just keep Western correspondents away. It also jealously guarded details of rebels' interrogations from the CIA and other Western intelligence agencies. Nobody in Riyadh wanted Saudi allies—or enemies—to know just how deep the rot went in the Saudi state. This again would be the pattern in future Saudi anti-terror investigations—including those of attacks in which Americans were the main targets and casualties.

TWENTY-NINE

Thousands of miles away, in snow-blanketed Moscow, Soviet officials watched the mayhem in Mecca in late 1979 with the careful
attention of a boxer who suddenly spies his opponent's unexpected
weak spot.

Already, Moscow felt empowered by the spiraling conflict between
America and Iran. "The Iranian revolution has undercut the military alliance between Iran and the U.S.," the Soviet leader Leonid Brezhnev
confided on a visit to East Germany. "Iran is now taking anti-imperialist
positions. The imperialism tries to regain influence in the region. We
are trying to counter these efforts."

The riptide of unrest caused by Juhayman's uprising took the Soviets' self-confidence to new heights. After the loss of Iran, the two other
linchpins of American influence in the region—Saudi Arabia and Pakistan—suddenly seemed on the verge of collapsing.

The destruction of the American embassy in Pakistan highlighted the
depth of anti-American sentiment there. Bloodshed in Mecca and Saudi

Arabia's Shiite heartland were even more gratifying for Moscow. After all, the kingdom was so fervently anti-Communist at the time that it even refused diplomatic relations with the USSR. In the zero-sum game of the Cold War, any weakening of the Saudi regime was perceived as an automatic boon for the Kremlin. This was especially so because the Saudis were backing their anti-Communist creed with weapons and money in one part of the Muslim world where the Soviets had a problem of their own—Afghanistan.

For several months now, an insurgency against the Soviet-backed government in Kabul had raged across that mountainous country, inflamed by the regime's zeal in rooting out religion and implementing Marxist-Leninist dogma in what was a deeply Islamic and essentially feudal society. In an alliance with Pakistani intelligence, Saudi Arabia's GID—led by Prince Turki—was at the forefront of funding and coordinating these rebels, who by now controlled an estimated 70 percent of the Afghan countryside. Saudi money talked so loudly that even Afghanistan's ambassador to Riyadh was convinced in late 1979 to drop his allegiances and switch to the guerrillas.

The CIA, allowed to provide only minimal, nonlethal aid to Afghan rebels at the time, deemed Saudi influence to be essential in holding back Soviet ambitions. "Unless the rebels receive more meaningful military support . . . and more financial backing from Saudi Arabia, their effort to bring the Soviet-equipped [Afghan] army to the point of collapse may lose momentum," fretted a classified CIA estimate issued in November 1979.

The Kremlin in those days was getting more and more anxious about the behavior of Afghan President Hafizullah Amin. In Brezhnev's opinion, Amin displayed "disproportionate harshness" and disrespect for Islam in the counterinsurgency campaign. Just as important, the KGB chief Yuri Andropov reported, Columbia University–educated Amin engaged in suspicious talks with American diplomats in Kabul. "There is no guarantee," Andropov warned as he suggested replacing the Afghan ruler with a more pliable client, "that Amin, in order to protect his personal power, will not shift to the West."

The Soviet military brass, led by the defense minister Dmitri Ustinov, was initially cool to such proposals of "regime change" in Kabul. But the generals' thinking was jolted by President Carter's decision to dispatch the USS *Kitty Hawk* battle group to the Persian Gulf on November 20— the day the Grand Mosque was seized, as U.S. officials believed at the time, by Iranian agents. "If the United States can allow itself such [a deployment] tens of thousands of kilometers away from their territory, in the immediate proximity of USSR borders, why then should we be afraid to defend our positions in neighboring Afghanistan?" is how Ustinov reasoned at the time. The surprising weakness shown in the Grand Mosque affair by Saudi and Pakistani regimes—the main backers of the Afghan insurgents—could only embolden the Kremlin.

On December 10, 1979—less than a week after Juhayman was captured in Mecca—Ustinov summoned the Soviet chief of staff and ordered him to begin assembling a force of 75,000 to 80,000 soldiers along the Afghan-Soviet frontier. Two days later, the most senior members of the Soviet Politburo gathered in the Kremlin. The meeting's top-secret, handwritten resolution was entitled simply "On Situation in A." It formally authorized a war that would transform the world of Islam and eventually cause the Soviet Union itself to disintegrate.

Soviet armies rolled across the Amu Darya River into Afghanistan on Christmas morning, December 25, 1979. In Kabul, a KGB commando force—dressed in Afghan uniforms and masquerading as Afghans— battled its way into the presidential palace and executed Amin. In his place, the Soviets installed another Afghan Communist, Babrak Karmal.

Bowing to the Islamic ardor sweeping the region, Karmal tried to sound like a pious Muslim in his first radio address to the nation. *"Bismillah ar-Rahman ar-Rahim,"* he began. "In the name of Allah, the compassionate, the merciful." The previous regime of "bloodthirsty butcher Amin," Karmal explained rather accurately, had been guilty of causing mass suffering through "imprisonment, deportation, barbaric and in-human tortures, martyrdom and killing of tens of thousands of our mothers and fathers, brothers and sisters, daughters and sons." The new Afghan government, Karmal pledged, would free all political prisoners and "respect the sacred principles of Islam."

Washington didn't pay much attention to such details, seeing the Soviet invasion as a direct threat to America's Persian Gulf allies—and to the West's all-important oil supplies. From Afghanistan, the U.S. Joint Chiefs of Staff warned at a White House meeting, Soviet fighter aircraft could fly all the way to the Gulf's choke point of Hormuz. So-viet land armored forces were now merely ten to twelve days away from reaching the shores of the Arabian Sea, and from the oil fields of Saudi Arabia and Kuwait.

"If the Soviets succeed in Afghanistan, and if Pakistan acquiesces, the age-long dream of Moscow to have direct access to the Indian Ocean will have been fulfilled," Brzezinski warned Carter in a Decem-ber 26, 1979, memo. "It could produce Soviet presence right down on the edge of the Arabian and Oman Gulfs."

The Saudis were even more frightened, seeing themselves as the next target. After all, the distance from Saudi oil fields on the Gulf coast to Afghanistan is roughly the same as the distance from these oil fields to Jeddah. "It was obvious," Prince Turki believed, "that the inva-sion of Afghanistan was one step toward reaching other countries, es-pecially Pakistan, and then moving on to the Gulf and the Arabian Peninsula."

Suddenly, Brzezinski's idea of a "Carter Doctrine" that would ex-tend an American security umbrella to Gulf allies like Saudi Arabia started to look much more attractive to its beneficiaries. As recently as mid-December, when an American delegation explored basing rights in Oman with Saudi officials, Prince Turki had poured cold water on the idea. The United States, he had suggested, should concentrate on build-ing up local self-defense capabilities instead. Anti-American "inflamma-tion" in the Muslim world, he had added, made any deployment of actual American forces in the peninsula undesirable.

Now, barely a month later, a visiting Brzezinski was "struck by the degree of apprehension [about the Soviet threat] among Saudi rulers." Crown Prince Fahd stressed to him the kingdom's new vulnerable position and was "much more prepared than before to consider, on a quiet basis, enhanced American-Saudi military cooperation." Pakistan's President Zia, too, was so scared of the Soviets that he dropped his flirting with Khomeini's Iran and sought American security guarantees. "Whatever we do, let us not create in Zia's mind the same ambiguity [about U.S. support] that clearly existed in the Shah's mind" before the Iranian revolution, Brzezinski advised the president.

In January 1980, President Carter officially committed America to defending these allies. "Let our position be absolutely clear," he pledged in the State of the Union address. "Any attempt by any outside force to gain control of the Persian Gulf region will be regarded as an assault on the vital interests of the United States of America and such an assault will be repelled by any means necessary, including military force." This doctrine has remained a cornerstone of American foreign policy ever since.

THIRTY

As the Soviet invasion sent shock waves through the region, Saudi Arabia's senior ulema gathered on January 2, 1980, to discuss the Mecca uprising, again. They were called by the House of Saud to deliver a binding opinion on the fate of Juhayman and other armed "renegades" who had been captured in the Grand Mosque.

Circumstances had changed dramatically since the clerics' previous meeting on the affair, in King Khaled's Maazar palace six weeks earlier. Back then, when the survival of the House of Saud seemed in doubt, the ulema chose to cast their lot with the government, disowning Juhayman. Now that formidable new perils to the Wahhabi order loomed from abroad, these clerics—led by Bin Baz—were even more determined to prop up the Saudi state. The House of Saud, once again, was seen by them as the only bulwark against the infections of Soviet Communism and the Shiite heresy from Iran.

Having examined Juhayman's writings, the Supreme Council of

Ulema reached that day a unanimous verdict: the wild-eyed guru now shackled to his prison bed was guilty of a "heinous crime" against the Islamic religion. "These leaflets are misguided and full of false interpretations which can be the seeds of discord and lead to chaos and disturbance," Bin Baz declared in the name of the gathering. "These leaflets make claims which may mislead some naive people although they contain much evil. Muslims should be warned against their evil intent and content."

Condemning Juhayman's heresies, the Supreme Council of Ulema refrained from issuing a formal fatwa on what should be done with the prisoners. Several individual ulema, however, quickly filled this gap, providing the government with theological verdicts urging that the rebels be "either killed, or crucified, or have their hands and feet cut in cross directions." This was enough for King Khaled. He was in no mood for pardons.

A few days after the ulema meeting, the Saudi monarch sent Prince Nayef a list of sixty-three prisoners, with an attached instruction: "Kill those whose names are appended to this statement, in order to please Allah, defend the sanctity of the Holy Kaaba and of his worshippers, and to vent the anger of Muslims." The morning of January 9, 1980, these sixty-three captives, shackled and drugged, were brought to face the long, ornamented steel swords of the executioners. The killings, following Saudi custom, were public. And, to make sure that the message of government firmness was heard far and wide, these beheadings occurred simultaneously in eight cities across the Saudi realm.

Juhayman's head was the first to roll into the sand, in the holy city of Mecca—the site of his crime. The alleged Mahdi's brother, who had been interviewed on TV, Sayid, was beheaded on the same spot minutes later. The heads of Mohammed Elias, the spiritual leader of Egyptian jihadis who had traveled to Mecca to join the uprising, and of the reluctant rebel Faisal Mohammed Faisal, were chopped off in Riyadh. Less important conspirators died in Medina, Dammam, Buraida, Hail,

Abha, and Tobuk—a total of thirty-nine Saudis, ten Egyptians, six Yemenis, and a handful of Kuwaitis, Iraqis, and Sudanese.

Their severed heads, according to custom, were sewn back onto the bodies for burial.

Those executed in public did not include the two African American converts who had joined the Mecca uprising.

United States embassy officials became aware of such American participation in Juhayman's rebellion on December 8, soon after Saudi security forces overran the Qaboo. This information was kept under wraps by the American and Saudi governments alike: a mere acknowledgment of American presence in the rebel ranks, after all, had the potential to reignite Khomeini's pernicious conspiracy theory.

There was another awkward detail. These American Muslims had converted to Islam because of the Saudi-funded proselytizing campaign and were drawn into radicalism on Saudi soil. Nobody wanted to throw a spotlight on the dark side of these missionary activities. In State Department cables, the two were described diplomatically as "missing Americans" who "could be victims of the insurrection that commenced at the Grand Mosque on Nov. 20."

It was only on December 30 that Ambassador West, after discussing American security help at a meeting with Prince Nayef, asked the Saudi interior minister for details. One of these two Americans, Prince Nayef replied, was "definitely a terrorist"—and no longer alive. The second American was still under investigation. "I believe that means a head will be lopped, but that's the best we can do," West noted dryly in his diary.

At another meeting with the American ambassador, on January 19, 1980, Prince Nayef mentioned again that the second American suspect remained in custody. Ambassador West was surprised. "I thought he had been hanged last week," the envoy wrote that day, in his diary's last entry on the issue.

In fact, most of the adult male rebels who had not been executed in public on January 9 were put to death, in secret, in the following months. The underage rebel supporters, including Samir—whose two older brothers had been beheaded—were thrown behind bars for years.

The State Department has invoked privacy laws in refusing to disclose the two African American rebels' identities, and the FBI, responding to a request under the Freedom of Information Act, has stated that it has no records on any participation by U.S. citizens in the Mecca takeover.

According to American officials deployed in Saudi Arabia at the time, however, the second prisoner was spared the executioner's sword. From the very beginning, he was jailed separately from other rebels, and eventually given the benefit of the doubt because he happened to carry an American passport. After a debriefing by the CIA, he was allowed to return home to the United States, a free citizen once again. He may well be alive and well today, resident in Anytown, U.S.A.

As King Khaled had promised to the ulema during the difficult talks in the Maazar palace on November 20, the Saudi state quickly moved to roll back the immoral liberties that had been tolerated in previous years. Anxious to maintain the loyalty of the ulema and to prevent another uprising, the House of Saud was determined to live up to its side of the grand bargain.

Just like Juhayman, Bin Baz and other senior ulema had long been upset with the gradual loosening of restrictions on Saudi women. In the weeks after the Mecca uprising, Prince Nayef ordered women announcers removed from Saudi TV. The restrictions on supposedly licentious pictures of women became so harsh that Jeddah's *Arab News* had to obliterate the face of the seventy-one-year-old actress Bette Davis from a photograph showing her with the TV interviewer Mike Wallace.

A parallel crackdown began on the employment of women, until then tacitly accepted by authorities. Even Western companies operating in the kingdom, including the Saudi branch of Lockheed, were forced to dismiss female personnel. A European manager of a Riyadh hotel was interrogated by Nayef's security services because he had hired a female secretary.

To appease the ulema, goons from the Committee to Promote Virtue and Prevent Vice were also given a free hand to raid Western enclaves that until then had been exempted from such visits. The U.S.-Saudi Joint Economic Commission offices in Riyadh were among those receiving attention from these bearded zealots on the lookout for un-Islamic behavior.

Alcohol—another target of Juhayman's railings—became much harder to obtain beginning in early 1980. Bootlegging networks, tolerated because they had been operated by prominent princes, dried up after the Mecca affair. The black market price of a bottle of whiskey shot up from as little as $75 to more than $120. American residents of the expatriate compounds in the Eastern Province oil areas got so scared of possible reprisals that many made quick trips to the desert in these weeks to smash up their treasured—and now incriminating—stashes of booze.

Prince Nayef provided a taste of the government's new attitude during a two-hour press conference he held in mid-January. A Western reporter, making an innocent assumption that Saudi Arabia would react to the Mecca uprising by cracking down on Juhayman-style religious fundamentalism, asked Nayef whether Saudi security services would now start arresting men with long beards. After all, expansive facial hair, an outward sign of Islamic piety, had been de rigueur among Juhayman's adepts.

"Certainly not. If we did this most Saudis would be in prison by now," a flustered Nayef responded. "Half the kingdom's population is bearded. We will always respect the marks of piety on a man's face."

The government's new determination to enforce Islamic behavior was combined with a giant influx of fresh cash to the Wahhabi ulema. Saudi petrodollars started to flow to the Islamic universities in Riyadh and Medina, and to missionary organizations that spread Wahhabi ideas around the world. Many of these official missionaries preached hatred of the infidel, dedication to global jihad, and rejection of anyone not sharing Wahhabi ideals as an apostate. The Mahdi issue apart, their ideology differed little from Juhayman's.

At the time, such an embrace of the Wahhabi orthodoxy seemed like a wise survival policy for the House of Saud. It was only after decades of this indoctrination produced a new generation of al Qaeda radicals that some senior princes realized the extent of the folly.

"I believe we have committed a mistake in this kingdom," Prince Khaled al Faisal, governor of the supposed Mahdi's home province of Asir, admitted in 2004. "We have eliminated the individuals who committed the Juhayman crime, but we have overlooked the ideology that was behind the crime. We've let it spread in the country, ignoring it as if it did not exist."

Prince Turki later explained that the Juhayman movement was viewed at a time as an aberration, a regurgitation of the Ikhwan past rather than a warning sign of future dangers. This was a perilous misjudgment, he now accepts. "Countries make mistakes," Turki said. "Societies make mistakes."

Americans weren't any wiser. The Mecca uprising—the first major explosion of Sunni Islamist violence in the modern world and a prelude to al Qaeda's outrages—was largely dismissed by Western policy makers, too focused on the Soviet threat and Iran. "In retrospect, the attack appears to have been the isolated act of a small group of religious fanatics," concluded a classified CIA intelligence memorandum entitled "Saudi Arabia: The Mecca Incident in Perspective." The present or future danger to the monarchy, the memo assured, should not be exaggerated: "Most Saudis appear to be outraged by the desecration of the mosque."

In a stunning cognitive failure, policy makers were so obsessed with Iran, and so wedded to the simplistic notion that Shiites were the West's enemies and the Sunnis, by default, allies, that many persisted in referring to Juhayman as a Shiite. The Grand Mosque affair was cataloged in the institutional memory as yet another exhibit of Iranian mischief. Even today, some American officials who were involved in that crisis recall a "Shiite uprising" in Mecca in 1979. The same goes for the French spymaster de Marenches, who wrote about "the Shiite assault on the sacred Kaaba" in his memoirs.

Once the Soviets invaded Afghanistan, there appeared a powerful new reason to consider Juhayman-style zealots harmless. White House officials, seared by the experience of watching American embassies burn across the Muslim world in previous weeks, saw a silver lining in the Soviet move. Global Islamic fervor that seemed to single out America as the main enemy of the true faith during the Mecca crisis, they reasoned, could now be redirected against another infidel power: the USSR. If it happened, all these young radicals yearning for the glories of the jihad could become a useful resource in the Cold War.

"World public opinion may be outraged at the Soviet intervention. Certainly Muslim countries will be concerned, and we might be in a position to exploit this," Brzezinski wrote Carter in the "Compensating Factors" part of a memo that analyzed American options a mere two days after the invasion. A more detailed analysis later prepared for Brzezinski by the National Security Council staffer Stephen Larrabee suggested that the United States should be "stressing [the] anti-Islamic element" of the Soviet move and aim to "isolate Soviets within [the] Muslim world."

The Saudis fully agreed with this policy, using their religious authority to secure condemnation of the Soviet invasion by the bulk of the Islamic world. Together with Egypt, the Saudis also saw the Afghan war as a perfect opportunity to channel away the energies of Juhayman-type Islamic zealots at home. In 1980, the gates of jihad were opened. With a fatwa by Bin Baz proclaiming jihad in Afghanistan an individual duty of every Muslim, mosques and universities across Saudi Arabia turned into recruitment centers for Islamic volunteers who thirsted for the blood of Russian infidels. Prince Turki, working together with the CIA, closely supervised this effort, personally shuttling to Afghanistan and Pakistan. Acting in parallel, senior Saudi ulema showered rivers of charity money on those Afghan warlords who agreed to abide by Wahhabi strictures.

One of the first Saudi volunteers who traveled to Afghan front lines, and who worked hand in hand with Prince Turki's intelligence services there, was a shy twenty-two-year-old named Osama Bin Laden.

THIRTY-ONE

At that time, just after the Mecca uprising, Bin Laden was still a loyal Saudi citizen. Brought up in a relatively modern household, he belonged to a different, more sophisticated generation of Saudis. Unlike Juhayman, Bin Laden had no problem with photography or television, viewing them as prized weapons of jihad. Most certainly, Bin Laden didn't share Juhayman's bizarre—and, after the death of Mohammed Abdullah, demonstrably wrong—theory about the arrival of the Mahdi in Islam's year 1400.

Yet, shocked by the ferocity of the battle in Mecca, and by the clerical approval for the military attack, al Qaeda's future founder couldn't help feeling sympathy for Juhayman and the rebel cause. In his only public comments on the Mecca uprising, made in 2004, Bin Laden reserved all his wrath for the behavior of the Saudi regime. "[Crown Prince] Fahd defiled the sanctity of the Grand Mosque," Bin Laden reminisced in an audio recording posted on jihadi Web sites. "He showed stubbornness, acted against the advice of everybody, and sent tracked and armored vehicles into the mosque. I still recall the imprint of tracked vehicles on the tiles of the mosque. People still recall that the minarets were covered with black smoke due to their shelling by tanks."

Speaking in a private circle, Bin Laden was even more explicit. "The men who seized Mecca were true Muslims . . . innocent of any crime, and . . . they were killed ruthlessly," one associate quoted Bin Laden as telling him in Peshawar in the mid-1980s.

According to some acquaintances, Bin Laden and his brother Mahrous had a personal run-in with the law in November 1979, when they were allegedly detained on suspicion of belonging to Juhayman's organization. Prince Turki says he has seen no information about such detentions, which, if they indeed occurred, could only have been very brief.

Once Bin Laden broke with the Saudi regime following the massive deployment of American troops in the kingdom in 1990–91, he started to repeat almost word for word Juhayman's repudiations of the royal family. Like Juhayman, he railed against the presence of non-Muslims on Saudi soil, against banks that violate Islamic prohibitions on usury, and against the royal family's dalliance with Christian powers. And, like Juhayman, Bin Laden poured scorn on Bin Baz, the head of the official religious establishment, who, after sanctioning an assault on the Grand Mosque, in 1990 formally approved the influx of U.S. soldiers. The blind cleric, Bin Laden complained, had been "weak and soft," allowing himself to be used by the House of Saud "as a cane to strike . . . honest scholars."

In many ways, Juhayman's multinational venture, which blended for the first time the Saudi militants' Wahhabi-inspired zeal and the Egyptian jihadis' conspiratorial skills, was a precursor of al Qaeda itself. It's these two currents—represented, respectively, by Bin Laden and his Egyptian second in command, Ayman al Zawahiri—that formed more than a decade later the kernel of a murderous network that has ravaged the world.

.   .   .

Juhayman's daring invasion of the Grand Mosque galvanized Muslim radicals around the world in myriad other ways. One of the pilgrims who watched the takeover in Mecca, and who brought Juhayman's writings home to Egypt, was a young student named Mohammed Shawqi Islambouli. An activist in the burgeoning Islamic revival, Mohammed shared this literature, and excited tales of the Mecca events, with his brother Khaled. A first lieutenant in the Egyptian army, Khaled Islambouli shortly thereafter began what he would later describe as an eighteen-month "path to martyrdom."

On October 6, 1981, marching past President Sadat at a military parade, Khaled Islambouli suddenly pointed his weapon at the VIP stand and unloaded several bullets into the "pharaoh" guilty of betraying Islam and making peace with the Jews. A main street in Tehran is still named in Khaled Islambouli's honor. The assassin's brother, Mohammed Islambouli, later continued this fight against apostasy and disbelief, joining Bin Laden in Afghanistan. He remains one of the top al Qaeda leaders, still on the run.

Juhayman's writings, meanwhile, have become a publishing success in Egypt. Assembled by an admiring Egyptian academic, a 438-page book of Juhayman's epistles and attached commentary is now in its third edition, gracing the windowfronts of Cairo bookstores.

Having survived Saudi jails, several of Juhayman's direct accomplices also joined al Qaeda after trekking to Afghanistan in the late 1980s. One of them, an Egyptian jihadi named Muhammad Amir Sulayman Saqr, arrived in Afghanistan around 1987, and then—working closely with Zawahiri—became one of al Qaeda's most prized document forgers, producing passports and other documents that facilitated terrorists' travel.

In the Afghan camps, where thousands of future terrorists were indoctrinated in radical Islam and taught how to slaughter the infidels, Juhayman's ideology was popularized with particular flair by a Palestinian preacher named Isam al Barqawi, alias Abu Mohammed al Maqdisi.

Born in the West Bank village of Barqa, this prolific theoretician of jihad—initially deemed too radical even by Bin Laden—grew up in Kuwait and lived in Saudi Arabia in the early 1980s. He had a personal bond with Juhayman's movement: Maqdisi's brother-in-law, Abdellatif al Derbas, had been among Juhayman's closest supporters and spent several years in Saudi jails.

Much impressed by Derbas's tales about Juhayman's unbending ardor, Maqdisi went as far as mimicking the rebel guru's appearance, growing long hair and a disheveled beard. Claiming kinship of blood, he argued—somewhat improbably for a Palestinian—that his own surname denoted a membership of the Barqa clan, a subdivision of the Uteybi tribal federation to which Juhayman belonged.

All this sentiment is obvious from Maqdisi's book, *The Clear Proofs That the Saudi State Is Infidel*, a piece of obligatory reading for generations of militants across the Muslim world. Even Maqdisi, of course, realized that Juhayman's designation of Mohammed Abdullah as Mahdi had been wrong. But, he wrote in the book, "it is nothing compared with the enormous crimes of the Saudi government: blocking people from the path of God, embracing disbelief, harming worshippers . . . and opening the doors of the country wide open to infidels of various faiths."

By sending soldiers against Juhayman's men, the Saudi state was the first to violate Quranic precepts that forbid waging warfare in the holy precinct, Maqdisi argued. "We ask God," he wrote, "to give mercy to Juhayman in exchange for all he has done to ensure victory for the religion of God, for his attempts to awaken people."

The new generation of jihadis learned from Juhayman's mistakes. Choosing a religious symbol such as the Grand Mosque as a target, Maqdisi wrote, betrayed the rebels' "simplicity, naivete and a lack of vision." Instead, the conspirators should have struck Saudi government installations or the royal palace itself. A confrontation between the House of Saud and Juhayman's group in Riyadh, Maqdisi lamented, "would have been to defend the government—whereas here [in Mecca] it could be portrayed as a defense of religion, of the House of God, and of the worshippers' freedom to pray." This error, Maqdisi explained, provided the House of Saud with a "golden opportunity" to eliminate the entire network of Islamic dissidence in one clean sweep.

One early reader inspired by this book acted on Maqdisi's advice in November 1995, planting a deadly bomb that destroyed a Saudi National Guard building in Riyadh, killing seven people—including five Americans.

By then, Maqdisi himself was already behind bars in Jordan, serving a sentence for involvement in a conspiracy to overthrow the Hashemite Kingdom. His cellmate, a co-conspirator and favored pupil, eager to learn about Juhayman's exploits, was not widely known at the time. Acting under an alias of Abu Musab al Zarqawi, a few years later he would create al Qaeda of Iraq, personally beheading infidel hostages and orchestrating almost daily massacres of Shiites. Unlike the rebels of Mecca, who—at least initially—tried not to harm civilians, the latest mutation of this virus would turn mass-murder into an art form. Yet, the roots were never forgotten: in his death, a suicide bomber dispatched by Zarqawi to attack the Palestine Hotel in Baghdad in 2005 paid a tribute to the original master, adopting the nom de guerre Abu Juhayman.

EPILOGUE

In the years after the Mecca uprising, the Saudi government tried its best to erase these bloody events from public memory. The subject of Juhayman remains taboo in the kingdom, strenuously avoided by Saudi historians and ignored by official textbooks. The one Saudi book published on the Grand Mosque uprising—a collection of articles from Saudi newspapers and official speeches unequivocally entitled *Death to Heresy!*—was withdrawn from libraries and placed on the list of banned publications soon after it was printed in Jeddah in 1980.

The Saudis' continuing sensitivity about events that happened nearly three decades ago is easy to understand. In the West, the politicians and public servants who were directly involved in the Mecca crisis are now out of office or dead. But the key players on the Saudi side are still there, occupying precisely the same jobs they held back in 1979. In the kingdom's gerontocratic hierarchy, Prince Sultan, now the crown prince, is still minister of defense and aviation. Prince Nayef is still minister of interior, in charge of internal security. Abdullah, now the king, is still the direct commander of the National Guard. Prince Saud al Faisal is still minister of foreign affairs. And his brother Prince Turki, who left the intelligence service shortly before the September 11 attacks of 2001 drew worldwide attention to his former protégé Osama Bin Laden, subsequently served as Saudi ambassador to the United States.

As it turned out, Prince Turki's belief in the French ability to keep secrets proved somewhat misplaced. In late January 1980, a French magazine, *Le Point*, published a report describing the GIGN involvement in wildly exaggerated detail—and claiming that French commandos fought Juhayman's men on the holy ground of Mecca. Saudi denials of any foreign participation in the affair were believed at first—until Captain Barril himself published his memoirs, *Very Special Missions*, in 1984.

This book featured on the cover a picture of Barril wearing a Saudi-style red checkered headdress atop the French uniform, a polished gun on his belt and a desert landscape shimmering in the background. Though the back cover warned that the captain's "passage through Mecca would not be discussed here," the text was peppered with vague references to Barril's combat exploits in the sacred city of Islam. One chapter lamented the poor performance of French flak vests against rebel bullets; another explained how Barril later got in trouble because a handful of detonators he had brought home from Mecca and passed to a fellow GIGN trooper ended up in the hands of right-wing extremists.

Many inside Saudi Arabia and in the wider Arab world took this book as proof that the French infidels indeed had stormed the Grand Mosque. A couple of years later, the GIGN commander, Prouteau, visited Saudi Arabia to share French intelligence warnings about Iranian plans for violent demonstrations in Mecca. Instead of inquiring about this looming threat, the Saudi religious affairs minister—who had not been personally involved in the events of 1979—first wanted to satisfy his curiosity about Barril's role in the past. Was it true, he asked, that the French gendarme had seen battle in the Grand Mosque?

Taken aback, Prouteau explained that he had issued specific orders for the French soldiers to stay in Taef and not to enter Mecca. The Saudi minister got up and extended his arms. "Thank you, thank you, for showing us this respect," he said beaming.

By then, Prouteau served as counterterrorism chief in the administration of President François Mitterrand, Giscard d'Estaing's Socialist successor. Barril followed his commander into the Elysée but didn't stay there long. In 1982, he was embroiled in the so-called Vincennes Irish scandal, accused of planting weapons and explosives in the home of Irish exiles whose arrest had been trumpeted by the Mitterrand administration as a major victory against international terrorism. As Mitterrand tried to quash the scandal, both Prouteau and Barril, according to French magistrates, participated in illegal wiretaps of French journalists and public figures on the president's behalf. After a long trial, in 2005 the two received suspended jail sentences for their role in the wiretapping affair; Barril is still appealing the verdict.

Forced out of government service in 1983, Barril in ensuing decades rented his security skills to Third World regimes of varying respectability. Barril's clients included the deposed emir of Qatar, who tried a countercoup from Saudi Arabia; and the Hutu regime in Rwanda just before the 1994 genocide. In 2002, the French commando advised the president of the Central African Republic, then busy suppressing a coup attempt by the opposition leader, François Bozizé. After capturing power the following year, Bozizé asked the International Criminal Court to arrest Barril for war crimes.

As of late, Barril has been providing advice to another embattled African president, Idriss Déby of Chad, increasingly undermined by the proxy war with Sudan in Darfur and tribal uprisings at home.

Barril's two comrades in arms were back in Arabia soon after the battle for Mecca. Lambert spent several months in the Saudi kingdom as an instructor seconded to the Saudi military. Wodecki was sent on a similar mission to the United Arab Emirates.

Among Americans involved in these events, Dan the chopper pilot declined to publicly speak about his role. He was last spotted flying for an oil company in Alaska. His relative, Mark Hambley, has retired in Massachusetts, in a house decorated with carved Arabian doors, after a brilliant diplomatic career that saw him become U.S. ambassador to Lebanon and Qatar.

Carter's presidency was fatally undermined by the 1979 meltdown in the Islamic world, and by his failure to secure the hostages' release. The American diplomats were freed from Iranian captivity only on January 20, 1981—a few minutes after Ronald Reagan was sworn in as president.

In Saudi Arabia, while most of Juhayman's supporters caught in the Grand Mosque itself were beheaded, the much larger number of sympathizers arrested outside Mecca ended up free after spending up to a decade in prison. Not all remained in radical opposition to the Saudi state. Some joined government service after their release. Others, such as Nasser Hozeimi—the youth who had fled with Juhayman through the desert from Medina—even switched sides. A chain-smoking journalist at *al Riyadh* newspaper, Hozeimi is nowadays one of Saudi Arabia's more outspoken liberals. By regional standards, the Saudi state was remarkably lenient to Juhayman's children: his sons were embraced by the National Guard, where they now serve with officers' ranks.

The soldiers and officers who fought in the Grand Mosque faced bloodshed again in the 1991 Gulf War. They were mostly retired by the time Juhayman's ideological heirs rocked Saudi Arabia with a wave of bombings and killings that reached a crescendo with murderous attacks on expatriate residential compounds in 2003. In early 2006, I sat down with Abu Sultan, the French-trained officer who had captured Juhayman in the Grand Mosque's underground. Over several cups of sweet tea in his villa along the Mecca-Jeddah highway, he recalled the horrors of that battle. "All the terrorists we see now are leftovers of Juhayman," he said.

It was a stroke of luck, Abu Sultan reminisced, that Juhayman seized the Grand Mosque just before the advent of mobile phones, the Internet, and live satellite TV news extended the reach of extremists. Back in 1979, the Saudi government managed to muffle Juhayman's message, containing the rebellion through an information blockade that would be unthinkable now. "If these people had the new technology that exists today," Abu Sultan mused, "they would have ended up conquering the whole world."

A Note to Readers

This book is a work of nonfiction and attempts to reconstruct—as faithfully as possible—the battle for Mecca, and for the soul of Islam, in 1979. The subject remains highly sensitive in Saudi Arabia, the government of which allows no access to its archives and discourages research on this topic. Many aspects of this crisis also remain classified in Western archives.

To put together a narrative of this battle and its repercussions, I traveled extensively in Saudi Arabia, Egypt, and the United Arab Emirates, as well as in the United States, France, Britain, and Turkey, interviewing several dozen eyewitnesses and participants in these events. In my research, I also drew on years of reporting from the Muslim world for the *Wall Street Journal*, and on relationships developed over the years in Saudi Arabia, Pakistan, Afghanistan, Jordan, Iraq, and other Muslim lands.

People interviewed for this book include former Juhayman adepts, among them former gunmen who actually took part in the assault on the Grand Mosque; Saudi security officers and senior commanders; prominent clerics and members of the royal family; former French commandos and government officials; and a number of American diplomats and spies who focused on Saudi Arabia and its neighbors in 1979.

Some of these sources—especially in Saudi Arabia—talked to me only on the condition of being granted anonymity. For them, fear of government punishment often mixed with concern about retaliation by radical Islamists supportive of Juhayman. One interview had to be carried out in the middle of the street in a militant neighborhood of Riyadh where foreign journalists were gunned down just months earlier, because my source said he had been specifically instructed by government officials to cancel my previously scheduled visit to his home.

It took a lot of sleuthing to track down Juhayman's former comrades in arms. At first, thanks to Saudi dissidents I had interviewed in the past, I managed to locate a few supporters of Juhayman who did not participate in the attack on the Grand Mosque themselves, either because they were in jail at the time or because they didn't believe in the Mahdi's arrival. With some of these men, the conversations were brutally short. "Are you a Muslim or a kaffir?" they asked, using the pejorative term for nonbelievers. After hearing that I was not a Muslim, they simply hung up and declined further contact.

But not all were so bigoted. Some went out of their way to be helpful, inviting me to their homes and treating me to lavish rice and lamb spreads. And, after getting to trust me, they provided me with mobile phone numbers of rebel survivors. Only a few of these are still around: most male adults captured in the Grand Mosque were executed. The ones that I managed to contact escaped beheading because they were age sixteen or younger in November 1979.

The first former rebel I reached, currently a government employee in Riyadh and a Ph.D. in Islamic studies, was a disappointment. He misunderstood me on the phone, thinking that I wanted to discuss a book *he* had just written about a battle between the Meccans and Prophet Mohammed in 624. Later that day, once I sat down in the man's home and showed him a picture of himself, shackled to other bloodied militants in the courtyard of the Mecca Hotel in December 1979, all color receded from his face. He started giggling nervously, fidgeting and looking for ways to change the subject. At first he claimed it was not him in the picture. Realizing that I didn't believe his denials, he sighed and just said: "Those who were there all either forgot or don't want to remember." Minutes later, he got alarmed that even such a sterile conversation with me would land him back in the torture chambers. The man demanded to see a government permit for researching this troubling chapter in Saudi history; he announced he would speak with me only if I returned with an officer from the Interior Ministry.

Luckily, the next former rebel I managed to contact proved a lot more talkative. The man—called in this book Samir, a pseudonym—agreed to drive down from Mecca and meet me in my Jeddah hotel. Too afraid to be seen with a foreigner in the lobby, he insisted on going up to my hotel room—where he kept recounting his dramatic experiences until the wee hours of the morning, emptying my minibar of its (strictly nonalcoholic) contents.

These kinds of encounters helped strip the veil of secrecy that the Saudi government had imposed on details of the warfare in Mecca. Another treasure trove of previously secret information came from hundreds of contemporary documents that were declassified and released to me by the U.S. State Department, the CIA, and the British Foreign and Commonwealth Office in response to my Freedom of Information Act requests; these documents included the diaries kept by Ambassador West.

In addition, I relied on scores of other documents from the White House and the National Security Council that were provided by the Carter Library, as well as previously declassified material gathered in other collections. I also had a chance to examine French documents directly linked with the GIGN mission to Saudi Arabia.

In describing contemporary news coverage of the crisis I made heavy use of the CIA's Foreign Broadcast Information Service's daily compilations of transcripts of relevant broadcasts and news articles from the regional media, as well as articles from the Saudi and Pakistani press.

These accounts were often mutually contradictory. In writing the book, I used what seemed to me the most likely version, based on the preponderance of evidence and the general credibility of the sources. When two differing versions of events seemed valid, I mentioned both in the text. On some aspects of this drama, the final truth may never be known. The notes, which begin on page 265, provide detailed sourcing of most assertions in the book.

Acknowledgments

This book wouldn't have been possible without the help of a great many people across four continents. Above all, I wish to thank those directly involved in the dramatic events of 1979. Dozens of participants and eyewitnesses set aside time to meet me, often for several hours and more than once, delving into painful memories. Those whom I can name are listed in the source notes at the end of the book. Thank you, and *alf shoukr.*

As always, my wife, Susi, and children, Jonathan and Nicole, had to put up with my long absences on reporting trips to Saudi Arabia, America, France, and elsewhere. The time I've taken from them is precious, and irreplaceable. I acknowledge the debt.

My agent, Jay Mandel, couldn't have played a more crucial role in conceptualizing this book, and expertly found it a great home. I can't thank him enough. His assistant, Charlotte Wasserstein, also provided invaluable support, making the reporting so much easier.

At Doubleday, I feel privileged to have worked with Gerry Howard, whose editing was superb and suggestions always spot-on. My thanks also go to his assistant, Katie Halleron, and to Alison Kerr Miller, who copyedited the manuscript.

I owe many, many other people for their help in completing this project. Because of space constraints, I'm mentioning only a few—and I'm equally thankful to those not on this list.

In Saudi Arabia: Sami Angawi and his son Ammar, who graciously introduced me to the people who mattered in Jeddah; Abdelaziz al Gassim, who opened many doors in Riyadh; Anees Qudaihi, whose time and generosity I abused without measure. I am especially indebted to Dr. Awadh Badhi and Dr. Yahya Ibn Junaid at the King Faisal Center for Research and Islamic Studies, which sponsored the visa for my most important trip to the kingdom and which hosted me as a visiting scholar in mid-2006. Any mistakes in the book are obviously mine, and I alone am fully responsible for its shortcomings.

Also in Riyadh, staff at the King Fahd National Library kindly dusted off old newspaper collections for me, letting me into storage rooms to study the 1979 coverage. Andrew Hammond of Reuters was a great dinner companion, listening patiently to my rants. In the Eastern Province, my thanks go to Jaffar al Shayeb, who made sure I felt at home while reporting in that part of the country.

In Egypt: Ahmed Salah, my indomitable fixer, was the best reporting companion one may desire. Thanks of course are also due to the inimitable Mandy Fahmy.

In the United States: My friends Debra and John Whelan, Roman and Chrystyna Czajkowsky, Philippe and Virginia Gelie, Ephrat and Tomer Levine, and Ian and Elke Johnson were great hosts during my reporting stays in New York, Washington, and Massachusetts. Ian's advice in particular is much appreciated. Thank you all.

Toby Jones read an early version of the manuscript and helped prevent numerous errors. For this, and for his kind introductions, many thanks.

In Washington, Dr. Mary Curry at the National Security Archive shepherded me toward a treasure trove of documents. Several key pieces of information in the book come from collections assembled by the archive. I am also grateful to staff at the libraries of George Washington University and Columbia University, the University of South Carolina, as well as at the New York Public Library, for facilitating my research.

At the U.S. State Department I owe a debt to Henry Clay Black, who skillfully guided me through the complicated process of requesting declassification of secret documents. The materials that I obtained as a result of this process form an indispensable part of the narrative in the book.

In Britain: Thomas Hegghammer helped me to a quick start by sharing dissident literature about the Mecca uprising. I also want to thank Robert Seely, James Buchan, and the staff at the British Library newspaper collection at Colindale.

In France: My friend Anne-Elisabeth Moutet's counsel and company made it all easier; Jihan Tahri so generously shared her time; and Christophe and Emma Boltanski were stimulating companions.

My thanks also go to Fidan Ekiz, Mehmet Ali Buyukkara, and Hugh Pope in Turkey; Simeon Kerr and Ana Romero in the United Arab Emirates; and to my colleagues at the *Wall Street Journal*—Bill Spindle, Alan Cullison, Gabriel Kahn, Alessandra Galloni, and Stacy Meichtry.

Last but not least, I'm forever grateful to my parents, Valery and Alevtina. They taught me to be curious, to question authority, and to be undeterred by frontiers.

Notes and Sources

INTRODUCTION

The narrative of the first day of the siege of the Grand Mosque is based on exten-
sive author interviews with eyewitnesses. These included Abdelazim al Matani
(Cairo, Egypt, Jan. 2006), Sheikh Abdulaziz Rafah al Suleimani (Jeddah, Saudi Arabia, Feb. 2006), Rida Bajamal (Jeddah, Feb. 2006), and others who preferred to remain unnamed (Jeddah, Sept. 2006). Some details are also based on a series of
interviews with pilgrims that were published in Mecca's *al Nadwa* newspaper on
Dec. 2, 1979, and Jeddah's *Okaz* newspaper on Nov. 30, 1979, and Dec. 2, 1979.

The author also obtained the recollections of the Grand Mosque's imam, Sheikh
Mohammed Ibn Subeil, via his son (Jeddah, Sept. 2006), who relayed questions and
answers. The imam also recounted his experiences in interviews with Saudi Arabia's
al Bilad and *al Jazira* newspapers, reproduced by Jeddah's *Arab News* on Nov. 25,
1979, as well as in a report by *al Riyadh* newspaper, *"Taalumat Mufassala an al
Khawarij,"* from Dec. 1, 1979.

Matani described the Mecca crisis in a 1980 book, *Jarimat al Asr ?!! Qissat Ihtilal
al Masjid al Haram* (*Crime of the Era*) (Cairo: Wahbah reprint edition, 2003), from
which some information is drawn in this and other chapters.

Juhayman's age and some additional descriptions in following chapters come from two books on the Mecca events, published clandestinely in Arabic by Saudi dissidents who didn't witness the uprising firsthand. These are *Ahdath al Haram bayn al Haqaiq wa al-Abatil* (*Events in the Shrine Between Truth and Lies*) (1980, publisher unknown), by Abu Dharr, a pseudonym, and *Zilzal Juhayman fi Makkah* (*Juhayman's Earthquake in Mecca*) (Munadhamat al Thawra al Islamiya fil Jazeera al Arabiya, 1987), by Fahd al Qahtani, another pen name. Other sources indicate that Juhayman was "in his late thirties."

The information that African American converts were present among the rebels is from author interviews with Nasser al Hozeimi (Riyadh, Saudi Arabia, Feb. 2006) and another former member of Juhayman's group (Riyadh, Feb. 2006), as well as an author interview with Mark Hambley, a political officer at the U.S. embassy in Jeddah at the time (Springfield, Mass., Sept. 2006) and James Placke, the U.S. deputy chief of mission in Jeddah at the time (via phone, Sept. 2006).

The number of gates at the Grand Mosque in 1979 is from *History of Makkah* by "A Group of Scholars Under the Supervision of Shaikh Safiur-Rahman Mubarakpuri" (Maktaba Dar-us-Salam, Riyadh, 2002), p. 105. Additional details on the mosque's layout and architecture are from the ArchNet Digital Library: archnet.org/library/sites/one-site.tcl?site_id=8803.

Rebels' announcement of control over Jeddah and Medina, and details about the timing of the assault, are from eyewitness accounts relayed in a telegram sent to the U.S. State Department by the U.S. ambassador to Saudi Arabia, John C. West. (American embassy Jidda cable 7993 of Nov. 20, 1979, "Occupation of the Grand Mosque, Mecca," originally classified "Secret," obtained by the author under a Freedom of Information Act request.)

CHAPTER ONE

Prophet Mohammed's hadith on the value of prayer in Mecca is quoted from *Mecca al-Mokar'ama, Medina al-Monaw'ara and the Black Stone: Secrets and Merits,* by Rashad Shaban Ramadan (Cairo: Dar al-Ghad al-Gadeed, 2001), p. 17. Other descriptions of the shrine are based on *History of Makkah* and *The Glorious Ka'abah and Islam* by Syed Farouq M. Al Huseini (Jeddah: Al-Medina Press, 2004).

The verse on the Army of the Elephant is 105.005 from the Quran's Fil Surah.

The account of Prophet Mohammed's life is drawn in part on *A History of Islamic Societies,* by Ira M. Lapidus (Cambridge: Cambridge University Press, 1988), pp. 21–37, and *Muhammad: A Biography of the Prophet,* by Karen Armstrong (HarperSanFrancisco, 1993).

The chapter's account of early Saudi history and Wahhabi ideology is based on following books: Madawi al Rasheed, *A History of Saudi Arabia* (Cambridge: Cambridge University Press, 2002); Alexei Vassiliev, *The History of Saudi Arabia* (London: Saqi Books, 2000), which served as the key source for passages on the Wahhabi attack against Karbala and Taef, as well as the general history of the Ikhwan movement; David Holden and Richard Johns, *The House of Saud* (London: Pan Books, 1982); Natana J. Delong-Bas, *Wahhabi Islam: From Revival to Global Jihad* (Cairo: American University in Cairo Press, 2005).

The history of previous desecrations of Mecca draws on F. E. Peters, *Mecca: A Literary History of the Muslim Holy Land* (Princeton, N.J.: Princeton University Press, 1994), pp. 38–40, 162–63, and on "Two Mecca Outrages in 1400 Years," by Aly Mahmoud, *Kuwait Times,* Nov. 24, 1979.

Juhayman's family history and descent from the Ikhwan is based on an account Juhayman himself provided to Nasser al Hozeimi, as recounted to the author. Other published accounts, based on secondhand sources, say that it was Juhayman's grandfather rather than his father who participated in the battle of Sbala and that he had been killed there. Hozeimi denies this. The battle's name is usually transliterated in Western literature as Sibila, which isn't how it is pronounced by Saudis.

CHAPTER TWO

Some dates and facts in this chapter are drawn from al Rasheed's *A History of Saudi Arabia,* Vassiliev's *The History of Saudi Arabia,* and Holden and Johns's *The House of Saud.*

The descriptions of the Grand Mosque's enlargement and the post-expansion size are based on *History of Makkah* and contemporary video footage viewed by the author.

The Bin Baz fatwa on the presence of infidels is quoted as translated by Gilles Kepel in *The War for Muslim Minds* (Cambridge, Mass.: Belknap, 2004), pp. 165–66.

Details on women's education are from "Women and Education in Saudi Arabia: Challenges and Achievements," by Amani Hamdan, *International Education Journal* 6, no. 1 (2005): 42–64.

Saudi oil revenue figures are from *The Saudis: Inside a Desert Kingdom,* by Sandra Mackey (New York: W. W. Norton, 2002), p. 7.

The "flush" quote about Saudi wealth comes from "Pakistan: the Middle East Connection," CIA National Foreign Assessment Center, February 1980, an Intelligence Assessment, originally classified "Secret." Saudi population figures in 1979 are from "As Mideast Heats Up, U.S. Frets over Peril to the Saudi Oil Fields," by Walter S. Mossberg, *Wall Street Journal,* Jan. 21, 1980.

CHAPTER THREE

Juhayman's activities and the inner workings of his group were described to the author by Nasser al Hozeimi in a series of interviews in Riyadh in February, August, and September 2006. Additional details were provided by group member Sultan al Khamis (author interview, Riyadh, Sept. 2006) and other former adepts who prefer to remain unnamed (author interviews, Riyadh, Feb. and Sept. 2006, Jeddah, Sept. 2006). The proselytizing trips to the desert were described to the author by Abu Sultan (Jeddah, Feb. 2006).

Some additional details on discussions between Juhayman's followers and establishment clerics were provided by Mansour al Noqaidan, a Saudi specialist in radical Islam (phone interview, Feb. 2006). Information on Juhayman's early religious ideas is also drawn from *Zilzal Juhayman fi Makkah,* which recounts the 1977 meeting, and from "Ahdath al Haram."

The Bin Baz fatwa on pictures is quoted from *Fatawa Islamiya Islamic Verdicts,* vol. 8 (Dar-us-Salam, Riyadh, 2002), p. 112. The fatwa on clapping is from the same volume, p. 126. The fatwa on barbers is on p. 103. The fatwa on smoking is from *Fatawa Islamiya, Islamic Verdicts,* vol. 6 (Dar-us-Salam, Riyadh, 2002), p. 337. The fatwa on women teachers is quoted from www.fatwaislam.com.

Juhayman's own writings are quoted from *Rasail Juhayman al Uteybi: Qaed al Muqtahamin al Masjid al Haram bi Makkah (Epistles of Juhayman al Uteybi . . .),* an edited compilation that includes the full text of the seven epistles and historical commentary by the Egyptian author Rifaat Sid Ahmed (Cairo: Maktabat Madbouli, 2004). The original version, published by Dar al Talia' around 1978 and viewed by the author, contains a virtually identical text of the seven epistles. The only difference is that Sid Ahmed's version ascribes all seven epistles to Juhayman, whereas his name is attached to only four of the seven in the original version. This chapter quotes mostly from the first epistle, signed by Juhayman and called *"Al Imara wa al Baya wa al Taa wa Keshef Talbis al-Hukam aal Talbat al Ilm wa al Awam"* ("The Power and the Oath").

CHAPTER FOUR

FBI files on the Nation of Islam are quoted from a collection posted on the FBI Web site. The documents that describe Fard's race as white include his LAPD and San Quentin records, reproduced in a March 5, 1955, memo. The memo is available at foia.fbi.gov/filelink.html?file=/fard/fard1.pdf.

Malcolm X on pilgrimage to Mecca is quoted from *The Autobiography of Malcolm X, As Told by Alex Haley* (New York: Ballantine Books, 1987), pp. 332, 246–47.

Information on Siraj Wahhaj being a student in Mecca at the time is from author interview with him (via phone, March 2006). Additional details are from "Spiritual Journey: One Imam Traces the Path of Islam in Black America—Baptist to Nationalist in '60s, Siraj Wahhaj Now Preaches Self-Help and Militancy—Defending the Blind Sheik," *Wall Street Journal,* Oct. 24, 2003. Mr. Wahhaj denied any personal involvement with Juhayman's supporters.

Mohammed Abdullah is described based on interviews with Hozeimi, Sultan al Khamis, Samir, and other members of the movement. The incident in the hospital is from Abu Dharr's book. Prince Nayef's conversation with Bin Baz was narrated to the author by the eyewitness (Jeddah, Feb. 2006).

Crown Prince Fahd is quoted from an interview to Lebanon's *al Safir,* as translated by the official Saudi press agency and published Jan. 14, 1980, in Jeddah's *Arab News.*

The Egyptian magazine *Dawad*'s article on Saudi Arabia is quoted from "Halte au porno en Arabie Seoudite," *L'Orient-Le Jour* (Beirut), Nov. 21, 1979.

Additional details on Islamic student activism in Egypt is from "Egypte: Les etudiants integristes s'agites," *L'Orient-Le Jour* (Beirut), Jan. 14, 1980.

The spreading of Juhayman's booklet in Cairo and Mohammed Elias's involvement in the movement are described based on author interview with Montasser al Zayat, a former activist of Gamaat Islamiya and a cellmate of Zawahiri (Cairo, Jan. 2006).

CHAPTER FIVE

Juhayman's ideas about the Mahdi are quoted from his treatise, *"Al Fitan wa Akhbar al Mahdi wa Nizul Issa aleyha as-Salam wa Ushrat as-Saa"* (*The Coming of the Mahdi and the Descent of Jesus and the Final Hour*), pp. 173–225 in Sid Ahmed's edition of *Rasail Juhayman al-Uteibi.*

Some additional details are drawn from "Sheikh Describes How Mahdi Will Appear," interview with Nasser Ibn Rashed, *Arab News,* Dec. 25, 1979, and from Joseph A. Kechichian's "Islamic Revivalism and Change in Saudi Arabia: Juhayman al'Utaybi's 'Letters' to the Saudi People" *The Muslim World* 80, no. 1 (Jan. 1990): 1–16.

The description of Saad's conversation with Hozeimi is based on the author's interview with Hozeimi. The dream pandemic among Juhayman's followers was recounted to the author by Hozeimi, Sultan al Khamis, and another former member of the group. It was also noted at the time by Saudi authorities. The hadith about dreams is Number 167 from Volume 9, Book 87 of Sahih Bukhari.

The gun-smuggling statistic is from "Naif Briefs Journalists on Renegades," an account of Prince Nayef's press conference, in the *Arab News* of Jan. 14, 1979. One of the several hadiths on the forecast swallowing of the army into the earth is Number 6889 from Book 041 of Sahih Muslim.

CHAPTER SIX

The descriptions of U.S. internal policy debates on Iran are based on the memoirs of Zbigniew Brzezinski (*Power and Principle* [New York: Farrar, Straus & Giroux, 1983]), and the National Security Council's principal officer dealing with Iran, Gary Sick (*All Fall Down* [New York: Random House, 1985]). Ambassador Sullivan's cable, "Thinking the Unthinkable," is quoted from both books.

Carter's "They have us by the balls" quote is from Sick (p. 209), while the president's quote about nonaligned Iran is from Brzezinski (p. 377). Brzezinski's description of his feelings toward "lawyers of the liberal bent" is from p. 355 of his memoirs.

The author also interviewed Gary Sick by phone in Jan. 2006.

Brzezinski's advice to Carter is from *NSC Weekly Report* no. 87, Feb. 2, 1979, section "Islamic Fundamentalism," originally classified "Top Secret." Held in the Carter Library.

Ambassador Young's words on Khomeini are quoted from "Young Praises Islam as 'Vibrant' and Calls the Ayatollah 'a Saint,' " *New York Times,* Feb. 8, 1979.

Carter on noninterference in Iran is from "A Transcript of President's News Conference on Foreign and Domestic Matters," *New York Times,* Jan. 27, 1979.

Khomeini's speech in the Tehran airport is quoted from "Khomeini Arrives in Tehran, Urges Ouster of Foreigners; Millions Rally to Greet Him" by R. W. Apple Jr., *New York Times,* Feb. 1, 1979.

Descriptions of gas shortages and Carter's letter to Saudi princes are drawn from *The Prize* by Daniel Yergin (New York: Touchstone, 1992), pp. 691–95.

Ambassador West is described in part based on an author interview with Hambley. The conversation with Prince Sultan is quoted from a Sept. 11, 1979, letter by West that is deposited in the Carter Presidential Library.

The CIA assessment is quoted from "Economic and Political Trends in the Arabian Peninsula, an Intelligence Assessment," the CIA's National Foreign Assessment Center, April 1979.

Descriptions of the CIA training program for Saudi Arabia are based on the author's interview with former station chief George Cave (McLean, Va., March 2006).

Ambassador West's conversation with Crown Prince Fahd is described based on

American embassy Jidda cable 7096 of Oct. 10, 1979, "Meeting with Crown Prince Fahd—October 2," originally classified "Secret" and provided to the author by the National Security Archive. The account of the hostage seizure in Tehran is based on, among other material, "Iran Leaders Back U.S. Embassy Seizure," *New York Times,* Nov. 6, 1979. Additional details are from an author interview with Charles Cogan, then of the CIA (Cambridge, Mass., Sept. 2006).

CHAPTER SEVEN

The narrative in this chapter is based in large part on author interviews with Hozeimi, Sultan al Khamis, Matani, and Saudi eyewitnesses. Between his arrest in early December 1979 and the beheading of uprising participants in January 1980, Hozeimi shared a cell with Faisal Mohammed Faisal in the Mecca prison. Faisal recounted his meeting with Juhayman in Amar and his reaction to the supposed Mahdi to fellow prisoners in those weeks. Khamis and other sources interviewed by the author also shared cells with direct participants in the uprising.

This chapter also draws on the author interview with one of these participants, identified in the book as Samir (Jeddah, Sept. 2006). The man, whose true identity is known to the author, requested that it be protected because of a high probability of retribution by Saudi authorities.

The 40,000-riyal bribe was mentioned by Prince Fahd in his interview with Lebanon's *al Safir,* as translated by the official Saudi Press Agency and published Jan. 14, 1980, in Jeddah's *Arab News.*

CHAPTER EIGHT

In addition to responding to the author's questions (Jeddah, Sept. 2006), Ibn Subeil described his own experiences in interviews with Saudi Arabia's *al Bilad* and *al Jazira* newspapers, reproduced by Jeddah's *Arab News* on Nov. 25, 1979.

The description of initial police reaction is based on Ibn Subeil's account in *al Riyadh* newspaper on Dec. 1, 1979. Matani's book, and in part on "Takeover of Grand Mosque Said to Be Political Act," by Steven Rattner, *New York Times,* Dec. 17, 1979.

Mohammed Abdullah's conversation with an Iranian pilgrim was recounted by the pilgrim in "Iranian Pilgrim Tells of Mecca Attack," *New York Times,* Nov. 22, 1979.

The *baya* speech is quoted from a partial transcript published by *al Riyadh* newspaper on Dec. 6, 1979. The entire speech was recorded by the Grand Mosque's automatic sermon recording system and subsequently broadcast in edited form on Saudi TV. The parts of the speech about the royal family were not reproduced, and are reported according to eyewitness accounts. Additional parts of the speech were reproduced in an anthology of documents and articles about the Mecca affairs, *Wa Tamut al Fitna!* ("Death to Heresy!"), that was compiled by the *al Nadwa* newspaper staff and published by the Tihama press in Jeddah in 1980 (p. 261). The book also contains an interview with members of the Grand Mosque police force (pp. 165–67).

Mohammed Abdullah's denial of Iranian links and the information on Ahmed Zaki Yamani's relatives is from American embassy Jidda telegram 8041 of Nov. 21, 1979, "Occupation of Grand Mosque, Mecca," which describes Ambassador West's conversation with Yamani and eyewitness reports on the subject. The telegram, originally classified "Secret," has been obtained by the author under a Freedom of Information Act request. A separate telegram, 8042, of the same day identifies Yamani as the source.

CHAPTER NINE

Descriptions of the Arab Summit in Tunis are based on the following contemporary reports: "Au sommet Arabe de Tunis: Les demandes d'utiliser 'tous les moyens' contre les Etats-Unis ont été repoussées," by Lucien George, *Le Monde,* Nov. 22, 1979; "La Ligue Arabe surtout preoccupee par Khomeini," by Philippe de Bausset, *Le Figaro,* Nov. 20, 1979; "Guards Bar Iranian Delegation from Summit," AFP, Nov. 21, 1979, as monitored by the FBIS Middle East report, Nov. 23, 1979, item NC211616; and Cairo Domestic Radio report 2000 GMT, Nov. 21, 1979, as monitored by the FBIS Middle East report, Nov. 23, 1979, item NC212038.

The descriptions of phone calls between King Khaled and Ibn Rashed are based on the cleric's own account: "Sheikh Describes How Mahdi Will Appear," *Arab News,* Dec. 25, 1979. Ibn Rashed recounted his concern about a possible takeover in Medina in a Saudi Press Agency dispatch of Dec. 11, 1979, published as part of "King Khaled Visits Soldiers Hurt in Mecca," *Arab News,* Dec. 12, 1979. An additional interview with Ibn Rashed is reproduced in *Wa Tamut al Fitna!,* pp. 187–88.

Additional details are drawn from interviews with Matani, Mohammed al Nefai (Riyadh, Aug. 2006), and American embassy Jidda telegram 7993.

American pilots in Mecca regularly briefed American diplomats about their observations. This information from the first day of the crisis is relayed in a telegram sent to the U.S. State Department by the U.S. ambassador to Saudi Arabia, John C. West ("Occupation of the Grand Mosque, Mecca," State Department telegram Jidda

7993, originally classified "Secret," Nov. 20, 1979, obtained by the author under a Freedom of Information Act request).

CHAPTER TEN

Faleh al Dhaheri's experiences the morning of Nov. 20, 1979, are described using Mr. Dhaheri's account of the day in Saudi Arabia's *Medina* newspaper, as reproduced by Matani in *Jarimat al Asr,* pp. 38–43. Mr. Dhaheri, reached by the author in Mecca, declined a request to be interviewed.

The narrative of Sami Angawi's conversation in the water and sewage department is based on the author's interview with Mr. Angawi (Jeddah, Feb. 2006).

Prince Turki's experiences are described based on author interview with the prince (McLean, Va., Oct. 2006). The hadiths on fighting and weapons in Mecca are Book 3, Hadith 112 of Sahih Bukhari and Book 7, Hadith 3144 from Sahih Muslim.

The tale of Prince Sultan berating troops is based on *Rasail,* p. 42.

The anecdote about the Moroccan intelligence agent is based on Alexandre de Marenches's (with David A. Andelman) *The Fourth World War* (New York: William Morrow, 1992), pp. 207–8.

CHAPTER ELEVEN

Details of the breakfast with Congressman Hall are from the November 20 entry in Ambassador West's diary, obtained by the author from the U.S. State Department under a Freedom of Information Act request.

Information about the first reactions of U.S. diplomats in Saudi Arabia comes from author interviews with then deputy chief of mission James Placke (Washington, D.C., March 2006) and American embassy telegrams Jidda 7981, "Occupation of Grand Mosque, Mecca," originally classified "Secret," and Jidda 7992, "Security Precautions Amembassy Jidda," originally classified "Confidential," of Nov. 20, 1979. The telegrams are kept in the Carter Presidential Library and were provided to the author.

American diplomats' contacts with "Dan" are recounted based on the author interview with Hambley and Ryer (Springfield, Mass., Sept. 2006), as well as American embassy, Jidda telegram 7993.

Details of the National Security Council meeting and the president's schedule are drawn from "The Daily Diary of President Jimmy Carter," Nov. 20, 1979. The diary is available on the Web site of the Carter Presidential Library.

Information on the "lucky thirteen" hostages and their treatment is based on "Hostages Recount Life as Embassy Captives: Bound Day and Night," *New York Times,* Nov. 20, 1979, and Gary Sick's *All Fall Down,* pp. 231–32.

Carter's quotes about his trip to Saudi Arabia are drawn from his memoir, *Keeping Faith* (Fayetteville: University of Arkansas Press, 1995), pp. 308–10.

Telegrams from Hamilton Jordan's file are kept at the Carter Library (Chief of Staff file, box 35, "Iran-Saudi Arabia, 1979, Seizure of Mecca"). Cited in the book are the following documents: DIA notice 2205, "Saudi Arabia: Violence in Mecca," Nov. 20, 1979, originally classified "Secret—No Foreign Nationals"; American embassy Jidda telegram 7993; American Consulate Dhahran telegram 1850, "Iranian Agitation of Saudi Shias and Mecca Mosque Agitation," Nov. 20, 1979, originally classified "Secret."

Hodding Carter III is quoted from State Department cable 301800 of Nov. 21, 1979, "Excerpts from Department Press briefing for November 20, 1979," unclassified. Initial U.S. government reaction on the Mecca siege is recounted from "Mecca Mosque Seized by Gunmen Believed to Be Militants from Iran," by Philip Taubman, *New York Times,* Nov. 20, 1979. The Israeli reaction is from "It Is Not Sign of Internal Unrest: Tel Aviv," *Kuwait Times,* Nov. 22, 1979.

Sir James Craig is quoted from "Disturbances in Mecca," Foreign and Commonwealth Office telegram 649 of Nov. 20, 1979, by Ambassador Craig, British embassy Jedda, originally classified "Confidential" and obtained by the author under a U.K. Freedom of Information Act request.

CHAPTER TWELVE

The ulema themselves described the circumstances of their meeting in the fatwa and an accompanying statement, distributed by the Saudi Press Agency and reproduced in the *Arab News* on Nov. 26, 1979. Some details on the Maazar palace interiors are from "The Majlis: Desert Democracy," *Time,* May 22, 1978.

Ibn Rashed outlined in more detail his views on the Mahdi in "Sheikh Describes How Mahdi Will Appear," *Arab News,* Dec. 25, 1979. Other details are from *Zilzal Juhayman fi Makkah* and *Ahdath al Haram,* and author interviews with Saudis familiar with these deliberations, as well as from Joseph A. Kechichian's "The Role of the Ulema in the Politics of an Islamic State: The Case of Saudi Arabia," *International Journal of Middle East Studies* 18, no. 1 (Feb. 1986): 53–71.

One Saudi prince who publicly observed that Juhayman's ideology was allowed to flourish after the Grand Mosque affair is Khaled al Faisal, King Faisal's son and the brother of the foreign minister Saud al Faisal and then GID chief Turki al Faisal. His statement, made on the Saudi-controlled Al Arabiya TV channel and reproduced later in the book, was also printed in the July 20, 2004, edition of *al Sharq al Awsat* newspaper.

The Saudi Interior Ministry statement is quoted from an SPA dispatch, reproduced under the headline "Official Statements" in the *Arab News,* Nov. 22, 1979. The time of the broadcast is from FBIS monitoring.

Details of rebel deliberations inside the mosque are from author interviews with Hozeimi, Samir, Sultan, and another member of the group. The information on rounding up African hostages is from author interview with Abu Sultan (Jeddah, Feb. 2006).

CHAPTER THIRTEEN

The ransacking of the American embassy on November 21 is described based on author interviews with Herbert Hagerty (Washington, D.C., March 2006) and Loyd Miller (Fredericksburg, Va., March 2006).

Hagerty himself narrated his experiences in a chapter of *Embassies Under Siege: Personal Accounts by Diplomats on the Front Line,* edited by Joseph G. Sullivan (Washington, D.C.: Brassey's, 1995), pp. 71–88.

Some details and facts are taken from *Time* correspondent Marcia Granger's eyewitness report "You Could Die Here," *Time,* Dec. 3, 1979.

Pakistani radio descriptions of the day's mood are from FBIS Middle East Report, Nov. 21, 1979, "Reaction of Populace," Karachi Overseas Service, Nov. 21, 1979, item LD211136.

The article in the *Muslim* newspaper is quoted from Steve Coll's *Ghost Wars* (New York: Penguin, 2004), p. 29.

Opinions of the Pakistani newspaper editor, accounts of student agitation on campus of Quaid-i-Azam University, and the quote of Commander Monaghan are from "Delay in Pakistan Rescue Is Criticized," by Stuart Auerbach, *Washington Post,* Nov. 23, 1979.

Khomeini's statement is quoted from FBIS Middle East Report, Nov. 21, 1979, "Khomeini on Mecca Attack," Tehran Domestic Service, 1030 GMT Nov. 21, 1979, item LD211058.

The Iranian foreign ministry statement is quoted from FBIS Middle East Report Nov. 21, 1979, "Foreign Ministry Statement," Tehran Domestic Service, 1030 GMT Nov. 21, 1979, item LD211302.

The CIA chief of covert action staff memo to Paul Henze, National Security Council, dated Nov. 21, 1979, is held in the Carter Library collection.

The narrative on Pakistani reactions and Zia's Rawalpindi visit draws on the following articles in the Karachi-based *Dawn* newspaper of Nov. 22, 1979: "US Embassy Set on Fire in Islamabad," by M. A. Mansuri; "Business Suspended in Karachi"; "President's Deep Concern over Mecca Incident"; and "Zia Urges People to Become True Muslims."

Zia's speech is quoted from FBIS Middle East Report, Nov. 21, 1979, "President Haq Describes Saudi Situation as 'Sad,'" Karachi Domestic Service, Nov. 21, 1979, item BK211017.

The involvement of the German ambassador is from "Des manifestants Musulmans ont attaqué et incendie plusieurs representations diplomatiques Americaines," *Le Monde,* Nov. 22, 1979.

Additional information is drawn from "Troops Rescue 100 in Islamabad; U.S. Offices Are Burned in 2 Cities," by Graham Hovey, *New York Times,* Nov. 22, 1979, and "Islamabad," by Stuart Auerbach, *Washington Post,* Nov. 22, 1979.

The identities of victims among the rioters are from "Carter, Vance Thank Zia," *Dawn* (Karachi), Nov. 23, 1979.

Carter on Zia is quoted from Carter, *Keeping Faith,* p. 474.

General Zia's CBS interview is quoted from "Protection of Foreigners: Zia's Assurance," *Dawn* (Karachi), Nov. 24, 1979.

Radio Pakistan in Arabic is quoted from FBIS Middle East Report, Nov. 26, 1979, "Karachi in Arabic Comment on Mosque Attack," *Karachi in Arabic to the Near and Middle East,* 0515 GMT Nov. 25, 1979, item JN251037.

Student demands for compensation and indictment of Hummel are from FBIS Middle East Report, Nov. 27, 1979, "Students Stage Brief anti-U.S. Demonstration in Islamabad," *AFP,* Nov. 26, 1979, item NC261140 and from FBIS Middle East Report, Dec. 3, 1979, "Students Demonstrate in Rawalpindi," AFP, Dec. 2, 1979, item BK021037.

CHAPTER FOURTEEN

The narrative of the summit in Tunis is woven using contemporary newspaper accounts and declassified documents.

The Saudi description of the siege in Mecca as a "domestic incident" is from "Storming of Grand Mosque Held Back," *Kuwait Times,* Nov. 22, 1979.

Crown Prince Fahd's comments on his attitude in Tunis are quoted from FBIS Middle East Report, Jan. 15, 1980, "Al-Hawadith Interviews Crown Prince Amir Fahd," *al Hawadith,* Jan. 11, 1980, item LD111653.

King Hussein's comments about Fahd's behavior are from American embassy Amman cable 7330, "Contingency Planning and Takeover of Mosque in Mecca," Nov. 22, 1979, originally classified "Secret" and obtained by the author under a Freedom of Information Act request. The cable relays conversations between the U.S. ambassador Nicholas Veliotes and Jordan's crown prince and armed forces commander.

Ambassador West described his meeting with Ahmed Zaki Yamani in American embassy Jidda cable 8042. The intelligence blackout quote is from his diary.

The second Saudi Interior Ministry statement is from "Official Statements," *Arab News* (Jeddah), Nov. 22–23, 1979.

President Chamoun and the mufti of Lebanon are quoted from "Inquiétude à Beyrouth à la suite des incidents de la Mecque," *L'Orient-Le Jour* (Beirut), Nov. 22, 1979. The Syrian radio and TV allegations are outlined in American embassy Damascus cable 7670, "Syrian Media Attacks Linking U.S. to Seizure," originally classified "Secret" and obtained by the author under a Freedom of Information Act request.

The Grand Sheikh of al Azhar is quoted from "Crucify Mosque Attackers, Says Cairo Grand Sheikh," *Kuwait Times,* Nov. 22, 1979.

James Buchan shared his experiences in an interview with the author (London, Feb. 2006). The article quoted is "Saudi Troops Storm into Mosque to Free Hostages," *Financial Times,* Nov. 22, 1979.

Angawi's tale is drawn from interview with the author (Jeddah, Feb. 2006).

The descriptions of planning by the Saudi task force are from author interviews with Nefai, Prince Turki, and other participants. Descriptions of rebel gunfire at choppers and F-5 overflights are from American pilot accounts described in American embassy Jidda telegram 8079 of Nov. 22, 1979, originally classified "Secret" and obtained by the author under a Freedom of Information Act request, and from American embassy Jidda cable 8039 of Nov. 21, 1979, "Occupation of Grand Mosque, Mecca," originally classified "Secret" and obtained by the author under a Freedom of Information Act request.

Matani's testimony is from an author interview and his book.

CHAPTER FIFTEEN

Details of the initial assault on the mosque were described by Ayed and other participants in a full-page interview with *al Riyadh* newspaper published on Dec. 18, 1979.

The account of the conversation between Prince Nayef and Colonel Homaid has been relayed by one of the colonel's relatives (author interview, Riyadh, Feb. 2006). Nefai says he is not aware of such a conversation. Prince Turki also denies it happened.

The battle in the Marwa-Safa gallery is reconstructed based on author interviews with Mohammed Nefai (Riyadh, Sept. 2006), Abu Sultan (Jeddah, Feb. 2006), and other participants, local newspaper accounts, and observations by Matani.

Lieutenant Qudheibi recounted his story and additional details about the deaths of Colonel Homaid and Major Useimi in an interview with *al Riyadh* newspaper, "Al Riyadh Yaqaddem Qissat al-Qital fil Masjid al-Haram," published Dec. 12, 1979.

CHAPTER SIXTEEN

The information minister Yamani's speech is quoted from FBIS Middle East Report, Nov. 23, 1979, Riyadh domestic radio, "Information Minister on Situation," item LD220944. Zia's message to King Khalid is from "Zia Greets Khalid," *Dawn* (Karachi), Nov. 23, 1979.

The USMTM assessment is related in American embassy Jidda cable 8032 of Nov. 22, 1979, "Occupation of Grand Mosque Mecca," originally classified "Secret" and obtained by the author under a Freedom of Information Act request. Ambassador West's perplexities about the mismatch of USMTM and pilots' accounts is from American embassy Jidda telegram 8079.

Ambassador West described his meeting with Ahmed Zaki Yamani in American embassy Jidda cable 8072 of Nov. 22, 1979, "Khomeini Statement on Events in Saudi Arabia," originally classified "Secret" and obtained by the author under a Freedom of Information Act request.

Cyrus Vance's message to Prince Saud is quoted from State Department cable 302568 of Nov. 22, 1979, "Allegations of American Involvement in Mecca Incident," originally classified "Secret" and obtained by the author under a Freedom of Information Act request.

Prince Saud's letter to Vance is quoted from American embassy Tunis cable 9013 of Nov. 22, 1979, "Allegations of American Involvement in Mecca Incident," originally classified "Secret" and obtained by the author under a Freedom of Information Act request.

Prince Nayef's statement denying U.S. or Iranian involvement is quoted from American embassy Jidda cable 8077 of Nov. 22, 1979, "SAG Disclaims Any U.S. Involvement with Seizure of Mecca Mosque," originally classified "Confidential" and obtained by the author under a Freedom of Information Act request.

Prince Nayef's criticism of the United States is quoted from FBIS Middle East Report Jan. 11, 1980, "Interior Minister Criticizes U.S. in Interview." Doha Qatar News Agency, Jan. 10, 1980, item JN101358.

The "criminal deed" comment is from a Tehran Radio International Service in

Arabic broadcast, as reported by FBIS Middle East Report, Nov. 23, 1979, item JN212001. Khomeini's speech to the Pakistani officers is quoted from FBIS Middle East Report, Nov. 23, 1979, Tehran domestic television, "Khomeini Addresses Pakistani Officers," item GF222200.

CHAPTER SEVENTEEN

The Saudi imams speaking out during the Friday sermon are quoted from "World Condemns Attacks," *Arab News* (Jeddah), Nov. 24, 1979.

Friday protests in the Muslim world are described based on "Anti-U.S. Demonstrations, Turmoil over Mecca Mosque Takeover Go On," *Washington Post,* Nov. 24, 1979.

The *Yanki* magazine comment is from the Dec. 3–9, 1979, issue. Agca's letter is quoted from the *Milliyet* newspaper, Nov. 26, 1979.

The first CIA memorandum is "Saudi Arabia: The Mecca Incident in Perspective," Nov. 1979, originally classified "Secret" (MORI DocID123290), obtained by the author under the Freedom of Information Act. The second CIA document is a secret briefing for Nov. 26, 1979, dated Nov. 27, 1979, MORI DocID123287, partially declassified and obtained by the author under the Freedom of Information Act.

Details on the SR-71 overflights and Mecca are from an author interview with Hambley and Ryer.

The "data point" description is from an author interview with Gary Sick. The Nov. 23 meeting and Vance's attitude are described based on Brzezinski's *Power and Principle* (pp. 483–84), Sick's *All Fall Down* (pp. 232–37), and Carter's *Keeping Faith,* (pp. 474–76). The Nov. 23, 1979, CIA memo, originally classified "Secret" (MORI DocID123286), was obtained by the author under a Freedom of Information Act request. The description of Vance's "grim and fatalistic" attitude is from Sick.

Laingen's telegram is number 34 of Nov. 22, 1979, transmitted to Hamilton Jordan, initially classified "Confidential—Eyes Only." It is held in the Carter Library and reproduced in *The Declassified Documents Reference System* (Farmington Hills, Mich.: Gale Group, 2006).

Vance's quote explaining the reasons for the evacuation of American personnel is from State Department cable 307611 of Nov. 29, 1979, "Possible Evacuation of Americans from Saudi Arabia," originally classified "Secret" and obtained by the author under a Freedom of Information Act request.

Bin Laden is quoted from the Al Jazeera interview recorded in October 2001 and subsequently broadcast by CNN.

Henze's memo is "The U.S. and the Islamic World," National Security Council memorandum for Zbigniew Brzezinski (number 6786), dated Nov. 27, 1979, initially classified "Confidential." It is held in the Carter Library and reproduced in *The Declassified Documents Reference System.*

CHAPTER EIGHTEEN

The fatwa of the ulema is quoted from a Nov. 25, 1979, Saudi Press Agency text, reproduced in the *Arab News,* Nov. 26, 1979.

The Quran verse quoted by the ulema is 002.191.

The shakeup at the task force is described based on author interviews with Nefai and Prince Turki.

Details of the military action are described based on author interviews with Abu Sultan, Nefai, Prince Turki, Samir, Hozeimi, and another former member of Juhayman's organization, and soldiers who declined to be identified. The narrative also draws on U.S. diplomatic cables and contemporary Saudi TV appearances by Dhaheri and Nefai.

Mohammed Abdullah and Juhayman are quoted by Samir.

Pilots' observations are drawn from American embassy Jidda telegram 8095, "Occupation of the Grand Mosque, Mecca: The Drama Apparently Ends," of Nov. 24, 1979, and telegram 8119 of Nov. 25, 1979, both originally classified "Secret" and obtained by the author under the Freedom of Information Act.

The recall of the Nadwa newspaper is also from cable 8119.

Secretary Miller's meeting with King Khaled is described based on Ambassador West's diary.

CHAPTER NINETEEN

Circumstances of Mohammed Abdullah's death were relayed to the author by Samir and other former members of the group.

Pilot accounts are from American embassy Jidda telegram 8095. The spotting of detainees in the airport is from American embassy Jidda telegram 8219 of Nov. 28, 1979, originally classified "Confidential" and obtained by the author under the Freedom of Information Act.

Prince Bandar on Bin Laden is quoted from Ambassador West's diary.

The British ambassador is quoted from British embassy Jedda FCO telegram 673, "Disturbances in Mecca," of Dec. 1, 1979, originally classified "Confidential," declassified and obtained by the author under the U.K. Freedom of Information Act.

The story of the conversation between King Khaled and the alleged Mahdi's mother, which may be apocryphal, has been recounted to the author by, among others, James Buchan (London, February 2006). It is substantiated in part by American embassy Jidda cable 8218 of Nov. 28, 1979, "Discussion with (blank): Mecca Event," originally classified "Secret," partially declassified and obtained by the author under a Freedom of Information Act request. It is clear from the declassified portion of the cable and Ambassador West's diaries that the information comes from Prince Bandar, who reported to Ambassador West that Saudi authorities had been able to locate and take into custody Mohammed Abdullah's family.

CHAPTER TWENTY

The descriptions of the cleanup work are from Matani's *Jarimat al-Asr* and author interview with Matani. The account of Prince Turki's visit to the mosque is based on author interview with the prince. Jizani's story is from his own account published by *al Riyadh* newspaper, "Al Riyadh Yaqaddem Qissat al-Qital fil Masjid al-Haram," Dec. 12, 1979. The size of Saudi armed forces at the time is from Mossberg, "As Mideast Heats Up, U.S. Frets over Peril to the Saudi Oil Fields."

The Tehran radio comment is quoted from a CIA cable, "Attack on the Grand Mosque in Mecca," Nov. 27, 1979, MORI DocID123287, obtained by the author under the Freedom of Information Act.

The Jordanian preoccupation with Saudi events and their offer to send troops are recounted in American embassy Amman cable 7330, "Contingency Planning and Takeover of Mosque in Mecca," Nov. 22, 1979, originally classified "Secret" and obtained by the author under a Freedom of Information Act request. The details of the meeting between King Khaled and King Hussein, and the Jordanian king's musings on the situation in the Hejaz, are described based on an account that King Hussein himself provided to the American ambassador in Amman, Nicholas Veliotes, on Nov. 30, 1979. It is contained in American embassy Amman telegram 7527, "Hussein's Views on Situation in Saudi Arabia," Dec. 1, 1979, originally classified "Secret" and obtained by the author under a Freedom of Information Act request. The information that King Hussein held a phone conversation with King Khaled is from "Leaders Laud Handling of Attack on Holy Haram," *Arab News,* Nov. 25, 1979.

Additional information on the Saudi reaction and the status of Jordanian commandos is drawn from author interviews in the region.

The Saudi Defense Ministry request for tear gas and smoke equipment is relayed by American embassy Jidda cable 8180 of Nov. 27, 1979, "Occupation of Grand Mosque: Situation as of 1300 GMT," originally classified "Secret" and obtained by the author under a Freedom of Information Act request.

The CIA involvement is described based on author interviews with Hambley and other U.S. officials in the region at the time. The station chief at the time, Charles W., declined to be interviewed for this book. The fiasco with tear gas use is based on author interviews with Abu Sultan and other Saudi sources. The Saudi expulsion of the CIA station chief is based on author interview with George Cave. Prince Turki's assessment of the CIA as "emasculated" is from author interview.

CHAPTER TWENTY-ONE

Information on Count de Marenches and on the Central African Empire raid is based on his two books, *The Fourth World War* and *Dans le secret des princes* (*Sharing Princes' Secrets*) with Christine Ockrent (Paris: Editions Stock, 1986).

De Marenches's opinion of Carter is quoted from *Dans le secret des princes*, p. 296.

The story of interaction between Prince Turki and de Marenches is based on the author's interview with the prince and de Marenches's account in *The Fourth World War*, pp. 206–9.

Details on the Moroccan offer of help are from American embassy Rabat cable 8731 of Nov. 28, 1979, "Moroccan Sympathy and Support for Saudis After Mecca Mosque Takeover," originally classified "Confidential" and obtained by the author under a Freedom of Information Act request.

Additional details on the history of French involvement in the Mecca crisis are pieced together based on author interviews with French chargé d'affaires in Jeddah at the time, Pierre LaFrance (Paris, Feb. 2006), Ambassador Michel Drumetz (via telephone, May 26, 2006), and the then foreign minister Jean François-Poncet (Paris, Feb. 2006).

CHAPTER TWENTY-TWO

The Shiite uprising in the Eastern Province is described in great detail in a chronological account and compilation of documents published clandestinely by Shiite Islamist exiles in the early 1980s under the title *Intifadha fil Mamtaqa al-Gharbiya* (*The Uprising in the Eastern Province*). This compilation, dedicated to "Mujahed Juhayman," served as the basis for my chronology of the uprising.

The number of American citizens in Saudi Arabia at the time is from State De-

partment cable 307611. General Malki is quoted from American Consulate
Dhahran cable 1872 of Nov. 26, 1979, "Tensions Rise Among Saudi Shi'as in Eastern Province," originally classified "Secret" and obtained by the author under a Freedom of Information Act request.

Descriptions of street protests are drawn from author interviews with Shiite militants who participated or witnessed the uprising, including Hamza al-Hassan (London, Feb. 2006), Dr. Fuad Ibrahim (London, Feb. 2006), and Ahmed al-Ali
(Washington, D.C., March 2006), who had shared a cell with a Juhayman follower.
Several additional interviews with several eyewitnesses and participants who declined to be named because of fear of retribution by the government were carried
out by the author on a visit to Qatif, Safwa, and Sayhat in August 2006.

This chapter also draws on Dr. Ibrahim's insights into the Shiite Islamic movement in Saudi Arabia, as described in his book *The Shi'is of Saudi Arabia* (London:
Saqi Books, 2006). Hassan al Saffar's writings in *Kaifa Naqhar al-Khawf* are quoted
from Dr. Ibrahim's book.

Valuable background details were provided by Toby Craig Jones, "Rebellion on
the Saudi Periphery: Modernity, Marginalization and the Shi'a Uprising of 1979,"
International Journal of Middle East Studies 38 (2006): 213–33.

King Khaled's telegram to Khomeini is quoted from "Saudi Arabia: Growing Shia
Restlessness," a CIA memorandum of Nov. 29, 1979, MORI DocID123288, originally classified "Secret," obtained by the author under the Freedom of Information Act.

The Shiite letters sent to Aramco employees are quoted in American consulate
Dhahran telegram 1956, "Anti-American Letters Being Sent to Aramco Employees,"
Dec. 9, 1979, by Ralph Lindstrom, originally classified "Confidential," obtained by
the author under the Freedom of Information Act. The intelligence report on Shiite
plans to blow up a refinery is mentioned in Ambassador West's diary.

CHAPTER TWENTY-THREE

The history of the GIGN is based on a series of interviews with the force's former
members.

Prince Nayef's visit to Satory is described based on author interviews with Paul
Barril (Dubai, Oct. 2005, and Rome, Dec. 2005) and the GIGN commander at the
time, Christian Prouteau (Paris, Feb. 2006, and via phone, Nov. 2006).

In addition to the interviews with Barril and Prouteau, the narrative of French
participation in the Mecca events is also drawn from author interviews with team
members Ignace Wodecki (La Farlede, South France, Jan. 2006) and Christian Lambert (Paris, Feb. 2006).

Prouteau provided the description of the meeting at the Elysée Palace. General Navereau, reached by the author, declined to discuss his role in these events.

Details of Barril's life are based on his autobiography *Missions très spéciales* (*Very Special Missions*) (Paris, Presses de la Cité, 1984).

Wodecki and Lambert showed the author contemporary mission documents and deployment orders.

CHAPTER TWENTY-FOUR

Ambassador West's reaction to suggestions of evacuating U.S. citizens from Saudi Arabia is based on his diaries.

In addition to sources mentioned for Chapter 23, the Shiite notables' meeting with Prince Ahmed is described in part using American consulate Dhahran telegram 1916, "SAG Attempts to Mollify Shi'as," Dec. 2, 1979, by Ralph Lindstrom, originally classified "Secret," obtained by the author under the Freedom of Information Act.

The comment on the *al Siyassa* article is from American embassy Kuwait cable 5422 of Nov. 29, 1979, "Booklet Attributed to Perpetrators of Grand Mosque Incident," originally classified "Confidential," obtained by the author under the Freedom of Information Act.

Details of the demonstrations in Kuwait are from FBIS Middle East Report, Dec. 3, 1979, "Use of Force Denied," Kuwait News Agency Report of Dec. 1, 1979, item LD011412.

Jack McCavitt described his role in the Tripoli embassy siege in a detailed account he e-mailed to the author in Feb. 2006. The former chargé d'affaires, William Eagleton, also described that day in "It's Better to Travel Light While Witnessing the History of the World: Peoria Native William Eagleton Has Made a Career out of Solving World's Problems," by Terry Bibo, *Peoria Star Journal,* Nov. 21, 1999.

Official Libyan comments and some details of the day's events in Tripoli are from FBIS Middle East Report, Dec. 2, 1979, "Tripoli Demonstration at U.S. Embassy Reported," Tripoli Domestic Service, Dec. 2, 1979, item LD021317, and "Toxic Gases Reportedly Used," Jamahiriya News Agency, Dec. 2, 1979, item LD022148.

CHAPTER TWENTY-FIVE

Dhaheri's statement is from an interview with Saudi media, reproduced by *al Jazira* newspaper on Dec. 6, 1979. Nayef's statement is quoted from FBIS Middle East

Report, Dec. 4, 1979, "Mosque Purged 'Renegades,'" Saudi News Agency, 2302 GMT, Dec. 3, 1979, item LD032316.

Abbas Ghazzawi is quoted from American embassy Jidda cable 8366 of Dec. 4, 1979, "Mecca Update: Situation as of 1030 Zulu Dec. 4," originally classified "Confidential" and obtained by the author under a Freedom of Information Act request.

The description of Juhayman's arrest is based on the author interview with Abu Sultan. Additional details are from author interviews with Nefai, Samir, Sultan, Prince Turki, and other participants and eyewitnesses, as well as from Saudi TV footage watched by the author.

CHAPTER TWENTY-SIX

Details of the final days of the French mission are from author interviews with Barril, Prouteau, Wodecki, and Lambert, as well as an account written by Wodecki for a GIGN veterans' newsletter.

Brzezinski is quoted from his Dec. 3, 1979, memorandum for the president, "NSC Agenda, December 4, 1979." The document, held in the Carter Library, was originally classified "Top Secret—Sensitive."

CHAPTER TWENTY-SEVEN

The description of the destruction in the Grand Mosque is quoted from "An Eyewitness Account: The Scene at the Mosque," *Arab News,* Dec. 6–7, 1979.

Prince Nayef's TV address is quoted from "Mosque Renegades Smashed: 135 Killed" in the same issue of the newspaper. The issue also contained several spectacular photographs taken in the damaged shrine by the *Arab News–al Sharq al Awsat* photographer Muhammad Ibrahim.

The scenes from Saudi TV are described from the footage viewed by the author. The diplomats' comparison of Juhayman to Rasputin and Charles Manson is from American embassy Jidda cable 8479 of Dec. 9, 1979, "Mecca Update: Prayers Resound at the Holy Ka'aba," obtained by the author under a Freedom of Information Act request.

Official casualty figures are from "127 Soldiers Killed, 461 Hurt in Mecca Siege—Naif," *Saudi Gazette,* Jan. 10, 1980; "Interior Ministry Statement," *Arab News,* Jan. 10–11, 1980; "King Khaled Visits Soldiers Hurt in Mecca," *Arab News,* Dec. 12, 1979.

American doubts as to the accuracy of official figures are quoted from American embassy Jidda cable 8429 of Dec. 6, 1979, "End of the Siege of Grand Mosque," originally classified "Confidential" and obtained by the author under a Freedom of Information Act request.

Prince Fahd's reply to President Carter's telegram is contained in American embassy Jeddah telegram 8742 of Dec. 19, 1979, "Crown Prince Fahd Reply to President's Message on Mosque Incident," originally classified "Confidential," held at the Carter Library.

King Khaled's comment about a possible attack against his palace is from Robert Lacey's *The Kingdom: Arabia and the House of Saud* (New York: Harcourt Brace Jovanovich, 1981), p. 512. According to Ambassador West's diaries, Prince Bandar made a similar admission, saying that had Juhayman attacked a different target, he "may have been able to have gotten support from other areas."

The demotions of Prince Fawwaz and Saudi generals are described based on "New Army Commander Appointed," Saudi Press Agency statement as printed by *Arab News,* Jan. 2, 1980; "Fawaz Quits; Air Force Chief Retired," Saudi Press Agency statement as printed by *Arab News,* Jan. 1, 1980; British embassy Jeddah telegram 10 of Jan. 3, 1980, "New Appointments in Saudi MODA," originally classified "Confidential."

CHAPTER TWENTY-EIGHT

Prince Bandar is quoted on the use of truth serum and interrogation methods by Ambassador West in his diary and American embassy Jidda cable 8218. Prince Turki's thoughts are described based on an author interview with him.

Fahd's interviews in December 1979 and January 1980 included those with Saleem Lozi of the Lebanese *al Hawadith* magazine, with the Paris-based *al Watan al Arabi* magazine, and with the Lebanese *al Safir* newspaper. The quotes on Juhayman's alleged inability to express himself and comparisons between the Mecca uprising and the Jonestown massacre are from the *al Safir* interview, reproduced by the Saudi Press Agency and reprinted by *Arab News,* Jan. 14, 1980.

The *al Hawadith* interview on the alleged Zionist conspiracy and U.S.-Saudi ties, as well as the lack of political aspirations among the rebels, is quoted from a transcript in FBIS Middle East Report, Jan. 15, 1980, "Al-Hawadith Interviews Crown Prince Amir Fahd," *al-Hawadith,* Jan. 11, 1980, item LD111653.

Prince Bandar's comments about South Yemen are from a chapter authored by James Buchan in Holden and Johns's *The House of Saud,* p. 521. The Saudi official on Russian involvement and Juhayman's alleged fondness for alcohol is quoted from

"Takeover of the Grand Mosque Is Said to Be Political Act," by Steven Rattner, *New York Times,* Dec. 16, 1979.

The *Washington Post* editorial "Battle in Mecca" ran on Nov. 25, 1979. The *New York Times* first reproduced Juhayman's writings in the Feb. 25, 1980, article by Youssef M. Ibrahim, "New Data Link Mecca Takeover to Political Rift."

CHAPTER TWENTY-NINE

Soviet documents cited in the chapter are from *Volume II: Afghanistan: Lessons from the Last War,* National Security Archive Electronic Briefing Book No. 57, edited by John Prados and Svetlana Savranskaya, October 9, 2001. The National Security Archive, www.gwu.edu/~nsarchiv.

Brezhnev is quoted from an archive copy of the transcript of his conversation. Andropov's letter to Brezhnev is from notes taken by A. F. Dobrynin and provided to the Norwegian Nobel Institute. Ustinov's reasoning is quoted from Georgy M. Kornienko, *The Cold War: Testimony of a Participant* (Moscow: Mezhdunarodnye Otnoshenia, 1994), pp. 193–95. Additional details are from Alexander Lyahovsky, *Tragediya i doblest' Afghantsa* (*Tragedy and Valor of an Afghan Veteran*) (Moscow: Iskona, 1995), pp. 109–12.

The CIA estimate of Saudi importance to the Afghan insurgency is cited from "Near East and South Asia Review," CIA National Foreign Assessment Center, Nov. 23, 1979. It is partially declassified and posted on the CIA's FOIA Web site, www.foia.cia.gov.

Prince Turki on Afghanistan is quoted from a six-part interview with the MBC television network and *Arab News* that he gave in 2001. The comment on the threat to the Arabian Peninsula appeared in the Nov. 9, 2001, issue of *Arab News.*

U.S. military estimates of the Soviet threat to the Gulf are from the Special Co-ordination Committee meeting minutes, a White House document created Jan. 14, 1980, and initially classified "Secret/Sensitive." It has since been partially declassified, and a copy is held in the Carter Library.

Brzezinski is quoted from the Dec. 26, 1980, memo "Reflections on the Soviet Intervention in Afghanistan," originally classified "Secret." A copy is kept in the Carter Library. His impressions of the Saudis' "apprehension" are from *Power and Principle,* p. 449. His advice on Zia is from the Jan. 11, 1980, "NSC Weekly Report #125" memo for the president, originally classified "Secret" and kept at the Carter Library. Turki's views on the Oman basing rights are from American embassy Jidda cable 8752 of Dec. 20, 1979, "Military Facilities Team Visit: Saudi Arabia," originally classified "Secret" and obtained by the author under a Freedom of Information Act request.

Carter's State of the Union speech is from the Carter Library Web site www.jimmycarterlibrary.org/documents/speeches/su80jec.phtml.

CHAPTER THIRTY

The ulema decision on Juhayman is quoted from a Saudi Press Agency statement reproduced under the headline "Ulema Condemn Mecca Renegades" in the Jan. 3–4, 1980, edition of *Arab News*. Details of the execution and King Khaled's decision are from a Saudi Press Agency statement reproduced under the headline "63 Renegades Executed" in the Jan. 10–11, 1980, edition of *Arab News*; "63 Grand Mosque Aggressors Executed," Jan. 10, 1980, *Saudi Gazette*; "Saudi Arabians Behead 63 for Attack on Mosque," *Washington Post,* Jan. 10, 1980.

The fate of American rebels in the Grand Mosque is described based on Ambassador West's diaries and author interviews with Hozeimi, Hambley, and James Placke (via phone, Oct. 2006), among others. The telegram quoted is American embassy Jidda cable 8450 of Dec. 8, 1979, "Missing Americans in Mecca."

The Saudi crackdown on women is described based on "Saudis Shy Away from Westernizing," by Christopher S. Wren, *New York Times,* Feb. 2, 1980, and "Saudis, Shaken by Mosque Takeover, Tighten Enforcement of Islamic Law," by Edward Cody, *Washington Post,* Feb. 5, 1980. Black market alcohol prices are from Mackey's *The Saudis,* p. 283. The smashing up of bottles is from "A Desert America Is Governed by Fear of Mideast Turmoil," by Walter S. Mossberg, *Wall Street Journal,* Dec. 20, 1979.

Nayef's quote on arresting bearded men is in part from "Naif Briefs Journalists on Renegades," *Arab News,* Jan. 14, 1980, and in part from Buchan's chapter in *House of Saud,* p. 514.

Prince Khaled, a brother of Prince Turki and, like him, the son of King Faisal, made the comments on Juhayman's legacy in an interview with the Dubai-based Al Arabiya TV network. The quote is from a partial transcript published in *Al Sharq al Awsat* newspaper on July 20, 2004.

The CIA memorandum "Saudi Arabia: The Mecca Incident in Perspective" was issued in Nov. 1979, originally classified "Secret," MORI DocID123290, and obtained by the author under the Freedom of Information Act.

Larrabee's memo "Soviet Intervention in Afghanistan" is dated Dec. 31, 1979. Originally classified "Secret," it is kept in the Carter Library.

CHAPTER THIRTY-ONE

Bin Laden's recording on Juhayman is quoted from Peter Bergen's *The Osama bin Laden I Know: An Oral History of al Qaeda's Leader* (New York: Free Press, 2006), p. 23. The recording was originally posted on the now disabled www.qal3ah.net Web site. Bergen used a translation provided by the U.S. government.

The account of the Peshawar conversation is from Jason Burke's *Al Qaeda: The True Story of Radical Islam* (London: I. B. Tauris & Co.), p. 58.

Bin Laden on Bin Baz is quoted from an interview published in the Oct.–Nov. 1996 issue of *Nida'ul Islam* magazine. It was retrieved by the author from www.fas.org/irp/world/para/docs/ladin.htm.

Islambouli's statement about the eighteen-month path to martyrdom is from his interrogation transcripts, as described by Youssef H. Aboul-Encin in "Islamic Militant Cells and Sadat's Assassination," *Military Review* (July–August 2004). The fact that Islambouli had received Juhayman's writings from his brother is from Mohammed Heikal's *Autumn of Fury: The Assassination of Sadat* (New York: Random House, 1983), p. 247, as cited in Joseph Kechichian's "Islamic Revivalism and Change in Saudi Arabia."

Maqdisi is quoted from his book, *Kawashef al jaliya fi kufr al dawla Saudiya* (*Clear Proofs of the Infidelity of the Saudi State*) (Minbar al Tawhid wal Jihad publishers (Internet version), Hijri year 1421. Details of Maqdisi's biography are from "Abu Mohammed al Maqdisi: al-Zarqawi 'Spiritual Godfather,'" by Mshari Zyedi, *Al Sharq al Awsat* (English Web edition), July 26, 2005.

Index